The
TWO
REFORMATIONS

The
TWO
REFORMATIONS

The Journey from the
Last Days to the New World

HEIKO A. OBERMAN

EDITED BY DONALD WEINSTEIN

YALE UNIVERSITY PRESS / NEW HAVEN & LONDON

Published with assistance from the foundation established in memory of
Oliver Baty Cunningham of the Class of 1917, Yale College.

Several chapters in this book have appeared elsewhere and may have been revised.
Chapter 1: "The Long Fifteenth Century: In Search of Its Profile," appeared in *Die
deutsche Reformation zwischen Mittelalter und Früher Neuzeit,* ed. Thomas A. Brady, Jr.,
with Elisabeth Müller-Luckner, Schriften des Historischen Kollegs, Kolloquien 50
(Munich: R. Oldenbourg Verlag, 2001). Chapter 2: "Luther and the Via Moderna: The
Philosophical Backdrop of the Reformation Breakthrough," is forthcoming in the
Journal of Ecclesiastical History. Chapter 3: "Martin Luther Contra Medieval
Monasticism: A Friar in the Lion's Den," appeared in *Ad fontes Lutheri: Toward the
Recovery of the Real Luther, Essays in Honor of Kenneth Hagen's Sixty-Fifth Birthday,* ed.
Timothy Maschke, Franz Posset, and Joan Skocir, Marquette Studies in Theology 28
(Milwaukee: Marquette University Press, 2001). Chapters 6, 7, and 8: "Toward the
Recovery of the Historical Calvin: Redrawing the Map of Reformation Europe," formed
a plenary address presented by Oberman at the International Congress on Calvin
Research, in Seoul, South Korea, in August 1998. Chapter 9: "Calvin: Honored,
Forgotten, Maligned," appeared in Oberman's *Calvin's Legacy: Its Greatness and
Limitations,* trans. John Vriend (Grand Rapids, Mich.: William B. Eerdmans, 1990).

Library of Congress Cataloging-in-Publication Data

Oberman, Heiko Augustinus.
The two Reformations : the journey from the last days to the new world
/ Heiko A. Oberman ; edited by Donald Weinstein.
p. cm.
Includes bibliographical references and index.
ISBN 0-300-09868-5 (alk. paper)
1. Luther, Martin, 1483–1546. 2. Calvin, Jean, 1509–1564. 3.
Reformation. I. Weinstein, Donald, 1926–   II. Title.
BR332.5 .O24 2003
270.6—dc21   2002153187

A catalogue record for this book is available from the British Library.

10 9 8 7 6 5 4 3 2 1

Burn after reading!
—Sixteenth-century epistolary postscript

Read them and weep.
—Sixteenth-century Dutch card-table proverb

Viele derjenigen, die unvorstellbar Furchtbares erlebt haben, schweigen.
Sie haben nicht überlebt.
—Wolfgang von Buch,
Wir Kindersoldaten, 1998

CONTENTS

EDITOR'S PREFACE

Until a few days before he died, on April 22, 2001, Heiko Oberman had been working on two books. One was a new appraisal of Calvin's career and thought, a labor of years of research, close study of Calvin's writings, and deep reflection. The Calvin book was part of a scholarly life plan: Oberman had carried the story of Reformation religious thought from its roots in the late Middle Ages (for example, *The Harvest of Medieval Theology, Forerunners of the Reformation,* and *The Dawn of the Reformation*) through Luther (*Luther: Man between God and the Devil* and *Masters of the Reformation*), and after Calvin, the City Reformation, and the Reformation of the Refugees, he intended to turn his attention to what is often called the Radical Reformation (although Oberman would not so call it) and then carry the story into modern times and across oceans.

With his Calvin still short of completion, however, Oberman learned that he had terminal cancer. About the same time he began writing another book, an extended essay comparing the respective contributions of Luther and Calvin toward the founding of the modern world. Clearly he regarded this as his last opportunity to place the Reformation in the larger perspective of European and American history. It was also the last chance he would have to express in print some of his deeply held feelings about such related matters as the influence of German nationalism on Reformation scholarship, the *trahison des clercs* of certain prominent twentieth-century German historians, and the Reformation and anti-Semitism (already addressed in his groundbreaking book *The Roots of Anti-Semitism*). The inspired energy that had driven Oberman's entire scholarly and teaching career was ebbing, but, with still more verve than most of us have at our peak, he persevered. In the growing shadow of death, Oberman worked furiously—often, as I was told by Mrs. Oberman, long into the night. Only when he began counting his life in days and when his strength was failing him did he seek help. Peter Dykema, one of his last doctoral students, would complete the Calvin book. I offered to do what I could, and Heiko asked me to edit and prepare for publication the chapters he had written for his second book in progress, on Luther, Calvin, and the onset of the modern world. I have undertaken this task as an expression of admiration for a great historian and wonderful colleague as well as a labor of love for a dear friend.

The material Oberman left consisted of a preface and dedication as well as several chapters that were in a state I regarded as a penultimate draft; that is to say, the chapters were virtually complete as to content but were uneven in footnoting and in need of some editing and light revision. Another section, indicated in the original table of contents as The Aggressive Reformation, with chapters on The Reformation in the Streets, The First Book Burnings in Europe, The First Martyrs: From Books to Bodies, and The Image as Battlefield: Competing for the Simple Folk, remained to be written. Because no one but Oberman—certainly not I—could write those chapters, they are lost to us, with one partial exception. It is a paper, "Der Bilderstreit im Zeitalter der Reformation," which he was preparing for delivery at the Interdisziplinärer Kongress, "Von der Macht und Ohnmacht der Bilder," subsequently held at the Universität Bern, from January 21 through 24, 2001. It appeared to me that he intended it as part of the chapter The Image as Battlefield, and although time ran out before Oberman was able to complete or revise it, I decided to include it. I have translated it and added some notes. My friend David Price, associate professor of history at Southern Methodist University, went over my translation with extraordinary care and expertise and made invaluable corrections and suggestions, just as he had already done for some other passages. It appears here under the title The Controversy over Images in the Time of the Reformation.

Although Heiko gave me carte blanche with the material, in editing the chapters he wrote I have tried to restrict myself to what he might have done to smooth out the text—so much of it produced at fever heat—to clarify a point, add a note, or check an American English idiom. Dutch-born and reared, Oberman commanded a remarkable English vocabulary and a writing style that must have been the envy of many a native American scholar. Only rarely did he fail to hit the nail squarely on the head, but it did happen, and I have tried to redirect those near misses. Heiko and I carried on a running debate about matters of style and tone: he loved alliteration, colorful similes and metaphors, and startling locutions. I prefer a more matter-of-fact style, and when criticizing other historians in print, I have tried (not always successfully) to maintain some measure of polite restraint; by contrast, Heiko, although he was very generous and fair, gleefully exposed and damned the scholarly shortcomings of fellow historians, especially when they committed the cardinal sin of anachronism, failed to work hard enough at their subject, or displayed an inadequate grasp of his beloved sources. Sadly, death has given me the last word in that friendly debate, and if I have betrayed my resolve not to leave my own fingerprints on Heiko's manuscript, it has been in yielding to the temptation to tone down a few of his more flamboyant images and in occasionally substituting a word or phrase with one that fits better what he meant to say. I have also made the decision (after some consultation) to present the surviving chapters as essays, each of which can stand alone as a scholarly contribution. This has little practical effect except to avoid giving the impression that they constitute the book that Oberman would have published had he lived to do it.

One of the last requests he made to me about the material he was leaving in my hands was that I include the four lectures in commemoration of Abraham Kuyper (which, although published in 1986, had not, he felt, reached the wider audience he had been aiming for) and also the article on Luther he had been preparing to publish in *The Journal of Ecclesiastical History*. Oberman frequently invited prominent historical scholars to his graduate seminar at the University of Arizona to address the question "What makes you tick as a historian?" What made Heiko Oberman tick as a historian—his passionate, inspired, personal engagement with the past—is nowhere better seen than in the Kuyper Lectures. It seems fitting that they close this book. With the permission of the respective publishers I have included both, in the case of the first (Calvin's Legacy), omitting a few passages that seemed more appropriate to the original audience and altering a few expressions, and in the second

(Luther and the Via Moderna), changing some wording and shifting some paragraphs. I have also translated some quotations and terms from the Latin. Finally, I trimmed Heiko's preface, Burn after Reading, of a few pages in which he expatiated on the difficulties of writing a book, particularly this book. In my judgment they reflect his impassioned, perhaps anguished, state of mind in those last days and not his considered thoughts about the problems of writing history. I think he would have edited them out had he had the opportunity for a final revision in calmer circumstances.

In preparing the book for publication, in addition to the aforementioned help of David Price, I have had the generous help and advice of Peter Dykema of Arkansas Tech University and John Frymire of the University of Missouri, two worthy laureates of Oberman's exacting doctoral program at the University of Arizona. Another student in the program, Joshua Rosenthal, has also been helpful. Two of my university colleagues lent me their expertise: Alan E. Bernstein, for some difficult Latin readings, and Jonathan Beck, for my queries about sixteenth-century French. Susan Karant-Nunn, director of the Division for Late Medieval and Reformation Studies at the University of Arizona, looked up material in Germany and answered my questions about German matters. Heiko's good friend, and mine, Thomas Brady of the University of California at Berkeley, offered general advice and encouragement. My dear friend Toetie (Mrs. Gertruida Oberman-Reesink), Heiko's beloved wife and companion, has always been available for consultation and information, as has Luise Betterton, program coordinator in the Division for Late Medieval and Reformation Studies at the University of Arizona. Last but not least, a special acknowledgment to Sandra Kimball, secretary in the Division, who has been extraordinarily willing and remarkably able in providing acute technical and editorial assistance. Her help in putting this book together has been indispensable. I thank them all.

Friends, though absent, are at hand; though in need, yet abound; though weak, are strong; and—harder saying still—though dead, are yet alive; so great is the esteem on the part of their friends, the tender recollection and the deep longing that still attends them.
—Cicero, *De amicitia*, 7.23

PREFACE
Burn after Reading

Among the thousands of letters I have read in the course of my Reformation researches, many contain a simple three-word postscript: "Burn after reading." The injunction conveys the need of sixteenth-century authors to conceal their identity and keep their ideas from falling into unfriendly hands. For similar reasons authors and printers commonly falsified or omitted names, places, and dates of publication in the thousands of pamphlets and tracts that circulated in Germany between 1500 and 1520. Those were dangerous times: dissent was a well-understood risk and public opinion a contested area, anxiously monitored by those who considered themselves the guardians of the public good. The tradition of evasion still pervades and influences Reformation studies. The entire field owes its rise and current renown to the art of concealment. The Reformation was understood as a German event, as indeed it was, in part, and German scholars have long been preeminent in it. So have German politics. The shifting fortunes of the Empire, Prussian rivalry with Vienna, Paris, and London, the split between the parties of Rome and Moscow, and above all, a German nationalism marginalized and rendered uncertain by the pan-European aspirations of the Hapsburgs, all these have inevitably influenced its German interpreters. These same scholars, however, have failed to consider how the historical, political, and social factors of German history have shaped their views, proudly offering their programmed and visionary findings as reliable results of scholarship. Whereas historians have generally become more sensitive to the distorting effects of confessional blinders, the influence of those wider cultural and national presuppositions on German Reformation scholarship remains buried and largely undetected.

More than anyone, Martin Luther, the key figure of the early Reformation, has suffered distortion from such practices of concealment. A combination of religious loyalty and national aspirations turned him into the first Protestant and a German prophet of global stature. How the kernel of truth has been stifled by myth in so much of Reformation history is demonstrated in the following reminiscence of a Holocaust survivor, who, as a little girl in February 1943 was on a train with her father, bound for Auschwitz. As the train passed Wittenberg, her father lifted her up so that she could see "the city of the greatest spokesman for freedom of all time." Our route back into the remote territory of the sixteenth century is therefore hindered by this founding myth of international Protestantism: the notion that Luther's call for liberation from the Babylonian captivity of the church led to a wondrous escape from Roman papal tyranny and a passage out of the dark Middle Ages. To be sure, Luther's destruction of the "three walls of the Romanists"—namely, papal claims to lordship over Scripture, synod, and state—inspired subversive movements all over Europe. Yet, although such struggles may inspire sympathy among modern constitutional democrats, they do not serve the project of a well-balanced reconstruction; Reformation liberation movements could not have been inspired by dreams of social and political emancipation that came into being only with the great revolutions of the eighteenth and nineteenth centuries.

Equally misleading is the perspective of Catholic apologetics. If the Protestant founding myth misguides us toward Protestant triumphalism, Catholic revisionism would turn the quest for origins back on itself. Revisionists have made salutary efforts to discern the hesitant beginnings of modernization amid the chaos of the papal exile from Avignon and the resulting Great Schism of the West; they have shed light on the humanistic resources of the early Jesuits who geared up in 1540 to extirpate heresy; they have dealt objectively with the horrors of the Roman Inquisition and explored the irenic efforts of the Council of Trent, especially those of its third session between 1561 and 1563. Perhaps their finest achievement was to recognize that the same *cri de coeur*, "Salvation at stake!" was to be heard from *all* the martyrs to sixteenth-century religious intolerance, whether Lutheran, Anabaptist, or Huguenot, *and* recusant Catholic. However, when we fail to find an entry for Counter

Reformation in the *Oxford Dictionary of the Reformation* (1998), we realize that the typically Protestant anti-Catholic paradigm—Inquisition, Jesuits, Trent—has been replaced by a bland and equally distorting revisionism. Those open-minded scholars who are "with it" have discovered an "it" that is not the historical past, but the ecumenical present. The brute facts of the Counter Reformation, best personified by the Carafa pope, Paul IV (1555–1559), who combined all the characteristics by which Protestants identified the Antichrist—suppression of lay Bibles, the Inquisition, the Index, and militant territorial expansionism—should not be glossed over, having played an important role in preparing the way for the Tridentine Reformation. The time has come for a transconfessional coalition of scholars who will avoid the smokescreens on both sides as they make their way back to the cultural and social milieu in which Reformation ideas and movements struggled for life.

Since I complain of Reformation scholars who have failed to examine their own presuppositions, I can do no less than try to lay bare the personal experiences that have influenced my own historical agenda. Human beings are not born just once, they are reborn in other times and seasons too. I am well aware that my first "birth" was privileged in many respects, above all because its circumstances identified an enemy who came from outside. When my father woke me at 5:14 A.M. on May 10, 1940, he pointed to a burning Junker airplane falling out of the sky after it had been shot down on its way back to Germany after fire-bombing Rotterdam. Of the preceding ten years I have no moving pictures, only a few stills; my historically conscious life began at that moment.

Scarcely two years later, in August 1942, I was born once more when my father was "lifted from his bed," as the persecutors euphemistically phrased it, in Utrecht, where as a Protestant minister he had set up a network for the redocumentation and flight of Jewish compatriots. My mother fared better that night because she was taken into "protective custody" in the same peaceful room in Holten where this book was conceived and where I am now writing. A loyal and courageous sheriff had directed four agents of the German SD (*Sicherheitsdienst*) to take a circuitous route to our house in the woods, then jumped on his bike and arrived there just in time to warn four fugitives sleeping downstairs. They escaped in the dark, but it was too late to alert the fifth man upstairs who was sharing my small bedroom. The command to show our papers awakened us. Fumbling to insert his glass eye (he had been blinded by the malfunction of one of the primitive Sten guns the Royal Air Force parachuted to our Resistance forces), the man produced his false documents—to no avail. Together with my mother, he was trucked off to prison. The experience colored for life my response to those two terms, *Sicherheit* (security) and *Dienst* (service), joined to such malevolent effect in the Nazi vocabulary.

In 1966, believing that the critical give-and-take of the international scholarly communities of Oxford and Harvard had rubbed out my wartime stereotypes, I dared to take up residence in Tübingen, already Europe's unrivaled center for Luther research. There I learned to distinguish war propaganda from postwar reality. For eighteen years I explored German history from the privileged observation post of a German academic civil servant and as director of the Institute for Late Medieval and Reformation History. If I had not lived in the land of the enemy, I could not have written this book, not only because its library holdings were so rich, but more important, because the Reformation tradition that survived there so remarkably intact fostered my own process of reformation. There I saw the day-to-day vitality and relevance of Luther's heritage, stimulated by the constant rivalry of a restored Catholicism and functioning as a beacon for a nation in a valiant search for identity after centuries of borderless ambiguity in middle Europe. Equally important was my slow, painful process of reexamining my entrenched generalizations about "Hitler's willing executioners." My stereotype of the typical German did not withstand the continued hammering of countless life stories, forcing me to distinguish between the weak and the courageous, the idealists and the opportunists. Just as I found unconverted Nazis and people who stuttered with a genuine sense of guilt, I found Bismarckians and democrats, anticapitalists and anticommunists.

My personal perspective may seem in some respects obtuse, but I think it has sensitized me to certain ignored or neglected aspects of the history I will be discussing. Perhaps living in Tübingen did not force me to revise all my wartime stereotypes, but it certainly made me see how the Reformation continued to echo during the Second and Third Reich and how it helped form the civic religion of the new Germany. Although in my own field I profited immensely from exchanges and debates with scholars, I was disappointed by the dearth of free collegial exchanges in German academe. By affiliating with a school of interpretation or by practicing loyalty to an academic faction, German academics seemed to find a measure of security against the divisive, unsettling past; but that same past was ever-present, and it turned lecterns into political platforms and scholarly essays into vehicles for shaping public opinion. What is specifically German about this is not the existence of scholarly dogmas and factions but the tendency to attribute the authority of prophecy to certain heroes of Germany's history. Martin Luther is a case in point. And, by extension, prophetic authority was subsumed by that too easily caricatured figure, the German university professor. Uncrowned king in his own domain, bulwark of hard and fast systems of philosophy, history, politics, and theology, he remains a major obstacle to that Erasmian critical vision that feeds on dissent.

Times are changing, however. The appeal to Luther as a national hero is losing its force and the so-called Luther Renaissance dominated by the patriot Karl Holl (d. 1926), the nationalist Werner Elert (d. 1954), and the Nazi Emanuel Hirsch (d. 1972) is finally on the wane. A new cohort of German scholars, refreshingly objective and undogmatic, has been using the methods of comparative and social history to reposition the Reformation in the context of early modern Europe. With a continuing high level of philological expertise and mastery of the sources, the new generation has succeeded in maintaining Luther's pivotal rule while ensuring that this crucial chapter in German history is understood as a part of the European-wide pursuit of holiness and reform that began in the fourteenth century and ended only with the eighteenth. Nonetheless, the icon of Luther-the-first-Protestant had dislocated Brother-Martin-the-historical-reformer so drastically that modern scholarship still has a considerable way to go—and to grow—before it recovers him. One aim of this book is to contribute to that growth; the other is to suggest where and to whom we should look to find the beginnings of modern Protestantism, and it is then that John Calvin will make his entrance.

Ekeby, Holten, The Netherlands
September 1, 2000

Massachusetts, as yet unaware that I would pass the next eighteen years in Tübingen, Germany. There, Reformation scholarship was still solidly in the hands of the students of Karl Holl, revered as an impeccable and infallible Luther interpreter.[2] Holl's favorite disciples, strategically appointed to such major chairs as Tübingen, Heidelberg, and Münster, had all evolved, as it too slowly dawned on me, into uncritical supporters of the Third Reich. In their ranks the German nationalist component in Hitler's message found fertile soil and fervent support (often in articles I found hard to trace because they had been ripped from journals dating from the 1930s and 1940s). The face-saving, apologetic cleansing and attempted rehabilitation of such unconverted Nazi Luther specialists as Emanuel Hirsch in Göttingen and Werner Elert in Munich should not be regarded as marginal, academic dramas.[3] They are part of a concerted effort to reestablish a nineteenth-century Luther-centered worldview. Erlangen's Berndt Hamm has courageously raised his voice, not by coincidence making a new exploration of the fifteenth century a priority in his investigation of the creative vitality of the later Middle Ages.[4] On the Catholic side, Nazi-oriented scholars included Joseph Lortz, who in 1939 made his name with a two-volume assault, to this day undocumented, on the church of the fifteenth century.[5] The Protestants who responded to Lortz romanticized his critique as an effort at "ecumenism," and in its place they set a benign rewriting of the pre-Reformation era. In this wide-reaching view it was an age of flowering piety without oppression, martyrs, or inquisition—a structural foreground for the Luther event.

A second, competing perspective on the fifteenth century derives from the new social history of early modern Europe, the most important and visible new direction of our field, with major representatives in the English-speaking world. By moving from established political history to cultural and mentality studies, historians reestablished the crucial importance of religion, although they frequently marginalized it under the misleading category of popular religion.[6] The latter concept, with its corollary of a two-tiered world upside down, could not stand up under the probing investigation of the past decade. Whereas Bismarckian Protestantism was dedicated to the Reformation miracle, with its perception of discontinuity, the best of our social historians have been working toward a paradigm of continuity that treats the Middle Ages and early modern times as one epoch, challenged but not disrupted by Luther and the Reformation. One of its finest spokesmen, Thomas A. Brady, Jr., is turning increasingly to the study of the resourcefulness and flexibility of the Holy Roman Empire, able to cope with the short-lived tragedy—as he is inclined to believe—of the Reformation. With his assumption that the rural Peasants' War was the most significant feature of the Reformation betrayed by Luther, Brady early on grasped the untenability of Bernd Moeller's romantic City Reformation thesis: a thin distillation of sixteenth-century religious propaganda and polemical sermons, it was unsubstantiated by archival reconstruction of social support among the citizenry.[7] In this second master narrative, the Reformation appears as an interlude, soon losing its potential, caught between the interests of lords and serfs, while weakened inside its own ranks by fighting between the two factions of zealots and *politiques*.[8]

A third grand perspective, whose most prominent spokesman is Heinz Schilling, would have been much easier for me to reject had not Schilling just published a comprehensive study of Europe from 1250 to 1750, which complicated matters.[9] Elsewhere I have expressed my considerable reservations concerning Schilling's structuralist view of history as an inevitable process, often attended by the connotation of progress. This appears to me to marginalize cultural history and *mentalité* and does not allow a place for religion other than as a subservient factor to state formation. In his new, broader vision of *Die neue Zeit*, however, Schilling succeeds in putting his process approach in better perspective. It is a comprehensive interpretation that deserves immediate translation into English.

In the meantime, however, a formidable number of German and American historians have followed the call of the earlier Schilling and continued to work within the confines of confessionalization and state formation, with such vigor and yield that this school should be addressed as a separate approach. It has the great advantage of bypassing the whole debate about continuity and discontinuity by taking Luther and the Reformation seriously as one of the confessions that will put an indelible stamp on seventeenth- and eighteenth-century Germany. Unfortunately, however, its very preoccupation with modernity feeds into a presentism that I regard as one of the major weaknesses of recent historiography.[10] A case in point is Richard Marius's book *Martin Luther: The Christian between God and Death*.[11] Instead of attempting to understand the time or thought of Martin Luther, Marius presents a series of revealingly modern reactions to Luther, basically casting him as a fanatical twentieth-century fundamentalist.

Although such presentism may entertain, it cannot sustain. As to the alluring notion of process, however, it has strongly influenced our understanding of the fifteenth century. When the so-called process is derailed or contradicted by the actual course of events, either a crisis or a failure is stipulated, depending on the metahistorical position of the author considering it. In spite of promising avenues of research as well as the sober reconstruction of gradual change, which other scholars as well as myself have amply documented, fifteenth-century studies are rife with crisis and failure theories, mistakenly cast in terms of a process that led from the end of the Middle Ages to the beginning of modern times.[12] Medieval legend knew it was the devil who wanted the chronicler to recount history as a process by presenting a straight line between cause and effect, between sequence and consequence. The fourteenth-century preacher's handbook *Fasciculus morum* taught that only the devil could measure the distance between heaven and earth, since he alone, in his fall, followed a straight line.[13] It is revealing that the Western mind has changed the original meaning of "devious" into "erring," so that which literally meant "departure from a straight line" took on the meaning of "deviant." Only by exorcizing this devil can we advance our understanding of history and recover a fresh awareness of unexpected turns of events on the contingent intersection of lines that are not straight. In short, the good historian is bound to be devious.

In what follows I intend to deal with four cultural clusters, which I will call "trends" so as not to fall into the terminological pit of describing them as a single dominant process. I will treat each of these trends equally rather than as subordinate elements in a preestablished grand narrative, and I will trace them through what is fashionably called the long fifteenth century. Some forty years ago, in order to gain an untrammeled perspective freed from Lutheran or Catholic confessional lines, one had to insist on the study of the later Middle Ages in its own right.[14] Today, however, we may draw on scholarly advances in all four of these clusters. With them we can stay on course without resorting to the blinders once needed for protection against the distracting glare of later events. By venturing well into the periods of the Renaissance and the Reformation—the long fifteenth century—the concept of the late Middle Ages is able to withstand partisanship and prejudice and establish its legitimacy. Late medieval studies have come of age.

Almost twenty-five years ago, I presented what I called a premature profile of major currents in the fourteenth century.[15] I intend to take up the same quest here by examining new challenges, events, and trends, taking into account the impact of the Black Death, the rise of the Third Estate, the decline and survival of conciliarism, the monastic mission to the masses, and the rising tide of anti-Semitism, touching finally on Renaissance humanism and the cutting edge of the New Learning.

THE DEVASTATING IMPACT OF THE BLACK DEATH

Although we no longer describe the impact of the Black Death on Europe in terms quite as stark as we once did, there is no disputing its severe demographic repercussions. In its first horrendous phase from 1347 to 1351, the bubonic plague raced through Europe from Marseilles throughout France, Italy, England, the Low Countries, Germany, and Russia, killing one-third of Europe's population of some 75 to 80 million people. Not until the end of the sixteenth century would the population return to its pre-plague levels. It is therefore understandable that historians like to refer to the aftermath of the plague in the fifteenth century as a period of demographic depression. The problems begin, however, when we have to specify the economic and social impacts of the steep decline in rural and urban populations. Even the effect on mentality as expressed in the *ars moriendi,* the dance macabre and *Totentanz,*[16] is no longer a matter of course in view of the findings of Jan de Vries that "death rates rose in a period that saw the final disappearance from Europe of the bubonic plague."[17] Recent scholarship has turned its interest to the patterns of recovery and accordingly has shifted its emphasis from doom and stagnation to the revitalization of Europe by innovative crisis management. As Bartolomé Yun put it, "From the vantage point of the rest of the world, this era marked the birth of Europe."[18] We are confronted with a whole complex of factors with widely differing regional variants and shaped by such historical contingencies as state formation and warfare.

With respect to our first cluster, the intellectual climate of the fifteenth century, it is helpful to take a closer look at a study of the plague by David Herlihy.[19] Herlihy deals successively with the medical dimension, the new economic and demographic system that broke the "Malthusian dead-lock," and finally, in the part which concerns us here, with the new modes of thought and feeling. Whereas the medical history of the Black Death would perhaps be written today with other nuances, the conclusion of the second part stands, accurately summarizing the salient characteristics of the post-plague recovery as a more diversified economy, an intensified use of capital, a more sophisticated technology, and a higher standard of living.[20] Problems, however, emerge when these new findings are grafted onto the old tree of Etienne Gilson's end-of-the-road notion of the late Middle Ages. Herlihy invokes a Saint Thomas–driven caricature of late medieval nominalism to explain the emergence of a new mentality: "The human intellect had not the power to penetrate the metaphysical structures of the universe. It could do no more than observe events as they flowed. Moreover, the omnipotent power of God meant in the last analysis that there could be no fixed natural order. God could change what He wanted, when He wanted. The nominalists looked on a universe dominated by arbitrary motions. Aquinas' sublime sense of order was hard to reconcile with the experience of the plague—unpredictable in its appearances and course, unknowable in its origins, yet destructive in its impact. The nominalist argument was consonant with the disordered experiences of late medieval life."[21]

Whereas David Herlihy is remembered with respect and gratitude for his signal contribution to medieval family history and, as in this case, for the all-too-rare effort to chart the interplay between intellectual and social history, his admiration for Thomas Aquinas as "this great Dominican" with his "sublime sense of order" may well explain why such an eminently critical scholar uncritically perpetuates assumptions of the past that in the past thirty years have been shown to be caricatures.[22] Ironically, Herlihy's final conclusion can readily be accepted: "The nominalist argument was consonant with the disordered experiences of late medieval life." The experience of the plague may in fact help us understand the fifteenth-century ascendancy of nominalism, its innovations in the whole field ranging from theology to science, and its successful invasion of schools and universities, where it was firmly established as the *via moderna*. What must have seemed to conservative Thomists of that time to be a threat to the hierarchy between heaven and earth was actually a fact-finding search for order by demarcating the distinct realms of faith and reason. In the domain of faith the epochal shift from God-as-Being to God-as-Person allowed for a fresh reading of the sources of the church in Scripture and tradition as attesting to the personal God of the covenant. At the same time, in the realm of reason the new quest for the laws of nature could be initiated once physics was liberated from its domestication by meta-physics, the speculative welding of Aristotle and the Scriptures. In any account of the transformation of the West, the crucial metamorphosis of the capital sin of curiosity into the nominalists' *bona curiositas* validated the exploration of the real world and is therefore to be given a high place in the range of factors explaining the "birth of Europe."[23]

Not even in the *Cambridge History of Late Medieval Philosophy* would Herlihy have learned of the new findings, for that authoritative work only occasionally touches on the fifteenth century.[24] In spite of the achievements of John Emery Murdoch in enlarging the scope of the history of science and of William Courtenay in tracing the antecedents of fourteenth-century philosophy, there has not yet been initiated a comprehensive study of the encounter between physics and metaphysics in the fifteenth century.[25] Only in its final section on the "defeat, neglect, and revival of scholasticism" does the *Cambridge History* cover the fifteenth century, whereas in the more substantial chapters on "happiness" and "conscience," the fifteenth century is ignored. This lopsided, old-fashioned preoccupation with the logical dimension of nominalism cannot help us understand such a card-carrying nominalist as Wessel Gansfort, who interpreted his move from Thomas and Scotus to the via moderna as a conversion and as the key to entering new intellectual territory, setting him on course toward a fresh and therefore challenging interpretation of Christianity.[26] Though developed in the rarified discourse of academic disputations and cast in the heavy language of terminist logic, the fundamental advance in shifting the terms of the centuries-old debate on universals was that radical turn from the deductive to the inductive method. This legitimized a new search for the laws of nature unencumbered by supernatural presuppositions. Whereas the many *incurati* who joined the cause made sure that theology would serve the *itinerarium mentis ad Deum,* the arts faculty was set free to pursue the *itinerarium mentis ad mundum.* It may not be a coincidence that works of Pierre d'Ailly, one of the masters of the via moderna in the tradition of Jean Buridan and Nicole Oresme, were found in the library of Nicolaus Copernicus. Rightly understood as the creative platform from which long-held, no-longer-tenable assumptions could be reassessed, the new critical spirit fostered by nominalism was part of the intellectual reorientation of the long fifteenth century. Whether and to what extent it was a factor in the pursuit of wealth and knowledge that drove the Age of Discovery is a difficult question for historians. It does not seem to be visible in the management of the crisis of the Black Death. Not only the stars but the whole realm of human society and nature could be investigated, as it were, with new eyes.

FROM PAPAL RULE TO POLITICAL CONCILIARISM

Conciliarism is perhaps the best-known and most intensely investigated aspect of fifteenth-century religious history. The Councils of Pisa (1409), Constance (1414–1418), and Basel (1431–1449) have long formed part of the canon in courses on medieval history. More important, perhaps, they were recognized as key events even as they were happening. Over the past thirty years, the study of conciliarism has taken on a new vitality and a novel direction, especially under the influence of Brian Tierney, Francis Oakley, and Antony Black—the first through his discovery of the antecedents of conciliar theory in canon law, and the latter two in drawing out the implications of conciliarism for constitutional and parliamentary history.[27] As Tierney makes clear, the new findings have not gone uncontested and have even found significant, indeed passionate, resistance.[28] This cannot surprise us when we consider the near reversal of the traditional roles assigned to papalism as the defender of orthodoxy and conciliarism as the at-least-potentially heretical alternative. Conciliarism proves to be the outgrowth of the earliest Decretist cohort in the evolution of canon law, whereas the doctrine of papal infallibility is shown to

8

have originated quite late in the circles of heretical Franciscans. *Structures of the Church,* with its proclamation of the superiority of the council above the papacy, perhaps the most lasting work of Hans Küng on the Council of Constance, gives this scholarly discussion the sharp edge of public controversy, fueled and intensified by the debate about the reception of *Lumen Gentium* in the wake of Vatican II.[29]

Understandable as this concentration on the decrees of the Council of Constance and the legitimacy of the conciliar claims may be, the relevancy of these issues for modern times led to a preoccupation with the rise and fall of conciliarism as an ecclesiological issue. This limited our purview and warped our understanding of what I would like to call political conciliarism. Studies on Pope Eugene IV (1431–1447) and Pius II (1458–1464), as well as the crossing of party lines by several leading conciliarists such as Nicolas Cusanus, have left the impression that the mere transferal of the Council of Basel to Ferrara and its continuation in Florence from 1437 to 1439 marked the end of conciliarism. The suspension of the meeting in Basel may well have derailed conciliar theory as envisaged by Constance, but it did not spell the end of conciliar reality. In the form of political conciliarism, it would shape the emerging nation states and remain an influential principle until thwarted—more by the growth of royal absolutism than by claims of papal supremacy.

In 1438, the French King Charles VII confirmed the liberties of the Gallican church in the form of a charter called the Pragmatic Sanction of Bourges, thus achieving one part of the conciliar platform concerned with curtailing papal jurisdiction. Bernard Chevalier has dismissed this charter as an illusion, arguing that "the French clergy escaped neither papal authority nor royal control."[30] If this had been the case, there would have been no need for Pope Leo X to seek the concordat with Francis I that was concluded in Bologna in 1516. And even this delineation of papal and royal rule over the French church did not prevent Henry II from seeing to it that the French prelates would vote during the Council of Trent on a Gallican platform in keeping with the liberties of 1438. Moreover, it has not been recognized that Calvin's campaign against the so-called Nicodemites had as its prime target the Gallican faction that hoped to combine new reformed ideas with the consolidation of their Gallican church. A number of well-placed, influential French bishops, among them Calvin's early school friend Gérard Roussel,[31] regarded themselves as leaders of the Gallican church. If Calvin had coopted their platform, it might have been broad enough to forestall the need to contain or exile Huguenots. As it happened, both the *Église prétendue réformée* and French political conciliarism saw their designs aborted not in papal Rome but in absolutist Versailles.

In England, the King's Great Matter allowed political conciliarism to bypass the formidable obstacle of royal supremacy that was to abort the movement in France. Notwithstanding certain queries and revisions in details, Geoffrey Elton has succeeded in reconstructing the achievement of Henry VIII's reign by reuniting the story of the establishment of the *ecclesia Anglicana* with the birth of the early modern parliamentary English state.[32] Nevertheless, our preoccupation with the question of whether it was a reformation from above or from below as well as with the question of continuity despite the "stripped altars" of the newly reformed English churches has not allowed us to see clearly enough the extent to which the Anglican church is a variant in the broader European story of political conciliarism. The Europeanization of English history, for which John Elliott called in his inaugural address as Oxford's Regius Professor of History, will permit us to get a firmer grasp of this aspect of the long fifteenth century.

A brief look at the German territories will complete this section. Again, political conciliarism supplies a hitherto unwritten chapter in the history of the Reformation in Germany. The Acceptatio of Mainz (1439) and the Vienna Concordat (1448) contain far less of the reform program of the Council of Basel than the Pragmatic Sanction of Bourges in France. Yet, once confronted with the challenge of Martin Luther, the formation of an *ecclesia Germanica* fell just one vote short of realization. In September 1524, the imperial Diet was cited to Speyer and was prepared to vote on the establishment of a German church with the full support of all imperial estates, including the anti-Lutheran prince bishops and the Emperor Charles V's brother Ferdinand. Our historians' preoccupation with what actually happened probably causes us to miss out on the significance of alternative paths that history might have taken. Such virtual history would illuminate the actual course of events.

THE MODERN DEVOTION: A TIP OF THE ICEBERG

For a long time the Modern Devotion was presented as the Renaissance north of the Alps and as the first stage in the liberation that was the Reformation in the Low Countries. Inspired by such scholars as Willem Lourdaux and R. R. Post, preoccupation with the Modern Devotion as the cradle of the Renaissance and the Reformation gave way to the study of the movement on the basis of its own testimonies. Post's richly documented, groundbreaking study, *The Modern Devotion,* was published in *Studies in Medieval and Reformation Thought* in 1968 and widely hailed because he approached the fifteenth century on its own terms. In our view of the long fifteenth century, we cannot avoid reengagement with the question of its relation to the coming of the Reformation, but we will do so in terms that Post's magnum opus already suggested in its subtitle: "Confrontation with Reformation and Humanism."[33]

For our approach to these questions we are greatly in the debt of two scholars who have recently produced critical editions of key documents. John Van Engen has deepened our understanding of the relation between the original vision of the Brethren and Sisters of the Common Life and the later regular canons of Windesheim.[34] Whereas Van Engen recovered the rich regional variants in the response to the steady pressure on the *devoti* to join the regular clergy, Kaspar Elm has presented the movement as placing itself programmatically, as he put it, "between the monastery and the world." By describing the *Devotio Moderna* as the tip of the iceberg of what he called *Semireligiösentum,* Elm liberated the devoti from the isolation in which proud Dutch scholars had placed "their" movement.[35]

The movement of the Brethren and Sisters of the Common Life was a striking success. Within the borders of today's Netherlands alone, there were two hundred foundations between 1380 and 1480, the heyday of the movement. Of this number, 35 monasteries and 30 nunneries belonged to the network of the Windesheim Congregation. It would be more accurate, however, to invert the traditional designation and call the movement the Sisters and Brethren of the Common Life, for the extent to which the Devotio Moderna was a women's movement has not yet been fully absorbed. More than 52 percent, namely 105 houses, were communities of the Sisters and only 15 percent, 30 in total, were establishments of the Brethren of the Common Life.[36]

On April 3, 1418, as the Council of Constance was in its last days, Jean Gerson raised his voice to defend the movement against the accusation of heresy by Matthew Grabow. The Dominican Grabow had charged the Sisters and Brethren with being a cover organization for Beghards and Beguines. Much has been made of Gerson's defense, for which the devoti considered him to have the status of a church father; nevertheless, a scrutiny of the history of individual convents shows that house after house was forced to accept an official rule, usually that of the third order of the Franciscans. Grabow thus proved to have a longer reach than Gerson. Notwithstanding this general trend toward regularization and remonastication in the direction of the Windesheimers, Geert Groote's original vision of the common life as the crucial alternative to the cloistered life was retained in the basic tenant that *religio* should not be understood as the monastic life but as Christian faith. For all three branches of the movement—the Sisters, the Brethren, and the Canons Regular of the Windesheim Congregation—*purus Christianus verus monachus* (the true Christian is the true monk).

In order to understand Erasmus's view of the early modern Christian city as a religious community, his *magnum monasterium,* and to grasp the impact of Luther's programmatic treatise *On the Monastic Vows* (1521), we will have to take into consideration that the Devotio Moderna in all its phases insisted that it observed the oldest rule, namely the Golden Rule, and acknowledged the highest abbot, namely Jesus Christ. As I read the evidence, the original intention of the movement is misunderstood when taken to be antimonastic. On the contrary, it should be entered under the rubric of "the pursuit of holiness" as a parallel phenomenon to the growing fifteenth-century Observantist movement. Only in the rhetoric of the defense against such attacks as Grabow's could the program of the Devotion be represented as serving a more general late medieval criticism of the friars.

The same caveat applies to the recent investigation into the late medieval roots of anticlericalism. Even if I assume the broadest definition of the term, I can find no trace of anticlericalism or of its related form, the disparaging of the parish clergy as irreformable. We find such sentiments not among the devoti, but in the sermons of the Observant friars. In fact, great awe for the office of the priest is evident in the diaries and chronicles recording the hesitation of Brethren urged to seek ordination. In this awe we touch on an essential characteristic of the movement, namely the *timor Dei,* in the Dutch chronicles usually rendered as *vrees* or *anxt.* According to Thomas à Kempis and Petrus Hoorn, the fifteenth-century biographers of Geert Groote, this anxious awe so dominated the movement's founder that he often abstained from the Eucharist, preferring to participate in the communion service *spiritualiter* rather than *sacramentaliter.* Although it would be interesting to consider how Groote's sentiment might feed into the discussion of the Ozment thesis of the Reformation as a response to late medieval anxiety and guilt, we will confine ourselves here to its relevance to our main subject, the long fifteenth century. The respectful awe that led Groote to distinguish between partaking of the Lord's body sacramentaliter and spiritualiter was already a long-established part of traditional church doctrine. In existentially mobilizing it, Groote alerts us to an unexplored aspect of the related *Corpus Christi* procession. This ritual was—among many other things—a form of spiritual communion, and its emphasis on spiritual eating did not challenge the significance of the Eucharist. On the contrary, it enhanced it.

The implied sufficiency of the spiritual eating is exactly the missing link to Cornelius Hoen's famous treatise of 1524. Probably connected to Wessel Gansfort, who was living in a sister house in Groningen and closely associated with the Brethren in Zwolle, Hoen's letter was spurned by Luther but became the basis for the famous symbolic interpretation of Huldrych Zwingli and the spiritualist left wing of the Reformation. Here the Eucharistic meal was highly honored as eating spiritualiter, regardless of the denunciation by all the critics including Luther.

Living between the world and the monastery did not imply any moral compromise. The chronicles attest to the fact that in housing, food, and dress, the devoti lived an ascetic life more rigorous even than that of the Observant friars. Augustine Renaudet has vividly described the rigor of life in the Parisian Collège de Montaigu, the most westerly extension of the movement and the training ground for Erasmus, Calvin, and Ignatius of Loyola. Jean Standonck, the Collège's *spiritus rector,* is characterized by domains were transformed into real estate and the church became a corporation subservient to its bankers."[39] Although he might be embarrassed to find himself associated with them, this modern author's sentiments are not far removed from those expressed by the devoti seeking to establish a viable counterculture of simple life between Church and World.

In this final section we turn from the sotto voce of the Devotio Moderna to Huppert's "thundering clerics," the itinerant Franciscan preachers north and south of the Alps. Their vociferous public platform of reform, quite different from that of the Brethren, and the astounding response it evoked reveal a development without which our characterization of the fifteenth century would be deficient. At the beginning of the next century, under the withering critique of Renaissance humanists and reformers, the status of the friars would be significantly diminished. Thus the success of the early Jesuits would be partly due to their careful avoidance of any form of association with the mendicant friars in dress, rule, or organization. In the fifteenth century, however, the friars were sought after by kings and bishops, princes and town councils, and urged to undertake preaching campaigns. They gathered masses of attentive listeners on village commons and town squares with widely reported miraculous healings and dramatic conversions. By carefully reconstructing the message and impact of two of the most popular of the thundering friars— Bernardino da Siena, who began his career as an itinerant preacher in Italy in 1405, and his spiritual successor, Giovanni da Capistrano, who started his trek north of the Alps in 1451—Kaspar Elm has made a valiant effort to overcome long-standing caricatures.[40] Understandably, there is an apologetic touch to Elm's defense against the charge of superstitious mass manipulation. But two precious, related insights emerge from his close scrutiny of the sources. In the first place, both men, strict papalists, opposed—and indeed persecuted—the Fraticelli, Franciscans who interpreted Saint Francis and his time as the beginning of the end time, bringing with it the end of established, papal Catholicism. Rejecting this apocalyptic reading, the two preachers called for immediate conversion of sinners in fear and trembling of the Final Judgment.

Elm's second insight is directly related to the theme of individual conversion: both Bernardino da Siena and Giovanni da Capistrano also insisted on a reform of society through the restoration of family, commune, and social peace in cities and territories. On May 18, 1451, in Villach, the first city on Giovanni's transalpine itinerary, he started his campaign "in the name of Jesus Christ and the Holy Bernadine of Siena." Trekking through Austria to Vienna and points north, he spoke with such fervor about social injustice that audiences in one place after another responded by heaping up piles of Fastnacht masks, dice, playing cards, jewelry, and fashionable shoes and dresses, and setting fire to them. As all reports make clear, their aim was to bring about a reordering of public life even before conversion.[41] What they were attempting to bring about can perhaps best be understood against the backdrop of the Benedictine vision of the *stabilitas loci* "in paradise," that is, within the walls of the monastery. The itinerant friars abandoned the ideal of the stabilitas loci for a ministry of begging and preaching, and thus exported the monastic experience and quality of life into the world by seeking to establish, as they put it, the *civitas Christiana* in secular space and time.

The story of itinerant Franciscan preaching has never made it to the list of key events of the century. Enlightenment-bred scholars have been embarrassed by the credulity of sources recording the fabulous deeds of the friars as faith healers. Historians of conciliarism were intent on the growth of the conciliar idea rather than on these preachers of papal supremacy; and finally, when these friars do appear in a central role it is as characters on the darkest pages of the books on the history of anti-Semitism. In his study of mendicant persecution of Jews, Jeremy Cohen concentrates on the thirteenth century and does not go beyond the fourteenth.[42] Had he done so he would have been little surprised by Giovanni da Capistrano's active role in the Breslau trial of 1453 dealing with Jewish desecration of the host: "Every Jew trembles at his very name!"[43]

The three themes of superstition, papalism, and anti-Semitism have kept our friars on the books, but only as exempla to prove the need for a Protestant or Catholic reformation in the century to come. Quite apart from the fact that exactly the same three ingredients provided continuity between the later Middle Ages and the era of Renaissance and Reformation, the key goal in the mission of the friars should not be overlooked. They were engaged in a concerted effort to defend and extend the boundaries of the civitas Christiana in a crusade against the devil. To them the

Evil One was no longer confined to the monastic inner hell of *tristitia* (melancholy), *acedia* (apathy), and the *Anfechtungen* (temptations) of the soul, but threatened public life in the form of the mammon of luxury and the might of the Jews. Bernardino da Siena and Giovanni da Capistrano were but two of an as yet uncounted army of friars plodding from village to village with their urgent message of conversion in the face of the coming judgment. Even more important, the preaching friars were spearheading a much larger campaign to reach the grassroots of society and protect them against contamination by the demons "of these modern times." As Robert J. Bast has shown, the invention of the printing press allowed for a widespread assault on ignorance: catechisms, long held to be the typical tools of the age of Renaissance and Reformation, were published, distributed, and debated throughout Europe.[44] The target group is not only the laity but the clergy as well. And Peter Dykema has carefully documented the concerted effort to provide the lower village clergy with hands-on instruction to help them execute their daily priestly and pastoral duties.[45]

I shall try to summarize. In the wake of the Black Death, the greatest natural disaster ever to strike Europe, and with the intensive efforts to cope with its effects, the centuries-old pursuit of holiness came into conflict with the new pursuit of profit. This called for new responses. In the domain of the intellectual life of Europe, the via moderna provided tools for discerning order in the chaos of unrealistic speculation. In the realm of polity and politics, conciliarism survived well beyond Basel, providing the constitutional solution of territorial churches. In the domain of mentalité and religious experience, the Modern Devotion and the preaching friars proved to be representative of a much more widespread effort to extend the communal life of the monastery into secular space and time.

All of this could be well established by looking only at the shorter fifteenth century. Yet, the view to the long fifteenth century reveals how important it is to disregard the artificial divide of the year 1500 and allows us to discern the innovations of sixteenth-century reform and reformation in the light of an unbroken continuity. Toward the end of the long fifteenth century, medieval Catholicism does not display any of the characteristics we have come to expect under the tutelage of Etienne

Gilson, Joseph Lortz, or for that matter, nineteenth-century Protestant historians. We could not confirm such general epitaphs for the age as philosophical skepticism, theological ambiguity, social dissolution, or moral dissipation. On the contrary, late medieval Christian society showed all the signs of the vitality and resourcefulness necessary for effective crisis management. The fifteenth century appears as a time of remarkable recovery from the onslaught of the Black Death, the confusion caused by the Western schism, the challenge of the Fraticelli, and the failure of the Hussite crusades. Even the sharp rise in the tide of anti-Semitism fits this general picture, insofar as not merely the annual period of Lent but especially the periodic waves of revival always spelled dangerous times for Europe's Jewish population.

There are fault lines to be noticed as well. With the emergence of the national states was a concomitant jockeying for power that resulted in near-incessant military conflicts punctuated by short periods of peace. Quite apart from the constant Turkish threat, the Hundred Years' War slid over into the phase of aggressive extension of the papal states and the colonizing aspirations of France and Spain in Italy. In reaction, nearly all of the emerging intellectual elite north of the Alps—be they an Erasmus, a Luther, or a Zwingli—went through a phase of pacifism that was to remain part of their dream of a new society even after the Turkish advance forced them to compromise their ideal.

A second fault line would prove to be more consequential: the spread of historical-critical testing of the foundations of faith, Scripture, and tradition. Lorenzo Valla's proof of the forgery of the Donation of Constantine enjoyed only a limited Italian circulation until the end of the fifteenth century. The prosecution of Wessel Gansfort for his biblical findings by the Inquisitors Jacob Hoek and Antonius de Castro, O.P., was not widely known until the documents were published in 1521. But the concerted effort of the Dominicans Jacob van Hoogstraten and Silvestro Prierias to achieve the condemnation of Johannes Reuchlin in a litigation process that stretched from 1514 to 1521 was notorious, pitting the highest echelon of the medieval teaching office against the most recent findings of a renowned biblical scholar. The *Letters of Obscure Men* (1515, 1517) was far more than a spoof of self-appointed defenders of Renaissance humanism.[46] In the form of satire, it confronts the puritan vision of the civitas Christiana propagated by our itinerant Franciscans, and it questions the very authority of the friars. Just as the Franciscan vision materialized into social control of the marginalized Jews, so the Dominican guardians of orthodoxy sought to mobilize the church against scholarly dissent among ranking members of the Christian intelligentsia. Turning from Wessel and Reuchlin to Erasmus and Luther, they met with varying degrees of success. Wessel died in 1489, and Reuchlin in 1523, just after his condemnation. Erasmus sought to defend the *consensus ecclesiae*, the Catholic middle ground between "the rabid friars"—with the Dominicans on the one hand and the Luther faction on the other.

It is therefore not by chance that we encounter, among Luther's first opponents, three battle-tested Dominicans: Tetzel, Prierias, and Hoogstraten. By that time, however, Luther could no longer be written off as just another irreverent intellectual. He had become a leader in the movement that, to his own surprise, developed an alternative vision of the civitas Christiana, hence initiating the end of the long fifteenth century.

With reference to Protestant triumphalism, I do not hesitate to uphold the lasting significance of Luther, broken, redirected, and constantly reemerging in a variety of new social constellations, at times perhaps more creeping than soaring, but always grounding the modern quest for moral man in an immoral world. Here I stand with Moeller. Yet Luther as Person der Weltgeschichte is a rhetorical claim beyond the scope of any serious validation: I fail to share the view of discontinuity that was embedded in Bismarck's anti-Catholic Kulturkampf and the Prussian Protestant claim to advance European civilization.

Double-sided must also be my assessment of the Brady vision. I see Brady as a partner in my own program of pursuing historical continuity; I see him as an opponent of my concomitant effort to identify more accurately the innovative dimension of early modern Europe, including the Reformation. I profit richly from Brady's work on Hapsburg German territorial holdings, with his sophisticated grasp of the institutional resources of the Empire. He shows how it was able to weather the storm of the Reformation, and he has a profound sense of the sustaining, inspiring force of religion. But he does not sufficiently relativize his thesis of continuity with an equal emphasis on the European-wide emergence of an antiabsolutist, antipapal republican countermovement—too easily ridiculed as Whig history. By positioning himself in Germany he gains a strategically placed, central observation post, but for our whole period this also has a major drawback. As I see it, the so-called Peace of Augsburg of 1555 caused Germany to implode by burdening it with the legally complex execution of the legally complex mandate to correlate *regio* and *religio*. The German *Sonderweg* did not start with Bismarck or Versailles but with Germany's withdrawal from European affairs after 1555. Henceforth Germany would be bent on securing the Teutonic walls against the Turks and establishing an internal balance of power while mortgaging Europe's future to the Roman Curia, the Jesuits, and the Huguenots. The European phase of the Reformation, for most of Europe the *first* Reformation, will have to be brought to the center of a truly grand narrative with a radical marginalizing of German political, cultural, and theological sentiment. The reformed Reformation of international Calvinism was, body and soul, programmatically carrying the burden of *Europa afflicta*. Spreading through France to the Low Countries, it thrived under the heavy hand of Philip II and the zealous cleansing of Alva's Spanish troops. Thus autocratic Spain produced refugee masses that were forced to abandon the medieval social contract of stabilitas loci. Driven spiritually out of the Middle Ages, they were to become settlers of new restless worlds beyond the ken of an Aquinas or a Luther.

Communalism, republican self-government, and the rejection of political and religious tyranny will continue to dominate our research agenda. The new millennium seems modern, but—and here I share the new epochal vision of Heinz Schilling—this very modern agenda can be seen emerging above the horizon of the very long fifteenth century.

II

LUTHER AND THE VIA MODERNA
The Philosophical Backdrop of
the Reformation Breakthrough

Bonaventura inter scholasticos doctores optimus est.
—Martin Luther, *Table Talk*

LUTHER AND THE NEW PHILOSOPHY

The idea of a *philosophia perennis* based on the explication of self-evident truths (*veritates per sese notae*) still had its adherents in the later Middle Ages, as did the related idea of philosophy as the ready handmaiden (*ancilla*) of theology. By Luther's time, however, they had been forced onto the defensive, surviving mainly in the Dominican network.[1] Against this fading background, Luther achieved his own redefinition of the range and role of philosophy (although Thomistic metaphysics reasserted itself in the wake of the Aristotelian renaissance and the Counter Reformation). Luther was an eager student of the tradition shaped by Occam, Gregory of Rimini, Pierre d'Ailly, and Gabriel Biel,[2] yet his insistence on learning to spell anew the grammar of theology[3] from God's own lips, as it were,[4] implied a new assignment for human *ratio*. Accordingly, the future reformer had first to campaign for a

21

redefinition of the relation of theology to philosophy, which he achieved by divesting the deductive method of its metaphysical foundations. No longer would deduction be the canonical means of reaching truth. Philosophical induction, from observed facts to legitimate conclusions, would take its place. Thus reason would assume its magisterial role in the formation of secular wisdom, transforming nature into culture: Reason is the principal and author of everything ("ratio omnium rerum res et caput . . . inventrix et gubernatrix").[5] An overlooked aspect of this formulation is that it assigns reason a specific role as the lord protector of a civilization threatened by the chaos of evil in the end time, the last days.

Not all interpreters would accept this view of Luther's quest for the unique grammar of theology and of his relegation of philosophy to a secondary role in the foundation of Revelation. The 1998 papal encyclical *Fides et Ratio* leaves the impression that Luther's concern to liberate theology and philosophy from their mutually suffocating embrace was not merely erroneous but redundant, because the right balance had already been attained in the thirteenth century.[6] It awards Thomas Aquinas the exalted title of "apostolus veritatis" (§44) because he achieved the highest standard of truth ("eo quod universalem, obiectivam et transcendentem veritatem semper asseruit") by reconciling faith and reason. Thus he bequeathed the perfect, unassailable, and ultimate "philosophia essendi et non apparendi dumtaxat" (§44). After Saint Thomas, however, tragedy struck: "Seiunctae a ratione fidei tragoedia." The bond between philosophy and theology was disastrously torn asunder: "Attamen, inde ab exeunte Medio Aevo legitima distinctio inter has duas cognitionis areas paulatim in nefastum discidium mutata est" (§45).

It is surprising that the encyclical can seriously put forward a view in which Saint Thomas stands at the peak (*culmen*) of medieval philosophy and the later Middle Ages as "the End of the Road."[7] This view has been disproved by some fifty years of new critical editions and detailed research. How can we understand Luther's laborious effort to find the distinction between the "areas of cognition in philosophy and theology" if that distinction had already been known since the thirteenth century?

At issue here are conflicting views of the Reformation. Either that movement was a collapse or it was a breakthrough. Either the Reformation is held responsible for the disintegration of the medieval synthesis and was, as the papal encyclical put it, the breeding ground of atheism and fideism, or it discovered the personal God of biblical revelation and ultimately made possible a secular culture no longer relegated to the realm of limited subsistence.

In the seventy years between the demise of the immensely learned Dominican Heinrich Denifle in 1905 and the death of the politically compromised Joseph Lortz in 1975, the treatment of Luther in Catholic research has been lively and at times sharp.[8] The shift in tone from Denifle to Lortz can easily lead the reader to underestimate what they had in common. Although Lortz loved Luther as much as Denifle hated him, both scholars used a common Thomistic standard in denying the legitimacy of Luther's Reformation. Stridently denouncing Luther as a scoundrel (*Schalk*), accusing him of lying, and generally condemning him for a debased character (*Gemeinheit*), Denifle, on the one hand, rises to Luther's own level of excited polemic. Lortz, on the other hand, seems to reflect a new ecumenical climate, indulging this eminently religious German (*homo religiosus*)—so unlike the indifferent Dutch Erasmus—for the unfortunate philosophical antecedents which led him astray.[9]

Although Denifle sees Luther as distorting the medieval tradition, Lortz thinks it *was* the medieval tradition, namely Occamistic nominalism, that distorted Luther. Luther has now been promoted from Halbwisser to Halbhörer, a dubious advancement perhaps not unrelated to the fact that while Lortz, albeit selectively, listened more to Luther, Denifle knew more about the scholastic tradition.

After Lortz, Catholic scholars of Luther went in two different directions. Whereas Erwin Iserloh and Remigius Bäumer continued the confessional approach of Denifle and Lortz, Hubert Jedin, and (with connections to the *apertura* achieved by Hans Küng) Otto Hermann Pesch, Peter Manns, and Jos Vercruysse followed a descriptive one.[10] Of course, confessionalism is by no means restricted to Catholic scholars of Luther. The philosopher Kurt Flasch equates Luther's rejection of the Thomistic philosophy of being with a rejection of philosophy as such: Flasch disparages Luther's attack on reason and his doctrinaire views on grace ("Luther's Schmähung der Vernunft und seine anknüpfungs—und vermittlungs-feindliche Gnadenlehre"). In surmising that Protestant intellectuals needed this Luther so they could cope with the shock of the demise of the

German "Staatsprotestantismus" after the Revolution of 1918, Flasch reveals his outburst to be a confessional exercise in psychohistory.[11]

Two other evaluations of late medieval nominalism occur in the work of Hans Blumenberg and Rudolph Lorenz.[12] Apparently unaware that the late medieval dialectic between God's *potentia absoluta* and his *potentia ordinata* indicates a paradigm shift in the conception of the God who acts in history, Blumenberg pitches nominalism against modernity by positing that the unpredictable freedom of the personal God necessarily crushes legitimate human self-realization and self-exploration. To be sure, self-realization and self-exploration are characteristic qualities of modern times, but Blumenberg's thesis, accepted in its own way by Lorenz, is based on the old misunderstanding of the nominalistic "Willkürgott," the notion that God's freedom implies an arbitrary suppression of human agency.[13]

Finally, Protestant Luther scholars of the nationalist Prussian school continue to display a marked interest in keeping Luther at a safe distance from the via moderna by reducing the broad movement of late medieval nominalism to Occamism, and by reducing Occamism to its doctrine of justification. By emphasizing Luther's rejection of the alleged Pelagianism of Occam they leave the false impression that Luther altogether severed his ties to nominalism.[14]

The Protestant dogmatician Eberhard Jüngel even goes so far as to regard Luther's doctrine of the hidden God in his *De servo arbitrio* (1525) as a complete rejection of his nominalistic heritage. Far from being an interpretation of late medieval nominalism, *De servo arbitrio,* he declares, is its "schärfste Kritik."[15] If the recent tendency of Protestant theology to reach back beyond the modernist Karl Barth to the Old Way of Friedrich Schleiermacher proves to be lasting, we will have come full circle to the status quo that pertained before the new Franciscan paradigm, once again in the domain of the *philosophia essendi* and its speculative assumptions.[16] And starting from the presuppositions of the Old Way, no amount of learning will give us insight into Luther's way of thinking.

With conflicting confessional and ideological claims as to the legitimacy of the Middle Ages and of modern times, we should try to recover the historical context of the via moderna and ask what its proponents themselves understood by the term.

SAINT THOMAS: THE FATAL FLAW

Students of Thomism need to realize that in the period after Saint Thomas a paradigm change took place, a momentous shift perhaps better regarded as dramatic than as tragic. The papal encyclical of John Paul II provides us with an excellent point of departure. Intending it as praise, the document accurately characterizes Aquinas's thought as a philosophy of being ("philosophia essendi et non apparendi dumtaxat"). Without knowledge of either Greek or Hebrew, Thomas could only assume that this philosophy of being had been authorized by God himself when Jahweh revealed his name to Moses (Exod. 3:14). As Erasmus put it in his preface to the *Novum Instrumentum* of 1516: "Without boasting, I dare to suggest that I have a better grasp of the biblical languages, 'most certainly better than Aquinas, who knew only Latin.' "[17] Thomas had to rely on the misleading Vulgate version, "ego sum, qui sum," which seemed to warrant the ontological connotation of being. He read, "I am who I am," instead of the intended promise, "I shall be who I shall be" (Exod. 3:14):[18] I am the reliable God of the covenant, the same yesterday, today and tomorrow (cf. Heb. 13:8). In the first French vernacular version, the so-called Antwerp Bible of 1530, Jacques Lefèvre d'Etaples, that farsighted biblical humanist who fell silent in his last years, succeeded in filling the old Latin form with new French content by the simple device of inserting "celuy": "Je suis celuy qui suis."[19] Luther rendered this verse in his Bible as: "Gott sprach zu Mose: Ich werde sein der ich sein werde. . . . Also soltu zu den kindern Israel sagen: Ich werds sein, der hat mich zu euch gesand." (God said to Moses: I will be who I will be. . . . Therefore say to the children of Israel: I will be who I will be, he sent me to you).[20]

For Thomas, "ego sum, qui sum" explicitly states that the Christian God is Supreme Being. It is often overlooked that the Latin version of Exodus 3 then serves as Thomas's biblical basis for the famous five proofs for the existence of God.[21] I need hardly point out that I use "Thomas" here as shorthand for a much broader tradition that goes back via Saint Anselm to Saint Augustine and gathers in neoplatonic and Dionysian influences. The axiom *philosophia essendi et non apparendi dumtaxat* characterizes not only Thomas's thought but a whole series of crucial earlier developments. Accordingly, although the presupposition of God as

highest being and the beautiful imagery of an overflowing of divine being in the world of mere appearances (*dumtaxat!*) might seem straight-
forward, they implied that: 1) there is a hierarchical relation between
heaven, church, and creation, 2) secular culture is part of the structure of
being, and 3) there is an epistemological conduit between creatures and
their creator, the so-called *analogia entis*.

A couple of generations before Thomas, Saint Francis of Assisi had
already envisioned a God who stood in a different relation to his creation
than what was taught in the platonizing theology of divine Being. In the
authentic *opuscula*, Francis frequently refers to God by the personal title
"Dominus Deus," or Lord God.[22] In the widely circulating treatise *Sacrum commercium S. Francisci cum Domina Paupertate*[23] (probably written in 1227, within a year of the saint's death and bearing the strong
impress of his thinking), God and his creatures are bound in a personal
covenant.[24] Developed by his early academic interpreters, Saint Bonaventura and Duns Scotus,[25] the two propositions, God as personal lord and
his action as covenant, became the two pivotal points of a surprisingly
cohesive new tradition centering on the Franciscan vision of history. The
Thomistic unmoved mover was becoming the highly mobile covenantal
God who acts, a God whose words are deeds and who wants to be known
by these deeds. When God is discovered to be the supreme person in his
aseitas and the lord of history in his *opera ad extra*—that is, a person both
in his inner council and his outer rule—the paradigm shift is in the
making. The immense literature on Saint Francis notwithstanding, some
stages of this discovery are better known than others because modern
scholars have, understandably, been preoccupied by the sensational rift
over Franciscan poverty (*usus pauper*).[26]

In the course of two centuries—roughly from the deaths of Thomas
and Bonaventura in 1274 to the official establishment of the via moderna,
particularly at the new German universities—the implications of this
discovery were pursued by an ever-growing number of magisters, variously inspired and challenged by the innovative findings of Scotus and
Occam, and including more and more non-Franciscans. Modern scholarship has made significant advances in detailing the various paths by
which this discourse came to dominate every known field of knowledge
from logic and dialectics to physics and natural philosophy, reaching well

into the higher faculties of theology, law, and medicine. Still, awash in such a vast amount of new information, it is easy for us to lose sight of the common thread that gave cohesion to this explosive period of fermentation and exploration. Once the new paradigm made it possible to shed the ontological cloak that covered experienced reality, reason could both submit to the rule of observation and rise to the objective status conferred by critical distance. We have come to regard these as the basic principles of all reliable investigation and sound scholarship.

Once words were understood as natural signs rather than as reverberations of the eternal *Logos,* scholarly vocabulary could be freed of its speculative connotations. "The content of words is a matter of choice" (*Nomina sunt placitum*) is the battle cry of liberation, a declaration of independence. Accordingly, in the field of linguistics the definition of terminology had to be newly sensitive to *modus loquendi* as *dicendi proprietas.*

In the hotly contested debate over universals, those former pivotal epistemological carriers of the hierarchy of being, we can discern a novel approach to accessing information. The new goal of observation was the identification of every object in its singularity (*cognitio particularis rei*). The concentration on finding facts demystified *experientia* and stripped it of its singularity, so that it became a synonym for authority. In the quest for objectivity in scholarly argumentation: *experientia docet!*

With the discovery of the God who acts, a new pride of place is given to the *causa finalis,* or ultimate purpose. The earlier, often platonizing, metaphysics of time and eternity is reoriented from a concern with the nature of time and timelessness to understanding the sequence of time by inquiring into the goals of history. Such questions as "Can God undo the past?" or "Can God 'in the future' save [accept] a reprobate?" may strike us as abstract but reflect a new existential interest in final causation: What does God want? What is history all about?

Perhaps the most significant effect of the new paradigm on the experience of everyday life is its correlation of *experientia* and *experimentum.* Besides providing the foundations of early modern science, it paved the way for a reassessment of such key concepts of the old metaphysics as material causality and motion.

The innovations in theoretical and practical experimentation outlined above ushered in the late medieval movement that is best called nominalism, since its spokesmen were increasingly referred to as *nominales.* Taking root as the via moderna in the academic institutions of the late fourteenth and early fifteenth centuries, it steadily defined its platform.[27] Occam was called the movement's Inceptor, a title more than an honorific since he was generally recognized as having "paved the path." Nevertheless, Stephan Hoest, vice-chancellor of Heidelberg, was able to assert in 1469 that the Moderns (nominales) did not recognize any one intellectual leader as *the* ultimate authority.[28]

In Paris, nominalism was associated with the names of Jean Buridan (d. ca. 1359), Nicolas Oresme (d. 1382), and Pierre d'Ailly (d. 1420); in Heidelberg, with Marsilius van Inghen (d. 1396); and in Wittenberg, with Gregory of Rimini (d. 1358). The Paris decree of March 1, 1473 (revoked in 1481),[29] reinforced the decree against Occam and his ilk (*et consimiles*) of December 29, 1340, and produced a wave of migration, thus contributing to the rapid spread of the via moderna. While dissemination was a sign of vitality and growth, the consolidation of the via moderna entailed a considerable loss as well. Scotus and Scotism, known in the language of the time as the *formales,* were driven into the arms of the *reales* to constitute, together with the Thomists, the *via antiqua.* This Old Road itself was in constant process of renewal. Even before Johannes Capreolus (d. 1444) had gained renown as *Princeps Thomistarum,* with his radical reorientation from the early Thomas to the mature author of the *Summa Theologiae,* the doctrine of Albertus Magnus, teacher of Aquinas, was attracting a growing following. The Old Way was a broad coalition of Albertinists, Thomists, and Scotists—in this respect not unlike the via moderna—its members, like those of its counterpart, more readily distinguished by contemporaries than they have been by modern scholars.[30] Studying them from the exclusive perspective of intellectual history is distorting: Scotists and Thomists were *not* driven into each other's arms by chance—they agreed in their rejection of contemporary morals, and they shared a common vision of social reform. As latecomers among the mendicants, the Augustinian Hermits, founded in 1296, tried from the outset to achieve a profile of their own, but in other respects they fit the mold perfectly. Moreover, it was not intellectual issues but the fierce competition between secular and regular clergy that would later array the nominalists—with their strong support among secular scholars—against the Fratres Minores, the order in which they had been conceived and nurtured. The common heritage of Franciscans and nominalists was all too easily forgotten in the division over doctrinal issues and in the public commotion that ensued. Scotists and nominalists were drawn together in a surprisingly effective alliance against Dominican opposition to the Immaculate Conception, a doctrine ardently supported by the Franciscans.[31] The intensity of the strife between the parish clergy (*curati*) and the intrusive *fratres* over the right of the latter to say mass, hear confessions, and raise money highlights the significance of the *Decisio* of Luther's vicar general and father confessor the Observant Augustinian Johannes of Staupitz, who, though himself a friar, took the side of the parish clergy.[32] Luther was one of the few who discerned the lines of continuity, and yet he said too little when he claimed: In moral matters Scotus and Occam are identical ("In moralibus Scotus et Occam idem sunt").[33]

Regrettably, the term *Bonaventurism* has not gained currency among modern interpreters, since Bonaventura escaped Scotus's fate of being identified with one philosophical type of scholasticism. The very name Bonaventura could have effectively reminded posterity of the importance of the paradigm shift, a momentous transformation misleadingly simplified in our textbooks to one of its aspects: the establishment of the priority of will over reason. Carried beyond the monasteries in the fifteenth century by the Franciscan preaching crusade,[34] it shaped the piety of Western Europe's laity in forms that Berndt Hamm has identified as a new constellation of *Frömmigkeitstheologie*.[35] A wave of devotional literature, in which the writings of Bernard of Clairvaux and Bonaventura mingled (often indiscriminately) with those of pseudo-Bernard and pseudo-Bonaventura, swept over the continent and unified Europe spiritually as it had never been—and never would be again. For his role in fostering and disseminating that devotion, Johannes Gerson was recognized as a father of the church.[36]

The paradigm shift legitimized and accelerated a radical reordering of society, dismantling what I have called its ontological scaffolding and toppling the hierarchy it shared with heaven and church. This coincided with Europe's political territorialization. In a fascinating essay, Constantin Fasolt traced this reordering in the period from the thirteenth to the seventeenth century as the context for the German Reformation. In his view, clergy, nobility, and burghers abandoned the hierarchical ordering of Christian Europe for a new settlement ("[sie] schlossen ein Art still-schweigenden Gesellschaftsvertrag miteinander ab"). These three power elites divided the hierarchical legacy of the church into territorial nations with absolute sovereignty over their respective subjects. This proves to have been the tip of a vast iceberg: all social relationships, particularly those between state and church, were radically revised. ("Das verlangte eine grosse Renovation im ganzen europäischen Haus, vom Keller bis zum Dachstuhl, im Garten und im Hof.") Casting his interpretive net well beyond the Reformation era to the seventeenth century and the Enlightenment, Fasolt concludes that liturgy, church, and hierarchy were now to be at the service of nature, nation, and the division of labor ("Der Gottesdienst wurde zum Dienst an der Natur, die Kirche zur Na-tion und die Hierarchie zur Arbeitsteilung").[37] Though the impact of the anti-hierarchical settlement observed by Fasolt is not fully felt until the eighteenth century, it does place our Franciscan paradigm shift in his-torical context, underscoring its social and political consequences and thus providing the medieval bridge to what we call today the era of *Konfessionalisierung*.

Although without this change the Reformation breakthrough would be inconceivable, it did not create an unbroken continuity between the discovery of the God as Person-acting-in-history and Luther's discovery of the God of covenant and promise (*Deus iustificans*). Luther's con-frontational *Disputatio contra scholasticam theologiam* of September 4, 1517, explicitly targets the whole preceding academic tradition, including Duns Scotus and Gabriel Biel.[38] Redirecting as well as elaborating the Franciscan vision, Luther confronts the philosophical theology which penetrates the being of God by means of concepts of substance and motion. Thesis Fifty puts this in succinct form: "In brief, all of Aristotle is to theology as darkness is to light. Against the scholastics."[39] Luther at-tacks what he sees as the Pelagianism of some of the leading nominalists within a larger frame of reference that, without the Franciscan paradigm, would have been inconceivable. New with Luther is the *theologia crucis:* the God who acts has become the God who acts in Christ, the God who is unpredictable and foils any systematic search, who contrary to reason and against expectation carries the cross from Christmas to Easter.

At the same time, we recognize the new paradigm in the concomitant attack on the *theologia gloriae*, which rejects the antiquated epistemology of hierarchical being. As Luther put it in 1518, the theology of glory seeks to grasp the mystery of God by rational analysis (*invisibilia Dei, per ea, quae facta sunt, intellecta conspicit*; cf. Rom. 1:20).[40] The vainglory of this natural theology is the delusion that by elevating our speculative reason, we can bypass the person of God to penetrate his being. Lutheran scholars are bound to misunderstand the meaning of Luther's *contra scolasticos* if they continue to ignore the significance of that other bold statement: "Bonaventura inter scholasticos doctores optimus est."[41]

PERSONALISM: THE PERSISTENT LEGACY OF SAINT FRANCIS

It is one of the ironies in the field of intellectual history that such terms as *Scotism, Occamism,* and *nominalism* tend to become ahistorical universals exactly like those Occam assailed.[42] Many of the underlying, long-debated questions can be solved, however, if we realize that the full implications of the personalism at the center of the new paradigm were not immediately apparent. They became so only through an arduous process of searching and discovery, of experiment, hypotheses, test cases, and new starts, which stimulated imaginations to identify evident laws of nature. For those historians who expect to find the virgin birth of a new *philosophia perennis,* the backing and filling, the shifts and novel insights involved in such a procedure are bound to be perplexing. Thus Duns Scotus could retain the ontological reality of such a universal as our "common nature," yet develop the doctrine of the *acceptatio divina* as the sovereign initiative of the personal God in predestination and justification just as he laid the foundation of a new theology of the Sacraments by turning from speculation about the elements of the *pactum Dei cum ecclesia.* This application of the covenantal God who acts to the whole realm of action in the world would become a characteristic tenet of the via moderna.[43]

All this is not to say that the new paradigm was without antecedents. The distinction between the absolute and the ordained power of God as a means for denying all necessity for God's action can be traced back to Thomas and to twelfth-century thought. With Occam, however, the invocation of God's absolute power assumes the systemic significance of establishing the contingent nature of history. A century later, Pierre d'Ailly clarified the meaning of the ordained power of God by defining it as the divine will revealed in Holy Scripture.[44] Whereas Occam had invoked the absolute power only to establish that what God actually did *de potentia ordinata* was not ontologically necessary, a hundred years later this very principle was applied to establish that any knowledge bypassing God's self-revelation is vain curiosity.[45] Moreover, whereas the Inceptor Occam intended the absolute power of God only as a theoretical principle, Gregory of Rimini and Marsilius of Inghen held that the absolute power of God can explain miracles as divine intervention in the actual course of history. For Luther, also, such miraculous intervention plays an important role. It has not so far been noted that Luther teaches an open canon insofar as he expects to find God's self-revelation not only in Scripture, but also in singular *signa or prodigia*—his terms for the signs of the last days.[46]

Those historical interpreters who like to work with clear school distinctions have found it difficult to understand how it is that adherents of the via moderna can cite Thomas with approval. Notwithstanding the marginalization of Thomism in the later Middle Ages, the *Secunda secundae* of Thomas's *Summa Theologiae* were still widely consulted for solving the ethical problems of everyday life. Contrary to the propaganda of early Renaissance humanists and reformers, late medieval theologians were eager to overcome school differences so that they could be as inclusive as possible. Thomas had elaborated a more extensive system of virtues and vices than any other medieval thinker, and so long as it was understood that God had his inscrutable reasons for choosing the present moral order, including the Ten Commandments, any self-respecting Franciscan might incorporate it without compromising the divine personhood.[47]

FROM DISSENT TO RESISTANCE:
LATE MEDIEVAL CHALLENGE TO THE INQUISITION

To assess the wider impact of nominalism in the late fifteenth century we must leave the realm of principles and platforms, the natural habitat of the intellectual historian, and move to the domain of the social history of ideas. We move to the arena where ideas prove to have legs and evoke social response, in this case, a response channeled via the Inquisition. Two thinkers bring us to the threshold of northern humanism and the early Reformation. They have often been confused because of the similarity in their names, John of Wesel (d. 1481) and Wessel Gansfort (d. 1489), but above all because both were controversial nominalists. The difference in their treatment is instructive. The first Inquisitor to investigate the Dutch theologian Wessel Gansfort was Jacobus Hoeck, who carried out a preliminary investigation. Hoeck, who between 1466 and 1476 had been twice rector of the University of Paris and twice prior of the Sorbonne, was a known representative of the Old Way, yet he treated Gansfort with due respect.[48] Whereas Wessel Gansfort remained uncondemned, John of Wesel was convicted of arch-heresy and died in prison. All the members of his Inquisitorial commission but one were Thomists.

Gansfort's discovery of nominalism was a conversion experience, a light at the end of a dark tunnel. From the Thomism he imbibed in Cologne, he had pressed on to Scotism in Paris, and it was also in Paris that he saw the light and become a nominalist.[49] Nominalism provided him with the truth he needed to avoid the basic fallacy of the old philosophy, namely, obfuscating reality with preconceived ideas instead of allowing experienced reality to shape thought.[50] His insistence on the authority of Scripture was part of a campaign against that vain curiosity which arrogantly penetrates the being of God, bypassing what he has decided to share about himself in his revelation.

As one of the first Christian Hebraïsts of his day, Gansfort programmatically identified with the new paradigm when he insisted that God revealed his name in Exodus 3 as "I will be who I will be" ("Ero qui ero . . . non dicit, qui est, misit me ad vos, sed longe et insolite aliter: Ero misit me ad vos").[51] In his commentary on the Lord's Prayer, Gansfort demonstrated the explosive nature of nominalist interpretations of Hebrew words. He pointed out that the Vulgate word *misericordia* (or *miserationes*), intended to render the Hebrew for "mercy," is dangerously misleading. The Hebrew original makes quite clear that there is a difference between *rechem* and *chesed*: whereas the first refers to motherly love and the maternal womb, the second has the connotation of male affection and fatherly care; so the one Latin word obscures the crucial gender difference. This observation had far-reaching consequences for theology and piety. Gansfort argued that one should not just pray to God as Father but, with the same biblical legitimacy, to God as Mother ("sicut Deus nobis pater, sic mater est").[52] However shocking this insight may still appear today, in Gansfort's age it must have been seen as a threat to the foundations of faith.

Wessel Gansfort's case not only alerts us to the fact that the demarcation line between late medieval scholasticism and northern humanism was permeable, but also leads us to see how ideas played out in institutional challenge and conflict. John of Wesel's heresy trial took place in Mainz in 1479. Wesel earned his doctorate in theology at Erfurt in 1456, and after a brief tenure as professor of Scripture at the newly founded University of Basel (May–October 1461), he held influential positions outside the academic world. Cathedral preacher at Worms from about 1461, he was dismissed in 1477 and became cathedral pastor (*Dompfarrer*) in Mainz until his trial, when he was forced to recant and saw his publications burned.[53] He died two years later in the Augustinians' prison at Mainz. We still do not have a clear grasp of the significance of these events. A major reason is undoubtedly that nineteenth-century Protestant historiography made Wesel into a forerunner of the Reformation, in the service of that kind of confessional reading of the historical record which has now become so suspect. An even more important reason, and decisive for the state of modern scholarship, is the fact that the task of editing and interpreting Wesel's legacy, those few fragments that survived the burning of his work, fell to Gerhard Ritter.[54] A decade before Lortz—though this time not from the explicit standard of Thomas but from the implicit perspective of Luther—Ritter presented late medieval nominalism as a period of utter lack of clarity. For him, Wesel's appeal to the authority of Scripture displayed the worst kind of late medieval fundamentalism ("spätmittelalterlicher Biblizismus in denkbar schroffster Form").[55] Moreover, Ritter regarded Wesel as a man who displayed "a high degree of naiveté," a typical product of late medieval thought with his Occamistic view of the complete "irrationability of the divine will."[56] Ritter's labeling of John of Wesel's soundly Scotist understanding of original sin as irrational and, more disdainfully, as the typical product of scholastic nonsensical irrelevancies is more than a naive error of judgment.[57] No one in the entire world of late medieval thought could have fared worse than Wesel at the hands of a spiteful humanist, or of a Luther. In charging that John of Wesel's biblicism makes Scripture into a new law, Ritter, although never explicitly saying so, is adopting the standpoint of Martin Luther. Ritter's concept of Occamistic irrationality is based on a misunderstanding of the dialectics of the potentia absoluta and potentia ordinata. Such was the prestige of Ritter's later scholarly oeuvre as to discourage a fresh approach to the late medieval via moderna in general and to John of Wesel in particular.

For our purposes it suffices to emphasize two characteristic points among the theses advanced by Wesel. In the first place, like Gansfort, he came into conflict with the Inquisition when in his reassessment of indulgences he dared to question the authority of the church to establish any such *lex divina* beyond the canon of Scripture. At the same time, one significant difference with the Dutchman should not be overlooked: Gansfort, the protohumanist, was able to base his arguments on a knowledge of the biblical languages, whereas John of Wesel had only the Vulgate Bible to argue against the claims of canon law and papal decrees. Nonetheless, both John of Wesel and Wessel Gansfort relied on the new paradigm for their shared conviction that the church is not vertically constructed, and hierarchically linked to God's being, but horizontally, functioning as the congregation of the faithful spread over time and space. To use the expression of that later student of the via moderna, Philipp Melanchthon, the church, they averred, is not a "Platonica civitas."[58] Accordingly, both men contested the claimed superiority and priority of the church over Scripture by insisting that the canon of the Bible is not created but received by the church.

Precisely this pitching of the Scriptures against the church sets the tone for Wesel's "Disputation against Indulgences." No simple biblicist, Wesel did not identify the Word of God with the Scriptures. Instead he found the Gospel in "the sermons of Jesus Christ" as recorded by the Evangelists. The preaching of Jesus contains "many and perhaps all the mysteries necessary for salvation."[59] This fundamental statement reveals a grasp of the original *viva vox evangelii* which does not easily fit Ritter's charge of a crude biblicism.

Wesel makes another crucial point in the sixth thesis of the same treatise: the will of God (*divina voluntas*) is known to us only from the

Gospel or through special revelation.[60] We encounter here the hermeneutical application of the shift from being to person: there is no reliable knowledge of God bypassing the Gospel as the authentic expression of his personal will. In keeping with the new paradigm, Wesel understands the sacraments as the covenant or *pactum* of the reliable God.[61] "Again, even if the blessed, while still in this life of misery, had deserved some merit, it would only be by the will of God, apportioned to them as it pleased him. For our merit is due to divine will, not to our own. No one may distribute those merits except God primarily. But if a human *could* distribute merits secondarily, like a priest, it would only be through a divine pact that god covenanted with men, as the doctors say of the sacraments. The gospel writings, however, have nothing of Jesus making such a covenant with priests."[62]

As if in a direct rejoinder, Johannes of Paltz, of the Order of Augustinian Hermits (d. 1511), uses the same pactum concept in his *Supplementum Coelifodinae* (1503) to defend the validity of papal indulgences as from Christ himself. ("Facit enim divina clementia pactum nobiscum in istis litteris, quod velit nos certissime exaudire secundum tenorem litterae. Quamvis enim papa dicatur dedisse istas litteras, tamen certissime credi debet, quod Christus dederit eas, qui dicit de papa: *Qui vos audit, me audit*").[63]

Gustav Adolf Benrath has provided a clear, only slightly abbreviated German translation of this disputation in *Wegbereiter der Reformation*.[64] Unfortunately his German rendering of "pactum" as *Vertrag* (contract) instead of *Bund* (covenant) tends to commercialize this biblical concept. Further, Benrath translates "incredibile" in Wesel's final sentence as if he had written "credibile," so that an important point is missed. The text reads: "non est incredibile, dominum erga sanctos suos mirabiliter operatum esse." (It is not unbelievable that God worked miracles for his saints.)[65] Wesel asserts here the possibility of an exceptional intervention by God, which we encountered in his view of special (post-biblical) revelation, and which in the tradition of the via moderna can explain miracles by God's potentia absoluta.[66] Compare Luther's *De votis monasticis iudicium* (1521): Christ neither taught nor lived the monastic vows, yet he worked and spoke through some holy monks, such as Saints Bernard and Francis, *mirabiliter* ("licet in sanctis sub votorum instituto captivis operatus sit et locutus mirabiliter sine votes").[67] Luther finds the biblical precedent for such miraculous intervention in the case of the three youths in the fiery furnace of Babylon (Dan. 3:19–27): "in qua electi miraculose . . . serventur."[68] Luther's point is that such a miracle as a truly Christian life-under-the-vows cannot be invoked to gainsay the revealed will of God. In nominalist wording: divine intervention "de potentia absoluta" does not delegitimize the established order "de potentia ordinata." Ergo, given Luther's understanding of the Gospel, *lege stante,* the monastic life runs counter to the will of God.

In this context Luther confronts the predominant (medieval and Protestant!) understanding of *sola scriptura.* The discovery of the God who acts in history leads him directly to the interpretative center of Scripture (that is, "was Christus treibet") as the clear expression of his saving will and at the same time opens the canon by pointing to the ongoing acts of God. ("In qua re nos erudimur, ut ubi scripturae testimonia non suffragantur, illic certis operibus dei nos niti oportere et vice testimoniorum ea sequi").[69] It is well known that Luther's insistence on the testimony of Scripture forced his early opponents to give less emphasis to scholastic authorities and appeal increasingly to biblical passages. The obverse consequence in this dialectical relationship has not been considered, namely, that Luther, intent on establishing the biblical basis of the Gospel, came to downplay the "extracurricular" acts of God "vice [scripturae] testimoniorum." Accordingly, this doctrine did not achieve confessional status in Lutheranism.

The Tridentine reception of the late medieval solution (in other words, the Bible supports post- or extra-canonical doctrine "implicite" or "silenter") by invoking the "sine scripto traditiones" (to be respected "pari pietatis affectu") assumes a continuous oral tradition reaching back to Jesus and the Apostles.[70] In contrast, Luther allows for ongoing new acts of God.

BIRTH PANGS BEFORE THE BREAKTHROUGH

Some of the most eminent specialists in the field of late medieval thought have been reluctant to allow Wesel any impact on the Lutheran Reformation.[71] This is understandable and must be respected as an effort to correct the distortions caused by Protestant confessional historiography's search for forerunners of the Reformation as *testes veritatis*. In considering this problem, however, we are well advised to distinguish between *initia Lutheri* and *initia Reformationis*—that is, between Luther's formation and Luther's impact.

Before I examine the significance of the new paradigm for the formation of Luther's thought, I wish to see what social history can tell us about the more daunting question of the impact and reception of Luther. The earliest published biography of Luther was by his fierce contemporary opponent Johannes Cochlaeus, who offers us a telling assessment of the mood of the times. In his historical diary, under the year 1518, Cochlaeus observes that Luther had so skillfully positioned himself as the victim in the indulgence debate that the cultural elites were swayed to take his side. They put their "tongue and pen" at Luther's disposal, influencing the unlettered laity by assailing the prelates and theologians not only as greedy and arrogant but also as ignorant and lousy Latinists: "incusans eos avaritiae, superbiae, invidiae, barbariei et ignorantiae."[72] As a matter of fact, leading German humanists had already formed a powerful pressure group when they joined forces on behalf of Reuchlin in the campaign against the "Obscure Men," the Thomist doctors of Cologne.[73] The powerful Dominican network reached well beyond Cologne to Louvain and the Magister Sacri Palatii in the Roman curia.[74]

Jacob Hoogstraeten had initiated the case against Reuchlin, while between 1514 and 1520 Silvestro da Prierio supervised the long, drawn-out curial proceedings and also opened the case against Luther.[75] Less well known is the screed against Wesel by Ortwin Gratius, one of the chief targets among the Cologne "Obscure Men."[76] In his preface to a new edition of the transcript of the Wesel trial (attached to a conciliarist history of the Council of Basel), Gratius confirmed his obscurantist fame as a rabid heresy hunter.[77] Just as the Cologne Thomists had tried to disparage Reuchlin as a philosemite, Gratius presents Wesel as warped by the Jews, tricked into a stinking mass of errors: "ab illis [Iudaeis] deceptum, in putidam errorum sentinam corruisse."[78]

The perfidy of the Jews must have seemed to Gratius a far more acceptable explanation of Wesel's condemnation than the one indicated in the first edition, published in 1521–1522.[79] In a short statement at the beginning and in a longer addition to the actual record of the interrogation (which lasted from Monday to Friday, February 8–12, 1479), the commentator, today known to be the Strasbourg humanist Jacob Wimpfeling, clearly partisan for Wesel, shows that the accused man had to fight an unequal battle. As an eyewitness (*interfui ego ipse*) he vividly reports how Wesel entered the Franciscan house in Mainz, marched in by two friars, "pale, more dead than alive, and walking with a stick" (*pallidus, silicernus, habens baculum in manu*). The five-day interrogation of the gravely ill Wesel was conducted by the Cologne Inquisitor, Magister Noster Gerhard Elten, O.P. Though the final adjudicating court appointed by Diether of Isenburg, Archbishop of Mainz, numbered six doctors, three from Heidelberg and three from Cologne, only one belonged to the via moderna. Had all the others not been of the via antiqua (*de via realium*), claimed Wimpfeling, the sentencing of Wesel would have been quite different—"mitius, humanius, et clementius benigniusque"! Two eminent, learned commentators, Engelin of Braunschweig and Geiler of Kaisersberg, made no bones about their sharp criticism (*vehementissime displicuisse*). Engelin declared that he himself could subscribe to many of the condemned articles and pointed out that the sentence was a move by the friars against members of the secular clergy and a typical Thomist ploy out of resentment against the Modern Way (*contra Modernos*).[80]

Within four years of the trial Wimpfeling wrote the treatise *Concordia curatorum et fratrum mendicantium,* ostensibly as a resolution of the long-standing rivalry between the secular clergy and the mendicant friars. In fact Wimpfeling defended Wesel and assailed the friars. It was published in Strasbourg in 1503 under a pseudonym, like so many other bold tracts of the times: Wesel, he wrote, was not condemned for heresy but for being a secular nominalist rather than a Dominican Thomist: "vehementer gauderent triumphare se posse contra secularem, contra nominalem, contra non Thomistam." We may conclude that well before Gratius cast him as a victim of the perfidious Jews, Wesel had been styled Reuchlin's forerunner and had become a hero of the fierce fight against Thomist "obscurantism." The establishment of the via moderna (*via Gregorii*) in the newly founded University of Wittenberg in 1503 (attested to twice in the statutes of 1508) and the appointment of Martin Luther in that same year must have seemed to Wimpfeling the fulfillment of his

deep gratitude for the fact that "you were the first to teach me that it is only to the Scriptures that we owe belief, whereas all other authorities have to be read with discernment."[82] Heinrich Denifle was not the only scholar to express surprise that Luther needed Trutfetter to discover the maxim of sola scriptura, which was after all the fundamental principle of the entire scholastic disputation tradition. However, before we accept Denifle's dismissal of Luther as a poorly informed "Halbwisser," it is crucial to realize that the paradigm shift implies a profound hermeneutical discovery: the Scriptures contain God's personal communication, which cannot be bypassed through an ontological analysis of God's being. This is exactly the basis of Luther's rejection of what he, later in the same year, would designate as the *theologia gloriae*.[83]

Luther found the interpretive center of the Bible in what is variously called pactum or *testamentum*, the promise of God, the foundation of salvation and the sacraments. This is far from a Biblicist identification of the Scriptures with the Word of God. As Kenneth Hagen and Berndt Hamm have shown, it is along the lines of the pactum tradition that Luther developed his doctrine of justification by faith alone.[84] Luther's inflexible rejection of Zwingli's "significant" is directly related to his conviction that the words of institution of the Eucharist were the reliable covenantal promise which cannot, without peril, be adjusted to fit the categories of human ratiocination. The God who acts cannot be figured out by reason but makes himself known in and through water, bread, and wine.[85]

Perhaps the most significant yield of the larger perspective provided by the discovery of the God who acts in history is the integration of an important element in Luther's thought that Luther scholars have long tried to marginalize as a medieval remnant—his realistic eschatology. Luther regarded himself as a forerunner of the Reformation—of that reformation which will be brought about by the coming of the new heaven and the new earth.[86] In contrast to Erasmus and Calvin, Luther did not believe that he was living at the beginning of modern times but rather that he was witnessing the end of time. The sense of eschatological urgency, which Luther knew he shared with Jesus and Paul, is present throughout his writings, both early and late. In 1521 he culminates his public letter to his father Johannes with the assertion: "I am convinced that the day of the Lord has drawn near."[87] And again in April 1544, looking forward to his death (*transitus*) and expecting it at any moment, Luther reiterated that the world was about to pass away: "mundus . . . mox mutandus, Amen."[88]

The discovery of the God who acts transforms the unmoved mover not only into the lord of history, but also into the divine timekeeper, who calls for the total mobilization of all resources in the service of the final battle against evil. As modern research has shown, it was the Franciscans who spread the millennial dream through Spain and carried it to the New World.[89] For Luther, Saint Francis did not initiate the new era of the *evangelium aeternum*.[90] His was the expectation of the long-awaited end of history which only God will bring about—soon.

This acute sense of time does not eclipse the role of philosophy. Precisely in the end time, false apostles will come—indeed they have arrived!—claiming all manner of visions and insights. Therefore it is all the more important to be alert and discerning. Though unable to grasp God's Being, the *ratio* can do something far more important, indeed essential, in the chaos of the last days. Reason may not know God, but it does know godlessness, the evil and injustice to be opposed. Though reason does not grasp the God of faith, it does recognize duplicity, murder, and revolt for what it is, and this *evidenter*.[91] During the confusion of the end time, therefore, it is the high office of reason to serve as a guide in the battle between God and the devil: in Luther's hands the new paradigm transported philosophy from the prayer stools of the theologians to the battle lines of "these Last Days."[92]

Even those Luther scholars who make a serious effort to include the via moderna as part of Luther's educational background describe his schooling as a phase left behind once the reformer had succeeded to the biblical chair of his vicar general, Johannes von Staupitz, in 1512. From that point on at least, Luther is for these scholars the single-minded student of Scripture setting his new course on biblical coordinates and leaving the medieval church together with the New Way behind on the shore, fading away in the sunset. That Luther underwent a reorientation of thought there can be little question. But the via moderna provided Luther with a philosophical orientation that continued to function for him as a guide and an eye-opener when thought turned into deed and his

Modern Way turned into the road to Reformation. In charting Luther's extended, painful process of emancipation from medieval monasticism, we need to keep in mind not only that the professor was foremost a friar but also that his schooling had provided him with modes of thinking which would sustain him in the battles ahead. When Luther the scholar emerged, reluctantly, from his study to enter the political arena, he had to draw on all his resources to survive the coming ordeal of opposition, criticism and, finally, condemnation. We may discuss in abstract terms the question of nominalism's lasting impact on Luther, but in the words of one of his beloved popular proverbs, the proof of the pudding is in the eating.

III

MARTIN LUTHER
A Friar in the Lion's Den

BARRIERS BEYOND THE BREAKTHROUGH

During the second part of the twentieth century a concerted effort was made to restructure the issues of the date and nature of Luther's Reformation breakthrough. Carefully steering a course between the Scylla of presenting Luther as a deus ex machina, the unprecedented discoverer of the Gospel, and the Charybdis of Luther as the latest link in a golden chain of medieval witnesses to the truth (*testes veritatis*)—the so-called forerunners—historians scrutinized his youthful studies to reconstruct the earliest stages in his development. Realizing that Luther developed his program in the course of fulfilling his duties as a professor of biblical theology, scholars including Heinrich Bornkamm, Martin Brecht, and David Steinmetz tried to place him in context by considering the scriptural commentaries that were—or could have been—at his disposal. They were able to do this successfully because Gerhard

Ebeling and Samuel Preus had already established the characteristics of Luther's new hermeneutics. Yet another major advance was achieved when Christoph Burger, Berndt Hamm, and Steven Ozment expanded the earlier limited canon of philosophical and theological academic authorities to include that wide range of devotional literature, not all of it mystical, that had been variously influenced by pseudo-Bernard, pseudo-Bonaventura, Gerson, Tauler, and the Modern Devotion.

Luther's development could be freshly charted by following in detail his exciting progress from the *Dictata super Psalterium*, the early Psalms commentary of 1513–1516, through the *Operationes in Psalmos*, the second commentary on the Psalms of the years 1519–1521,[1] as he grew increasingly aware that the books of the Bible were intended primarily as texts for meditation rather than as sources of doctrinal information. Luther was forced to break off this line of investigation abruptly when his case (*causa Lutheri*) had become so politically explosive that he was cited to appear in April 1521 before the emperor in Worms. As for the continuing debate over whether the Reformation breakthrough should be dated as early as 1514 or as late as 1518, no agreement has yet been reached.[2] Nevertheless, all scholars involved in this exacting and meticulous research project agree that between 1513 and 1519, Luther developed a new biblical lexicon by investigating what he called the "theological grammar" of the Scriptures.[3]

Trained in Erfurt in the tradition of William Occam, Gregory of Rimini, Peter d'Ailly, and Gabriel Biel, Luther as reformer stood on the shoulders of innovators who had declared the words of human language to be natural signs rather than reverberations of the eternal Logos. These *nominales* or *moderni*, generally known today as the nominalists, had undertaken to eliminate all speculative connotations from the scholarly vocabulary. In their slogan "words are free" (*nomina sunt ad placitum*) they sounded a battle cry of liberation that should be heard as a declaration of independence. Accordingly, in the fields of philology and linguistics the definition of terminology in context had to be attended to with a new insistence on precise formulations and forms of argumentation (the *modus loquendi* as *dicendi proprietas*). This ingenious plank in their platform made the nominalists welcome allies of the Renaissance humanists in their campaign to vindicate rhetoric—and the attraction was mutual.[4]

It is this search for the unique vocabulary of Scripture that set Luther on a path to ever new discoveries. He became increasingly aware that the biblical God communicated with the prophets and apostles in ways and through words not respected or reflected in the traditional scholastic speculative grammar, saturated as it was with definitions drawn from Aristotle. This is what Luther meant when he insisted on the need for the "eyes and ears of faith." God's words and ways are so unexpected and so far beyond our ken that without the spirit "no human being will be able to grasp them."[5] In his earliest autograph notes of 1509, Luther had already dismissed Aristotle as an unreliable Schwätzer or fabulist (*fabulator*)[6]—not as concerned his impressive, wide-ranging analysis of the physical world but as an authority when the word of God is being cited.[7] This Augustinian tenet, which was in keeping with the *via Gregorii* (named for Gregory of Rimini and his nominalist program), did not fail to cause tensions between the theological and philosophical wings of Erfurt's nominalists. In his letter of May 1518 to his former teacher of philosophy, Jodocus Trutfetter, Erfurt's prominent nominalist logician, Luther roundly faulted him for a serious lack of critical distance from Aristotle. Luther had already launched his attack against scholastic theology on September 4, 1517, writing Aristotle out of the book of theology even more resoundingly than any of his Augustinian predecessors with his simile of light and darkness.[8]

Luther's critique of Aristotle could not have come as a surprise to Trutfetter, because he had already made his views public before writing the letter. His expression of lasting indebtedness to his former schoolmaster, therefore, is all the more noteworthy: "You were the first to teach me that it is only to the Scriptures that we owe belief, whereas all other authorities have to be read with discernment."[9] This statement should not be understood as the later Protestant maxim of "Scripture alone"— after all *sola scriptura* is the fundamental principle of the entire scholastic disputation tradition. What Luther intended here was something else and, for our purposes, far more important: in the Scriptures God defines his own vocabulary or—to coin a phrase not used by Luther—*nomina sunt ad placitum Dei* (God defines his own terms). The conscientious interpreter will attend to his way of speaking (*modus dicendi*); only the

Scriptures can introduce the grammar of God to the reader who expects to crack the code of key terms, the kernels of biblical theology. For this reason Luther prized Reuchlin's 1506 introduction to Hebrew as a valuable tool and ten years later hailed the publication of Erasmus' groundbreaking *Novum Instrumentum* as a signal event.[10]

Several historians working independently on both sides of the Atlantic share the credit for pinpointing the terms *covenant* (*pactum*) and its variants, *testament* and *promise,* so crucial to the new theology Luther developed in his lectures on the Letter to the Hebrews between April 1517 and March 1518.[11] By focusing on covenant, Luther was able to proceed to his discovery that God is not the Thomistic highest being but the bonding God who acts in history, not an unmoved mover but the highly mobile grantor of testament and promise, the God of faith and fidelity.

Today we see clearly the extent to which this covenant theology was firmly rooted in the thought of the earliest Luther, and how, as he explored the testament of God, he came to discover the doctrine of justification by faith alone, as well as its ecclesiological and sacramental implications.[12] Traditional scholarship treats Luther's doctrine of justification under one heading and presents his teaching on the Eucharist under another; but this is a mistake. Luther's passionate rejection at Marburg in 1529 of Zwingli's interpretation of *significat* in the Lord's Supper as symbolic was directly related to his interpretation of the words of institution of the Eucharist: the trustworthy covenantal promise cannot, without peril, be adjusted to fit the categories of human ratiocination. The God who acts cannot be figured out by reason but makes himself known in word and deed, through preaching, absolution, water, bread, and wine.

The interconnection between Luther's confrontations with Erfurt's Trutfetter and Zurich's Zwingli should alert us to the considerable limitations of the time-honored concept of the Reformation breakthrough. My reservations are unrelated to the question of whether it was closer to 1514 or to 1518, and irrespective of the argument I have made elsewhere that the so-called breakthrough is properly described as the transformation of the justice of God (*iustitia Dei*) into the justice of Christ (*iustitia Christi*).[13] Rather, they stem from my conviction that the concept of a one-time breakthrough is romantic and unrealistic, summoning up an image of a mighty divine bulldozer smashing through all barricades on the road to Reformation—once and for all. Misled by this notion, scholars have paid too little attention to the other momentous developments in the reformer's thought that were to follow. After that awesome turning point in his quest for the merciful God, some major decisions still awaited Luther. One of the most important of these was also the most existential, namely, whether he was leading the right life, the life of an Observant Augustinian friar dedicated to serve God under the eternal vows of obedience, poverty, and chastity.[14]

TO BIND FOR LIFE IS TO BLIND FOR LIFE:
THE MONASTIC VOWS

It has long been assumed that Luther's reconsideration of monastic vows in 1521 marks a watershed in Europe's religious and cultural life. Indeed, his rejection of eternal vows in *De votis monasticis iudicium* of that year cannot be understood except as a frontal assault on the monastic life. It implied a complete reinterpretation of the moral fiber of medieval Christianity, of its high road to perfection, of the safer way (*via securior*) to salvation in the ordered life of untrammeled dedication to the service of God.[15] In recent research this treatise of Luther has even been held up as "the most radical critique of monasticism ever formulated" and is said to have unleashed a "mass movement" of monks, friars, and nuns who experienced a second conversion: the monastic vision which once had been the very raison d'être of their way of life had become obsolete; indeed, to combat it could now be embraced as the "new vocation."[16] The claim, especially when dramatized as a clean and clear-cut break with the past (*klarer Schnitt*), sounds very much like the righteous assertion formerly in vogue among Protestants. But was it so? Before Luther's *apertura*, his breaching of the monastic walls, can be properly assessed, we must look at the stages in which he came to terms with the cowl covering his own body. It would be three more years before he was prepared to shed it (October 9, 1524). On closer examination the heralded klarer Schnitt is not so clear but shot through with intriguing opaque streaks.

"irrational fury," he psychologized—and therewith trivialized—the voice of prophetic protest against the systemic fury of the anti-Church.[21]

If Luther had left the matter with this attack on divisive self-righteousness, we might well conclude that in 1519 he was merely extending the range of his initial targeting of the opponents of some extremely observant friars. For the Augustinian vicar, the Frater Martinus of 1515, this was a fanatical group of pharisees, anxiously and therefore aggressively sticking to the letter of the *Constitutiones*—the regulations defining everyday monastic life for his Augustinians.[22] Deviating from the Rule, they clung to the rules. In that case, we would have readily granted that by 1519 the previous demarcation line had stiffened and sharpened into a radical rift between the godless (impii) and the faithful (pii), with the miserable deviators becoming mighty demons. We would not, however, have dared to go so far as to suggest that Luther's criticism could be interpreted as an assault on the monastic life. Yet Luther himself felt that he had come so close to giving this impression that he had to deny explicitly that he was implying a total dismissal of monasticism: "I do not say this because I object to the rules and rituals (*caerimoniae*) of churches and monasteries. To the contrary, from the very start it has been the essence of the monastic life that one enters a monastery in order to learn obedience by sacrificing one's own will, prepared to serve everyone in every respect. The monasteries were the very training centers to learn and grow in Christian liberty, as they still are today (*sicut adhuc sunt*) wherever they serve this original intention."[23] Sicut adhuc sunt—"as they still are"—is still emphatically conservative as compared to some of Luther's later statements. Yet the appreciation and legitimation implied in this statement does not warrant the conclusion that he regards monasticism to be an essential feature of Christianity, to remain a part of Christian life forever. Monasticism can be abolished, just as the ceremonial part of the Old Testament law was abrogated: "After all, the ceremonies of the Old Law were eminent forms of practicing true and genuine piety. Yet when by evil design they started to undermine freedom and when, under the pretext of sticking to ceremonial propriety, they started to douse the flame of true piety and consequently perverted liberty into slavery, it became necessary to abolish all such ceremonies—just as today every faithful pastor will do away with that rage of rules (*tumultus caerimo-*

niales), wherever these become traps of souls and scandalous obstacles to genuine piety."[24] In 1519, however, they still are centers of inspiration: the monastic life is still functional and functioning.

The Prophet of the Last Days

By 1521 the time of that faithful pastor had come. Vows had to be abolished because they proved not to be based on God's word; on the contrary (*immo*), they "militate against the word of God."[25] *De votis monasticis* is so rich that Luther scholars understandably have had their hands full to summarize its contents. However, if we want to do more than merely chronicle Luther's doctrinal positions, we must discover what exactly caused him to change his mind on such an existential issue as the monastic life. In general terms, we know that it occurred sometime during those two decisive years of mounting confrontation, between the end of 1519 and November 1521, when he committed *De votis monasticis* to paper at the Wartburg. Fortunately, we can be even more precise, indeed, quite definite. Though there may well have been a variety of factors unbeknownst to him, or us, one was of overriding significance to Luther—the ticking clock of eschatological urgency. Once this is clear, we can come closer to the time that this occurred to him: it is toward the end of February 1520 that Luther had become acutely aware of living "in these last days."[26]

Reformation scholars bent on establishing Luther as the father of international Protestantism have highlighted his message of religious and social emancipation from the medieval two-tiered morality which held that the general standard of Christian decency (*praecepta*) sufficed for common folk, whereas for those under vows, the heroic counsels (*consilia*) of the Sermon on the Mount obliged them to obey the call to turn one's cheek and to go the extra mile (Matt. 5:39, 41). According to these scholars Luther provided future humanity with its emancipated awareness of prime responsibility to a needful society, the world outside the monastic walls: thus he lifted medieval Christianity over the threshold to modern times. But Luther did not live on the eve of modern times; he lived at the end of time.[27] With a sense of extreme urgency the reformer leaps to the defense of the Church Catholic, now caught "in these last days" in the Babylonian cage, enslaved and suffocating under the yoke of justification by works. This new urgency is for Luther confirmed by the fact that vows prove to be devastating weapons of the devil assailing church and society at the end of time. The Evil One perverts the best we have, our highest aspirations, deceiving us with his semblance of a highway to heaven.

The climax of Luther's preface to his father, Johannes, is his statement that "the Day of the Lord is near."[28] To bring this message home he goes right to the top, to the Apostles Saint Paul and Saint Peter. He invokes Saint Paul to show that we live in "dangerous times" (*periculosa tempora*) (2 Tim. 3:1).[29] Saint Peter is his prophet of the horrible chaos to come "in the last days" (*in novissimis diebus;* 2 Pet. 3:3): in the end time we will be misled by deceivers (*illusores*) who undermine the Gospel.[30] Whereas Luther had long since identified Aristotle as the illusor, the perverter of scholastic theology, this deception has now come to include all the diabolical forces that subvert Christian freedom and suppress the Gospel. There is no time to be lost: the good pastor is to be the prophet of the end time. The dialectic of 1519, softened by the "not yet" (*adhuc*), has grown into the clarion call for full mobilization and become the platform for resistance.[31] The demonic threat of "these last days" forecast by Saints Peter and Paul first dawned on him horribly in February 1520, and he spelled it out in November 1521. Luther wrote this manifest in Latin, so it initially reached only the educated elite; yet even a mediocre Latinist was bound to be mesmerized by the force of his impassioned prose.[32]

Notwithstanding all the innovative features of these developments, we should keep in mind that Luther continued to believe a genuine evangelical monastic life was possible—he himself would stay on in the cloister for another three years. Provided the conscience is free from seeking gain before God, he thought, one can embrace the vows. It is to be absolutely clear, however, that the monastic life is in no sense a higher state than any secular profession. And as soon as Christian love (*caritas*) calls you to duties outside the monastic walls, "you would commit a grave sin if you would cling to your vows."[33] One could indeed make a conscientious decision to stay or to enter the monastery for schooling and discipline, in keeping with the original foundation of the monasteries. It is, however, difficult to be certain that one enters—or stays—without ulterior motives.

Indeed, "in these dangerous times," to attempt to draw the right demarcation line is extremely risky.[34] Yet one thing should be clear to everyone: vows by their very nature are temporary. Beware—be prepared! To bind for life is to blind for life.

Open These Gates: *Sola fide*

In 1528, Luther's gestation was definitely completed. His fifteen German theses on the monastic life (*Das Closter leben unchristlich sey*) come down to us in a single manuscript carrying the date 1528 and presenting itself as an extract from *De votis monasticis.* The title of the three early imprints of 1531 suggests that someone else may have drawn up this list of fifteen propositions, but, as its editor properly points out, the 1528 theses contain too many fresh formulations to think in terms of a mere scribal extract. The occasion may well have been a widely broadcast event, the dramatic decision of Ursula, duchess of Münsterberg, to leave her Saint Magdalen Cloister in Fribourg on October 6, 1528. Luther wrote a postscript to her apologia *pro vita sua.*[35]

Yet even if he wrote it to sanction the duchess's Klosterflucht, to use that loaded term for the escape from the monastery into the world, it is clear that in 1528, Luther not only reinterpreted his own vows but also abandoned the "not yet" (*adhuc*) of 1519. The evangelical option of risking the monastic life by entering or staying in good conscience has been left behind as well. All the arguments of *De votis monasticis* are here refashioned into fifteen sharp hammer blows against the monastic life. In one formidable summation of his entire position, Luther throws the whole weight of the doctrine of justification against the vows: contrary to faith "they rely more on the quality of their life than on Christ."[36]

The year 1521, then, had not brought the surgical removal for which it is all too readily acclaimed. We encounter Luther in *De votis monasticis* set upon a path of clarification on which he has made enormous strides— its ultimate destination, however, is still shrouded in the expected, yet unpredictable clouds of the end time. By dramatizing the klarer Schnitt, even when we do it admiringly, we do not enlarge the stature of the towering, real historical person who groped for answers before acting on his convictions; on the contrary, we diminish it. Throughout most of

1524, three years after his frontal assault on the vows, Luther was not yet ready for what should have been a ceremony of triumph, a celebratory farewell to arms. Notwithstanding his growing convictions, Luther was not yet prepared to shed his cowl, nor would he be for a long time to come. At the Sunday service on October 9, 1524, he appeared for the first time in public without his Augustinian robes and after another week he would never don them again.[37]

Martin Brecht is prepared to accept Luther's explanation that he had retained his cowl "out of consideration for the weak." This may well be part of the reason; the other part Luther recalled later: he had found it "difficult to shed his habit" (*difficulter cucullam meam deposui*).[38] That he hesitated before taking such a momentous step is all the more credible in view of Luther's other declaration, that he had entered the Order not for gain, but for his soul's sake. For twenty years he had been a highly motivated friar, living "in every respect conscientiously in keeping with our *Constitutiones*" (*salutis meae causa vovebam et rigidissime servabam nostra statuta*).[39]

The correct understanding of Luther's crucial May 1524 letter to Wolfgang Capito, the Strasbourg reformer, and indirectly to Martin Bucer, proves to be more complex than the clear Latin would lead one to expect. On first reading, the central clause seems to support verbatim the interpretation that Luther, though long clear about the "right attitude" in his own mind, retained the cowl out of pastoral concern lest the "weak" might be scandalized. However, the apologetic context of this statement should not be overlooked. Realizing that he must seem slow compared to the quickly evolving, robust evangelical movement in southern Germany, Luther has to explain the advance of the Reformation at two different speeds, so much faster abroad and, measured in terms of the issue of the vows, so obviously successful in Strasbourg. This is the context for his admission: "We have long enough catered to the weak." Luther goes on to agree that it is time for action: "Accordingly, even I myself finally begin to stop wearing my cowl. I kept it on to respect the weak and ridicule the pope."[40] Only then follows the phrase that will not have convinced any of the southern reformers—nor should it mesmerize his modern interpreters. The very choice of words "even I myself" (*et ego*) and "finally" (*tandem*) alerts us to the fact that Luther belonged to those weak ones himself. Even at this late date, it took him another half year to make good his intention "to stop wearing my cowl" in public.

This conclusion removes the reformer from the lofty perch of neutral umpire where he has been placed and restores him to the ranks of actual participants in a fast-moving series of contingent, constantly surprising historical events. Ultimately, far more important than the rejection of the "weak" who hesitated is Luther's ridicule of the pope. Capito and Bucer will not have been impressed even by this explanation, since they were already well on the way to Protestantism, intent on organizing a new church and combatting the medieval Antichrist who blocked access to modern times. The prophet of the end time is convinced that only the Gospel can slacken the hold of the Evil One: at stake is the defense of Catholicism, and the mightiest weapon is the only one left—the irony of truth.

THE SACRED WAY: FROM SAINT ANTHONY TO SAINT FRANCIS

What made the last days seem so dangerous was the total loss of moral orientation and the inversion of all values. An especially pernicious case in point was the exploitation of the intimate connection between saint and monk in such exemplary persons as Saint Anthony, Saint Bernard and, above all, Saint Francis. Their very lives were constantly cited to prove that God himself legitimized monastic vows and approved their path to perfection. Luther's progress from 1519 to 1521 could not have been achieved without scaling a formidable barrier—the authority of precedent established by those great saints who had written rules and established the mighty, omnipresent orders.

The easy part was the acknowledgment of the value of monastic houses as gymnasia for the youth. In 1519, Luther had expressed his appreciation of their important pedagogical and societal function; in 1521 he still maintained his respect for their original intention with its programmatic goals. Luther's own order had cherished this educational role (*docere verbo et exemplo*). Today regarded as a characteristic of the *Praemonstratensian* renaissance during the extended incubation period of the Augustinian hermits, it was to become an essential part of the dowry for their Great Union, approved in 1258.[41] Accordingly, the monastery as a center of learning and discipline might need reform, but it could be retained without any need for concession or compromise.

The Holy Fathers, the *sancti* who had established rules and lived accordingly, were a problem of quite a different dimension, and in 1521, Luther had to come to terms with them. The religious world in which he himself had been reared was saturated with the lives of saints, notably the *Vitas Patrum* and the *Legenda Aurea*. His own order had extended these two rich collections of saintly lore with the stories of Saint Augustine's miracles, performed by their *pater noster,* as well as the great deeds of the later "sons of Saint Augustine," forming together the true City of God. In Luther's own *studium* in Erfurt, Jordan of Quedlinburg had completed his *Lives of the Brothers* in 1357, making them available to the lectors who read them aloud to the monks, silent at their meals in the refectory.[42] In his daily study of his Bible, Luther was surrounded by that living voice of the Gospel, the cloud of witnesses stretching from the desert fathers to his own times, all of them in unison proclaiming the high road to perfection. To crack the code of the saints was no mean task. In 1521, Luther labored page by page to solve the mystery of the monastic rule, trying to come to terms with the evident power of the spirit flowing in that mighty monastic stream from Saint Anthony to Saint Francis and to his beloved vicar-general, John of Staupitz, self-confessed forerunner of the Gospel (*precursor evangelii*), who died in 1524.[43]

The golden thread of *De votis monasticis,* the theme to which Luther returns ever anew, is the miraculous operation of the spirit calling forth saints to live the life of the Gospel. Accordingly, he chose as his point of departure Saint Anthony, the very father of all monks and founder of the monastic life. Saint Anthony withdrew from the world and lived a spotless life in keeping with the Gospel.[44] His successors, however, turned the Gospel into the law and insisted on a rule instead of obeying the command "listen to Christ" (Matt. 17:5). In a next step Luther turned to Saint Francis, that truly great man deeply driven by the spirit (*vir admirabilis et spiritu ferventissimus*). Citing the rule confirmed in 1223, Luther points out that Saint Francis wanted no rule other than the Gospel,[45] but decided nevertheless to give a rule to his *minores.* This, he observed, was a human error: a Franciscan friar cannot pledge more than what he already vowed in his baptism, namely the Gospel (*nempe Evangelium*). If, then, their rule is declared to be the Gospel, and if following this Gospel is claimed to be typically Franciscan, what else are they saying but that Franciscan friars are the only Christians![46] The loss of Christian liberty that this entails is pernicious, and particularly so in the case of the Observant Franciscans. For this group Luther created the special derogatory term of "super-Franciscans" (*Franciscanissimi*). He had debated the Observants two years earlier in a dramatic Wittenberg disputation;[47] now he anathematized them in uncompromising terms: "No one is today less like Saint Francis!"[48]

In order to cope with Saint Francis—as well as Saint Bernard and Saint Anthony—Luther invoked the precedent of Daniel in the lion's den, the Babylonian pit of destruction.[49] There the great saints survived by divine intervention (*miraculose*).[50] Saint Francis and his fellow saints erred in claiming the Gospel for themselves; yet at the same time they were driven by such a power of the spirit that "though they might not have possessed the Kingdom of God in word, they did so in deed."[51] Saint Bernard and many other great monks were so full of the spirit that the poison of the vows could not touch them (*venenum hoc non nocuit*).[52] In short, Luther does not question that "these saints lived under the vows"; his point is that "they did not live *out* of them."[53] They survived in the lion's den thanks to the miraculous intervention of God.

The imagery of the Babylonian den came readily to mind for Luther and for his readers as well. As one of the mnemonic devices popularly employed in sermons, stained-glass windows, and catechetical instruction, the connection was obvious: the seven mortal sins corresponded to the seven temptations of Christ, with the seven sacraments—and the seven lions in Daniel's den. The life-context of the friar in the den was crystal clear—the early humanists would be quick to call it *luce clarius*—as immediately understandable as a modern lampoon.[54] The theme of the prison in the den set Luther free from his holy past; thus empowered he could take a major step ahead on the winding road to Reformation, the Day of the Lord, the final remnant of the Church Catholic. It was a step not easily taken. Even three years later, it was with difficulty (*difficulter*), or as he put it elsewhere in the Table Talk, "with pain in the heart" (*aegre*) that he shed his cowl. He himself had been a friar in the den and there discovered God's sustaining intervention, a place not easily erased from memory—or ripped away like rags from the body.[55]

OPEN THE SCRIPTURES: *SOLA SCRIPTURA*

We have followed Luther well beyond the so-called Reformation breakthrough as he struggles with and finally resolves the wrenching question of the monastic vows. In *De votis monasticis,* that rich, private, yet candid treatise crowning a year's Reformation writings, other surprising discoveries await us.[56] In campaigning to open the monastic doors for service to the outside world, Luther elaborates the religious and social implications of his doctrine of justification by faith, the so-called formal principle of the Reformation. At the same time, he redefines "Scripture alone" (sola scriptura), often called the material principle of the Reformation. And with this theme we return to our point of departure, Luther's quest for the grammar of God. In his effort to come to terms with such saintly heroes as Saint Francis, Luther pondered the story of the friar in the den: Saint Francis survived the poisonous condition of the monastic life, thanks to God's mighty intervention. All those assiduous monks lived under extremely dangerous conditions, and out of this den of evil God salvaged them miraculously (*in qua electi miraculose . . . serventur*).[57] Though Christ neither taught nor lived the monastic life, he spoke and lived through his saints so powerfully (*mirabiliter*) that, although under the vows, they lived without vows.[58] The exceptional survival of these great saints cannot establish a precedent for the Christian life; they are extraordinary, living acts of God (*nam sanctos semper excipio in suis mirabilibus*).[59]

The three vows do not lead to a higher Christian life, Luther insisted: they create obstacles that hinder us from reaching it. With regard to poverty, the proverb "desperation makes the monk" applies.[60] The vow of obedience Luther already addressed in the Latin preface to his father Hans. In the German vernacular he shows at greater length how it undermines the cornerstone of societal cohesion by subverting the Fourth Commandment.[61] Yet the reformer still has to deal with the most dangerous question of all, the emotionally and socially precarious issues raised by the vow of lifelong chastity. Addressing a sexual taboo unflinchingly, he draws on Saint Paul to argue that the desire indelibly graven in the law of our body's members wars against the law of the spirit.[62] Saint Paul himself is a witness that God forgives libido and accepts it as part of the life of faith.[63] Hence it cannot be legitimate that a vow of chastity, which is after all a human invention and not part of the law of God, cannot be broken without the penalty of mortal sin.

Now Luther takes another decisive step. As we know from the Book of Acts, during the Council of the Apostles,[64] the Apostle Paul supported Peter's plea for baptizing Gentiles without circumcision by invoking the mighty acts of God, "all the signs and miracles through which God had worked among the Gentiles."[65] Luther points out that Saint Paul thus legitimized the revolutionary move to universalize Mosaic Judaism by opening the doors of the church with reference to God's miraculous mass conversion of Gentiles. Such disregard for the law of Moses could not but appear to deviate from the truth: "Against nearly the complete— and completely erring—earliest Church, Peter, Paul, and Barnabas stood shoulder to shoulder in upholding the doctrine of freedom by appealing to the liberating acts of God."[66] They spoke up "against everyone" (*adversus omnes*)—exactly the formula Luther had used to abjure scholastic theology four years earlier (1517).[67]

Then follows Luther's momentous conclusion: "From this we learn that in cases where there is no evidence of Scripture to appeal to, we should rely on certain works of God and accept them in place of the testimony of Scripture."[68] Luther had already touched on the issue of new revelation in arguing that the vows had neither a basis in Holy Scripture nor the support of "any sign or miracle to establish that they carry divine approbation."[69] This time he invokes God's revealing intervention as explicit proof and decisive evidence. We do not want to overlook Luther's proviso that such divine acts must be "certain" in order to be understood and obeyed as if they were Scripture. Nevertheless, as early as 1519, during the Leipzig disputation, he mentioned the possibility of a new revelation, adding that any such revelation stood to be tested and approved (*nova et probata revelatio*).[70] Now, returning to this idea, he is much more emphatic, arguing his case against "nearly the complete Church" on the basis, we must assume, of the amazing acts of God in the course of the

Reformation. He must have been particularly mindful of the wave of monks even then flooding out of his Wittenberg monastery.[71] This exodus was not the acclaimed "mass movement" unleashed by *De votis monasticis*. Once again the Reformation movement is ahead of Luther's thinking.[72] The exodus began before Luther wrote that treatise and it spurred him to arrive at his stunning conclusion.

The parallel is too striking to ignore: just as Saint Paul read the mighty ingress of Gentiles into the church, Luther is here legitimized to read the amazing exodus from the monastery—both are significant liberating signs from God. His fear (*timor*) is that this configuration may not be properly understood or all its implications fully grasped. One of the implications is that the canon is open inasmuch as the acts of God recorded in Scripture continue to occur and are to be reckoned with. Luther does not elaborate on the safeguards implied in the word "certain," but it cannot be wrong to say that such new guidance is to be accepted when in keeping with the acts of God as revealed in the Scriptures.

As is well known, Luther's insistence on the testimony of Scripture forced his early opponents to reduce their dependence on scholastic authorities and turn more frequently to biblical passages. The obverse consequence in this dialectical relationship has not been pursued, namely, that Luther, determined to augment the biblical basis of the Gospel, came to downplay the "extracanonical" acts of God. His concern was to protect that crucial twofold function of sola scriptura, namely that of interpreting itself (*sui ipsius interpres*) *and* of testing (*lex divina*) the validity of all ecclesiastical legislation. Undoubtedly, any appeal to "new" acts of God (*vice testimoniorum*) might all too readily be used to legitimize either the "inner word" of the Radical Reformation or the "outer word" of the Counter Reformation.

What Luther came to downplay, Lutherans erased and Protestants dismissed. In the very process of dissemination, the full scope of Luther's stance on the vows was severely curtailed. Whereas his platform—far more daringly innovative than hitherto supposed—called for opening not only the gates of the monasteries but also the canon of the Scriptures, this second aspect of his *apertura* did not outlast his lifetime. Luther's attack on the vows, originally addressed in Latin to sophisticated, well-trained *confratres* in 1521, was divulged to the German-speaking world in the vivid vernacular of the *Weihnachtspostille* in 1522 and the *Predigten von Advent bis auf Ostern* in 1525. By 1544 it was promulgated in more than twenty-three editions. The 1540 Wittenberg edition of Hans Luft and the 1544 edition of Nikolaus Wolrab, however, omitted two crucial sections, that is, the explicit discourse on the three vows (and precisely here the message of God's ongoing acts was embedded) as well as the extensive elaboration of Luther's vision of the end "in these last days."[73] If it is correct to define a biblical prophet as an interpreter of divine intervention in history rather than as a forecaster, we must conclude that these omissions, in a single, fateful stroke, obfuscated, if they did not erase, the mighty prophetic message of Luther's eschatology *and* his extension of the prophetic canon. In short, we witness here the emergence of an expurgated Luther that would shape his historical profile down to our own day.

The Tridentine reception of the late medieval solution, namely that the Bible supports post- or extracanonical doctrine implicitly (*implicite*) or silently (*silenter*), would elevate the "unwritten traditions" (*sine scripto traditiones*) to a respect equal to that of the Bible itself (*pari pietatis affectu*). Thus the Council of Trent proclaimed a continuous oral tradition reaching *back* to Jesus and the Apostles.[74] In contrast, Luther looks *forward*, to embrace the ongoing postbiblical acts of God.

Such extracurricular interventions of God do not convey a new gospel but provide marching orders for the Church Militant. They are misunderstood—and will continue to be ignored—as long as we overlook the realistic eschatology at the very center of Luther's prophetic faith. The new acts of God serve to protect the Church Catholic "in these last days," amid the struggle for survival in the decisive battle between God and the devil.

IV

REFORMATION
End Time, Modern Times, Future Times

MODERN WAY VERSUS OLD WAY

One of the foundation myths of the Reformation pertains to the term *reformation* itself. When I use it in the singular, I am referring to the movement originating in Wittenberg to acknowledge that novel forms of thinking and experiencing, of seeing the surrounding world, and of interpreting the course of events were fundamentally shaped and informed by Martin Luther. As even his staunchest critics and more distant observers have noted, we can speak of a mentality before and after Luther, ante- and post-1519–1520, those crucial years when the authority of councils and popes was put on public trial by the "true Gospel." In the plural, I mean to remind readers that before, with, and after Luther, competing movements emerged from which only confessional partisanship withholds the designation *reformatio* as if it were a badge of honor to which only Luther is entitled. In fact Luther so clearly rejected the emerging late-medieval program of reform that despite the power of entrenched tradition his Protestant movement might be better termed a Counter Reformation. Certainly it was counter to the reform position in the medieval debate between the *via antiqua,* the Old Way, and the *via moderna,* or Modern Way, the *antiqui* and the *moderni.* The Old Way approached reality with universals in mind, the preconceived ideas which—and herein all agreed—select, interpret, and order the chaotic messages transmitted by the senses. But from here on the Ways split: for the Moderns, these universals are concepts produced by the human mind, a means to access knowledge, to store, and to discern similarities in the surrounding world—and above all to discover the unique characteristics of each individual person or object. For the Ancients, the universal by definition transcends the singular; it possesses an ontological payload that increases along a hierarchical path toward the origin of all that is and has being.

In modern terminology the Ancients were idealists, although from their own perspective they were realists insofar as their universals were not conceptual but real tools through participation in God's order of creation. Fundamental for its treatment of all aspects of metaphysics, this philosophical universalism appealed to sacred Scripture to prove that God is the highest universal—sheer Being. It insisted that the vocabulary of the Scriptures reflects the eternal Logos, so that the grammar of truth can be spelled by ascending the ladder of meditation to God as supreme speaker and highest universal.[1]

The medieval advocates of the Modern Way argued instead that universals are man-made adjustable models to be defined and redefined in terms which receive exact and ever new meaning depending on the context in which they are used. Thus reclaiming secular responsibility for human discourse, they accused the Old Way of creating a world of make-believe in terms beyond the rule of logic and critical control. However academic and technical the controversy may seem, for both Ways the interpretation of the Scriptures and thus ultimate authority was at stake. For this reason the debate could not be limited to an abstract disputation about a theory of linguistics, logic, or epistemology, although these are aspects of the controversy that fascinate us today.

The program of the Modern Way set up lasting shock waves in the foundations of knowledge. In the fifteenth century, moderni clashed with late-medieval Thomism and fell afoul of the Inquisition. As late as the nineteenth century, in the heyday of idealism, they confronted the German system builders. Latter-day universalists—New Thomists and their neo-Protestant confessional opponents—found themselves shoulder to shoulder in an unintended coalition in defense of a world of harmony and regularity. The moderni, guardians of contingency, reappeared in a new role when the battle lines shifted from metaphysics to science and history; whereas the latter-day moderni had originally been concerned with logic and with defining meaning in context, they used their critical observational tools to separate scientific fact from fiction. As they saw it, their charge was to demonstrate the futility of trying to domesticate contingent events by enclosing them in generalizations claiming the status of eternal law.

When the Age of Reason reached Germany, the Old Way reemerged with new force. The three great deviators—Søren Kierkegaard, Friedrich Nietzsche, and Karl Barth—although separated in time and by fields ranging from literature and philosophy to biblical studies, each with his own vision, testified by their individual revolts to the might of the system builders of their day. Their voices were effectively drowned out by the sweet music of harmonious reason, the leitmotif of modernity. Increasingly dominating historical discourse, the Old Way rearranged the chaos of the historical drama into a self-evident chain of events and jubilantly announced that full understanding (*Durchblick*) had been attained. Lost was the element of wonder; amazement was an uncouth sentiment betraying the untutored mind of the common man and the uninitiated.

This history of the battle between the Ways shows how the Middle Ages remain with us. In 1494, Sebastian Brant sent his *Ship of Fools* coursing through the German territories. In 1511, it was joined by its Latin counterpart, *The Praise of Folly*, haltingly written by Erasmus in his carriage en route from Milan to London. These bestsellers skillfully employed ironic humor to sensitize the fast-growing reading public to the hypocrisy of everyday life. But real change needed more than laughter on the road to Reformation. The Modern Way set itself to dig deeper to the metaphysical foundations, so long deemed untouchable, of the God-ordained structures of church and state. After the initial clashes with the

Old Way in the fifteenth century, the moderni found an unexpected spokesman in Martin Luther, who joined it with a platform all his own. Unlocking the Scriptures, the reformer of Wittenberg raised hell to fight the devil, with all the more force because he knew time was running out. Moreover, he knew why.

Yet Protestant history takes its cue not from the Luther of flesh and blood but from the Luther icon sitting at his desk, reading his Bible, making the grand discovery justly depicted as a breakthrough. It was not as the man of the end time but as a man of all seasons, the icon of triumphant Protestantism, the steadfast hero of the Wartburg, that Luther was to bless the founding of the Second Reich in 1817 and legitimize the Third in 1933, henceforth to be ignored or camouflaged in a patriotic cloud of glory. Ours is a rough story, not only because of the furious struggle of the sixteenth century but also because the historical record itself must be wrested out of the hands of the record keepers who naturally abhor the subversion of the Modern Way. By concentrating on the growth of the mind as though it were protected from the mud and bustle of the street, oblivious to the raucousness and smell of the marketplace, we can easily lose sight of the historical Luther who lived, as his compatriots did, among the harsh realities of everyday life. In such settings are ideas born, or, as in this case, particular scriptural passages appear suddenly to speak out loud and clear. At the same time, those in stations of authority from emperor to city councilors, from prelates and nobility to local bailiffs—all those charged with the responsibility of responding to the challenge of change, often dismissed as the "ruling elite"—could not but regard challenges to religious and social authority as threats to societal cohesion and communal values. Only by entering into the social history of ideas, combining in thick description the mud and the marketplace, the guildhall and the council chamber, can we possibly overcome confessional triumphalism and pursue the critical task of even-handed adjudication, considering the stake of all parties in the unavoidable clash we call Reformation.

Prepared by Oxford and Harvard to develop into a medieval intellectual historian, I brought with me to Tübingen files filled with evidence of the Reformation's deep indebtedness to medieval thought—in Luther's case, to his nominalist training in the Modern Way, the via moderna. I also knew that this approach would not be hailed by all German Reformation scholars, a perception soon confirmed. I was wrong, however, to assign this disinclination only to the vested confessional interest in a "Man without Beginnings," admired for his fresh start and break with tradition. The problem proved to be far more fundamental: the Old Way, the via antiqua, regarded by Luther as the dark side and burden of the medieval tradition, had become the dominant feature and common thrust of German philosophy between Immanuel Kant and the early Martin Heidegger. The ideal of consistency called for a single point of departure, the highly revered *Ansatz*, with monism celebrated as the condition of proof and truth. Closed systems were the aim; plurality the condition of uncertainty. This mentality had decisive implications for historical interpretation as well as for religious thought in the nineteenth and twentieth centuries. Whereas the Modern Way designs flexible models to be tested by experiment, constantly adjusting to new data, the Old Way embraces fundamental axioms to explain experienced reality by *deduction*. The modern pursuit of the principle of induction, in the English-speaking world the overriding reality check for scientists as well as historians, remained alien to the disciples of German idealism.

As they always do in a favorable cultural climate and conducive economic conditions, these ideas grew legs. The nineteenth-century ideology of the German elite had a deeper impact on politics—perhaps as much by its withdrawal as by active participation—than has ever been admitted. The recently renewed investigation of the passivity of German academia during the demise of the Weimar Republic and of the rise of Adolf Hitler has begun to look beyond Heidegger into the ranks of the great masters of the critical 1830s who failed to mobilize public opinion. One of the underlying weaknesses of German culture, its intellectual subservience to the Old Way, still awaits exposure. By providing metaphysical legitimization to such universals as national destiny, racial identity, and *Volkstum*, it was an easy victim for Nazi ideology. In Reformation history, this mentality was widespread and equally pernicious. For the way Luther and his role in Reformation history were interpreted in the first half of the twentieth century, it is essential to realize that in its heyday, German thought had fallen in step with a medieval past it claimed to have left behind forever. With the national fervor which welcomed the founding of both the Second and Third Reichs, favoring a progressive German Luther separated from his medieval roots, the reformer could be made to spring full-blown from native soil, obscuring the complex genesis and growth of his thought.

John Calvin fared decidedly much better. Whereas the challenge of the historical Luther cannot be understood without an awareness of his modernist roots, one of the most influential movements inspired by him followed an altogether different trajectory. The Reformed Reformation never distanced itself from the Old Way with Luther's sense of achievement and relief. This is due partly to Calvin's humanist confidence that all of scholasticism was too outdated to salvage anything from it, but even more to the social matrix conditioning his movement. As early as 1536, John Calvin designed the first version of the *Institutes,* which later grew to massive proportions, as a concise manifesto, a simple summary of the essentials of faith. But hard and fast systems are helpful for teaching basics to students and eager disciples of visionary founders of schools. To provide clear guidance to his daring emissaries to France, Calvin developed an exquisite system, choosing a path that was also in this respect different from the modern Luther. Though insisting time and again that he had merely provided this manual of scriptural doctrine "for teaching purposes" (*docendi gratia*), his followers, increasingly set upon by a revived Tridentine Catholicism and under the duress of persecution, came to embrace a system of doctrine—unintentionally perverting the aim of their leader. Thus Calvinism would carry across Europe to the shores of the New World a clear summary of the truth in the fundamentals of Scripture. Henceforth, international Protestantism turned Luther's defense of Catholicism into a decidedly anti-Catholic manual for life and thought.

Lutheranism had to strive for doctrinal consensus and stability. It had been left by its founder without a systematic guide, and though his successor, the *modernus* Philipp Melanchthon, had the title of "Germany's Teacher" (*Praeceptor Germaniae*), he was never actually entrusted with that role. The precarious Peace of Augsburg of 1555 and the devastating Thirty Years' War (1618–1648) were followed by what Heinz Schilling has called the Era of Confessionalization, a time when the mood was for peace and order in all realms of life. The same abhorrence of heresy that demanded a stabilized papacy and sparked the Tridentine Reformation induced German Protestantism to give profound credence to its professors and entrust its universities with powerful authority. In need of systems, Protestantism assailed the moderni as relativistic skeptics who would deny religion the status of experienced knowledge and relegated the open-minded, critical stance of the Modern Way to the sciences. Thus, the academic elite was prepared to welcome German idealism, resuscitating the Old Way of closed systems, hailing it as offering intellectual certainty.

The result was a Protestant schizophrenia that combined a genuine admiration of Luther's thought with the rejection of Luther's way of thinking. Although undiagnosed, this in itself is neither exceptional nor necessarily detrimental: in all cultures, East and West, philosophical schools come and go, having made incremental and, in that sense, lasting contributions. But such progress demands that historians be reliable stewards of the past, not partisans of given systems. When the record keepers are also the system builders, the historian easily assumes the stance of prophet. In the mighty shadow of Friedrich Hegel intellectual pluralism was first suspected, then disparaged and, finally, during World War I, dismissed as Western and un-German. Thus the German intelligentsia was ill prepared for the advent of democracy, which could not but appear to be chaotic and the voice of the people vulgar by definition. In the turbulent 1930s the fate of the nation was at stake, but lofty, respected professors failed to support the Weimar Republic, instead succumbing to the allurements of the Führer.

Germany has been much applauded for its remarkable economic recovery (*Wirtschaftswunder*) after World War II. Even more remarkable was its political renaissance, making it first in Europe in the stability of its democratic institutions, responsible political parties, firm trade unions, and the rich pluralism of its informational media. By contrast, the universities have been satisfied to be observers, concentrating, after the brief interval of the student revolution in the 1960s, on preservation and restoration, relieved to return to their nineteenth-century role. To the extent that the academic view of the Reformation still claims to be the orthodoxy of today, the universities will struggle to make lasting progress.

Old wounds easily begin to fester in a climate of societal isolation. In the world of German Luther scholarship, there are some incipient signs that the past may be in process of reclamation. Thus a group of admirers of Emanuel Hirsch and his legacy have not only gathered to commemorate his contribution to Luther research but have also proceeded to edit his scholarly work in Reformation history. However, in the mistaken conviction that scholarship and politics can or should be separated, they are intent on bypassing Hirsch's invocation of the authority of Luther to support his stance in the Third Reich. As the editor of the project had it in his postscript, contemporary theology "cannot ignore" the voice of Hirsch, which, except for unidentified details, deserves to be heard today "as every objective reader will conclude."[2] Emanuel Hirsch was not a marginal figure in the campaign to turn Germany in Hitler's favor; he put his full authority as Luther scholar behind the demise of the Weimar Republic and the rise of Adolf Hitler.[3] Hirsch's reading of the signs of the times fed into the doctrine of providence which paved his way to a Nazi ideology he would never forswear. The key sign of such divine intervention (*Gottes Lenkung*) was the national rebirth (*nationale Wiedergeburt*) which produced the unique phenomenon of *Deutsche Humanität*, a typical universal of the Old Way not easily rendered into English but amply broadcast throughout Europe. It is ironic that Emanuel Hirsch saw more clearly than these admirers that politics and scholarship are closely, in this case indissolubly, intertwined. Without a sense for the biblical Luther of the end time, Hirsch made the darkest epoch in German history into a vessel of divine revelation. He tried to give an honest account (*Rechenschaft*) of his past.[4] We own the same honesty to the next generation.

FROM THE END TIME TO MODERN TIMES

The prophet Zechariah, whose preaching and writing we can date with rare precision from 520 to 515 B.C.E., is not known as a "minor prophet" because of his lesser signifance but because of his acute awareness of the approaching Day of the Lord; no time was left for such sizable books as Isaiah or Jeremiah. In this sense, Luther is a minor prophet, to be understood from his proclamation of the end time. The shift of Luther's Reformation to early Protestantism is the history of the transformation of this belief into the expectation of modern times.

Libraries have to be built to contain all the books written on the character and the beginning of modern times. As with all such momentous questions, the answers vary with time and place and reveal as much about the author as about the subject. Good arguments can be advanced for a "modern" person anywhere on the time line between Columbus and Napoleon, for Elizabeth I of England as well as for Philip II of Spain, for Descartes as well as Spinoza, for Copernicus as well as for Kepler and Newton. The major characters in Reformation history, however, rarely appear in such lists except for reasons of confessional pride. But modern is not what it once was boasted to be. The emergence of the critical term *postmodern* coincides with a global fundamentalism that combines the protection of past values with a deep suspicion of all manifestations of modernity. The left and the right form a rare coalition in energetically chipping away at the statue of modernity.

Our task is not to join in this ideological warfare. For the scope of this book, there is no need to establish the beginnings of modern times or to trace its profile. We want to look for implications of what it meant to have any future at all, for the existential expectations attached to modern times. Where are we on the time line of history?

Two of our major actors, the German Luther and the French Calvin, often subsumed under the same title of reformer, were ages apart in their answer to that question. Accordingly they presented very different platforms for reform. However difficult to conceive, the sense of the future inspires the mobilization of social groups and guides their selection of political strategies and agendas. Prophets who envision the imminence of The End can neither mince their words nor compromise their programs with an eye on long-term gains.

In discussing the eschatology of Luther and Calvin I will begin with the younger man because his vision is easier to grasp and closer to our twenty-first-century sense of past, present, and future. Though the Erasmian era is passing, some of its basic assumptions have survived, and for this we have Calvin, in many ways our contemporary, to thank. The locution "Erasmian era," however, slights the French contribution of ingenuity and originality. The Parisian humanism that shaped the mind of John Calvin was as much at home in France as the country's early evangelical movement: both Erasmus and Luther were latecomers to the

French scene, although Erasmus studied in Paris between 1495 and 1499. In 1523, the translation of a Luther text brought imprisonment and, in 1529, martyrdom at the stake to the French evangelical Louis de Berquin. In the long run, however, Erasmus outshone Gillaume Budé and Jacques Lèfevre d'Étaples in their home country just as he had displaced Johannes Reuchlin in the Empire. No doubt this is due to his amazing creativity, his wide network of correspondents and admirers, his two-front war with Luther and the Sorbonnists, as well as to his careful preparation for *fama,* or posthumous renown.

Erasmus came to symbolize a European cultural tradition that retained its viability until it disintegrated under the onslaught of two world wars. The Erasmian canon incorporated a vision of renaissance (*renascentia*) through the recovery of ancient wisdom, equating good letters (*bonae literae*) with Greek and Latin authors and teaching that the study of the classics provided the best school for life. Not only was the study of the classics (*paedeia*) indispensable to a well-functioning society, but the ideal citizen was the informed Christian (*philosophia Christi*) who combined true learning with authentic humanity (*humanitas*). Today Greek, Latin, and ancient history have become esoteric, and few traces of the Erasmian tradition remain. We ought not to forget, however, that such modern achievements as basic civil rights had to be wrested from a humanistically educated Christian society, nor that Erasmus himself was an anti-Semite and supported Christian war against the Turks as just (albeit after some soul-searching). At the same time, we express Erasmian optimism when we elect our presidents and popes and when we teach that communal happiness can be achieved by sound schooling and responsible behavior (a combination of private and public discipline). While we may contest the details of this formula, it has served us as the foundation of the social contract in our modern democracies.

Although the ideal of equality owes more to the French Revolution than to the Dutch Erasmus, this exquisite scholar was impatient, at times disdainful, of the ritual and external ceremonies that sustained and displayed the imperial and papal hierarchies. In this he was deeply indebted to the tradition of the Modern Devotion. He did not envision a classless society, yet he suffered rather than sustained the structures that later revolutions were to assail. By mocking social distinctions as the games of fools, he caused many—including those associated with the Inquisition—to fear that he was shaking society's foundations.

In all these respects John Calvin was an Erasmian. His confidence in individual growth (*sanctificatio*) is as amazing as his belief in the future growth of the true church (*regnum Christi*). He respected the inventions of the mind as the yield of good schools, and in explaining the six-day creation story as the adjustment of God to the mindset of Moses (*accommodatio Dei*) he showed respect for scientific evidence. Finally, he believed that the reform of Christianity required not only religious piety but public service in order to save a Europe corrupted (*Europa afflicta*) as much by royal absolutism as by papal dominion (*dominium antichristi*). Thus Calvin should be ranked with Erasmus among those sixteenth-century opinion makers who regarded the tragedies of the present as obstacles to a better future, to be overcome in a war to end all wars.

Apart from speaking different tongues and longing for different homelands, Erasmus and Calvin had different conceptions of the Church Catholic. Although Erasmus criticized certain popes—most famously Julius II—his loyalty to the papal office survived periods of doubt so that in the end, tested but unbroken, he deserves to be called a Roman Catholic. Calvin, however, radically reconceived the true church along biblical lines in theology, governance, and liturgy so that the designation "Protestant" is fitting. And, as the effective organizer of the Reformed churches, he deserved to be called the first Protestant.

Both Erasmus and Calvin were pilgrims without a fixed abode. Whereas the erudite Erasmus could claim to be "at home where my library is," the persecution that drove Calvin from his homeland forced him to seek the meaning of the Christian pilgrimage more deeply. Abraham's trek to the promised land (Gen. 12:1) became for him as much a key narrative as was the certainty of being inscribed in the book of God (*praedestinatio*), a seal of identity no country was prepared to supply. Whereas Erasmus would be hailed as the Prince of Humanists, John Calvin became the leader of the Reformation of the Refugees, who were harassed and driven from coast to coast throughout the Old World and across to the New. In all of this, he and his followers were sustained by the belief that time was on their side—much time, the future.

Calvin's distance from Luther is apparent in that whereas for Luther

the church was one, undivided, Calvin assumed the reality of two Western churches, one Christian, the other papal, an anguished situation best
compared to the clash of twins in Rebecca's womb, struggling for the
right of the first born (Gen. 25:23). The contrast is stark. Martin Luther
lives in a radically different world, thinks and speaks his own language,
feels and fights his own demons—as a matter of fact, the devil himself.
In the past, German Reformation historians sought to praise Calvin as
Luther's most obedient disciple, on the assumption that obedience is the
highest virtue. Yet nothing could be more misleading. Luther did not
live—as both Erasmus and Calvin lived—on the threshold of modern
times but in the last days (*finis mundi, Endzeit*): Luther experienced the
very last stage in the history of this world. Because the acute awareness of
the ticking world clock survives today only in marginal groups and is
learnedly dismissed as Jewish apocalypticism, Luther scholars intent on
ensuring the relevance of their hero marginalized this central focus of
Luther's thought and action. By missing a major component of his authentic message they have failed to resolve the mystery of Luther's impact.

Modern Christianity, eager to extend the umbrella of ecumenicism,
has deconstructed heaven and hell, further distancing itself from the
historical Luther, a man who lived between a real God and a real devil.
Those who esteem Luther's message as a lesson for today must take a
prodigious step back in time if they are to rediscover and absorb his
growing conviction that the end of history was rapidly approaching. If
scholars find his real devil an embarrassment, they remain completely
silent when they encounter his belief that the world was in its terminal
phase (a conviction Luther shared with Amos, Zechariah, Jesus, Peter,
and Paul, all of whom measured the future in months rather than centuries). With the best intentions and no doubt unconsciously, even the
best Luther scholars have muffled his apocalyptic voice.

In May 1523, defending the right of a congregation bereft of the
Gospel to call its own preacher, Luther proclaimed the priesthood of all
believers. In a meticulous recent edition (Berlin, 1983) the editor seems
embarrassed by what he calls Luther's "utopian conception" of congregational rights despite the plain anti-utopianism of his warning that the
mighty Antichrist[5] is silencing the Gospel "in this damned Last Time" (*in
dieser verdampter letzten Zeit*).[6] Luther saw unfolding the exact scenario

foretold by the apostles Peter ("in the last days" [*in novissimis diebus*]; Vulgate, 2 Pet. 3:3) and Paul ("those dangerous final days" [*periculosa tempora*]; Vulgate, 2 Tim. 3:1). Although Luther repeated this warning tirelessly, early and late, Luther scholars who read his words do not receive his message.

Why were these times so dangerous? In February 1520, it begins to dawn on Luther that the Evil One, the Antichrist, has penetrated the center of God's house, the Roman see. The old prophecies of the apostles Peter and Paul are being fulfilled "in these days": the Catholic Church itself is threatened and occupied from within. In 1520 Luther's pen explodes with a fervent appeal to the Christian nobility to mobilize for the coming struggle. The biblical sacraments necessary for salvation initiated a life dedicated to the gathering and protection of Catholic treasures, which were under such dire threat of extinction that "these days" must be the end time.[7] Luther's realist eschatology—a term perhaps less loaded than "Jewish apocalypticism" but describing the same scenario of the end—qualifies him to be called Catholic. As Luther's teachers in the Modern Way discovered, words are not immutable reflections of an eternal grammar but human tools to be carefully chosen (*nomina sunt ad placitum*) for clear communication. In this light, Catholic is exactly the right term.

Luther's place in the history of Christianity lies between the Roman Catholic Erasmus and the Protestant Calvin. While the famous words "Here I stand" may never actually have been uttered by Luther, it should be clear that Luther was taking his stand on the Church Catholic—neither to the left nor to the right of it, but exactly there. For him Roman Catholicism had become a contradiction in terms. In the midst of the "darkness at noon" (Matt. 24:29), the prophet perceives clearly and thunders that the papacy's intention is to disparage the older catholicity of the Eastern Church, claim infallibility, create its own saints, and dominate the world in the name—O travesty of travesties—of the suffering servant, Jesus of Nazareth. Under the threat of such "devastation" (Matt. 24:15), the true catholicity of the church has to be defended mightily and uncompromisingly. In the end time no one may give an inch or lose a precious day.

The Antichrist occupied holy territory (Matt. 24:15). The exodus from captivity spelled Catholic survival, though at the high cost of leaving behind the see, once the authoritative ear-listening post for the voice of God (*vox Dei*), now in the hands of the enemy. The Vicar of Christ has usurped the place of Christ: the Day of the Lord cannot be far (1522).[8] Luther's hope for reformation was not a counteroffensive to recover this lost territory. As a matter of fact, "Luther's Reformation" is as much a contradiction in terms as Roman Catholicism: reformation was no longer a matter of human initiative but of God's, soon to be realized with the arrival of his kingdom. Insofar as the Antichrist threatened not only the church but all of human life, public peace and order were urgent matters. Yet the hope for a Germany at peace as the fruit of reformation (*restitutio reipublicae*), as envisaged by Melanchthon, Martin Bucer, and Calvin, is a dream scholars of the Reformation projected onto their German hero.

Still another obstacle stands in the way of recovering the historical Luther. Today the greatest challenge may not be that of grasping the horrors of the last days—our century lives under the constant threat of nuclear disaster and silent springs. More puzzling than any specter of horror is Luther's sense of the rapidly approaching Day of the Lord. As he put it in the 1521 preface to his revolutionary reformulation of Christian ethics: "I am certain that the day has drawn near" (*Confide enim instare diem illum*).[9] And again at the end of his career, believing himself to be near death, he was equally explicit: "Soon this world is to pass away. That is certain" (*mundus . . . mox mutandus, Amen*).[10] Our modern sense of time more easily corresponds to a secularized sense of the liturgical phrase "World without end. Amen." To truly grasp the meaning of the "Day of the Lord" is not a novel challenge; the early Christian community, to a large extent Jewish and schooled in the rabbinical teachings of the minor prophets, faced the same problem. The first missionaries sent out to convert the hellenistic world had problems rendering *Parousia*, or Advent, a key messianic term in the gospel of Jesus for which there was no current (nor is there a modern) word. The idea that the Messiah would come at the end of time to establish the Kingdom of God and initiate the new heaven and the new earth draws on pre-Christian Jewish thought without an equivalent in the Greek Septuagint.[11] The early Christian missionaries had to struggle to create a language in which Gentiles would understand this unfamiliar message. The most effective solution was to denied the achievements of the Renaissance: he even broadened the scope of the movement from the usual "good letters" to global trade, painting, sculpture, and engraving, as well as movable type and artillery.[12] Those achievements, he said, were unequalled by anything seen since the birth of Christ: "Today a young man of twenty can do and know more than twenty doctors in the past." Yet he thought that this explosion of feverish progress in worldly matters was as clear a sign of overheating as the explosion in the spiritual domain where the Gospel was condemned and the abominations stank to high heaven: "I do not doubt that this cannot last any longer: it will be all over before you know it. Amen."[13] It is clear that if Luther had given a lecture course on "Renaissance and Reformation History" it would have had little resemblance to anything offered today—particularly one given by a modern Luther scholar. More to the point: such a course would be very different from one given by Calvin or any of the Protestants influenced by him.

Of all the ways in which Protestantism has distanced itself from Luther, none is so revealing as its shift away from his designation of the pope as Antichrist. For Luther, long a convinced Roman Catholic, "Antichrist" as a warning call is the heaviest weapon in the medieval arsenal of fury, a shout of horror signifying that the inconceivable has happened: that Man of Perdition, the Evil One, had penetrated the center of the Church, the most holy see of Rome. The Antichrist has established his diabolical presence in the conclave of the cardinals (2 Thess. 2:1–4). The message of the Gospel "in these last days" is the rallying call for the mobilization of catholicity. Although the faith of the church, its values, its learning, and its governance no longer sufficed to keep the ship of Christianity afloat, only one chance to make land remained, namely, the marshaling of the Catholic treasures entrusted to the church—the promises of God, his Word and Sacraments. Insofar as Luther is the first to unmask the Evil One who has gained his foothold in the Roman curia, he is the first Catholic fighting the papal waves engulfing Western Christianity. Almost ten years after the colloquy at Marburg, where he became aware of the distance between his own Catholic and the new Protestant views of the Eucharist, Luther replied to the last and most generous overture of his evangelical opponents as follows: "There is an insuperable difference between you and me, in mind and heart" (*sensu et affectu sumus dissimiles;* Zurich, May 14, 1538). This was far more than the difference exposed in the stormy debate over the Real Presence; Luther's sense of catholicity was his own, and it was fundamental to his understanding of reformation at the end of time. While both Calvin and Bucer sought unity in compromise so as to serve the future, Luther took his stand "here," because the future had become the present and there was no time to lose, or to negotiate.

The Reformed Protestant tradition also employs the term *Antichrist* widely, but with a different sense. There it characterizes any evil strategy, whether of sinister papal politics, the counteroffensive of the Jesuits, the devastation of the Netherlands by Philip II, or the invasion threat of the Spanish Armada. The Reformed still understood Antichrist as the empire of evil, but one that was bound to fade in time. While the machinations of the Antichrist might lead to temporary setbacks, on a larger scale of faith they were seen as interventions of the lord of history who by such instruments of discipline (*flagella Dei*) guides his people to the promised land. At times the present may look bleak but, far from signaling the end of time, such trials are the divine road signs to a happy destiny for Europe, and soon for the New World.

We get close to the matrix of early Calvinism in a letter written by Wolfgang Capito, who for years, together with Martin Bucer, served as the leading reformer of Strasbourg. It is the momentous year in which Capito provided refuge to Calvin, who had failed in his mission of transforming Geneva into the city on the hill, unable to overcome the resistance of the city fathers to returning to the burden of clerical rule. Dismissed from Geneva, Calvin would find Strasbourg the right place at the right time. Far more than a temporary refuge, it proved to be a laboratory where he could rethink and refine his missionary tools. In the sobering assessment of Strasbourg in his letter, Capito does not embellish the fact that the Reformation of the City has resulted in magistrates and pastors alike abandoning their layfolk. Yet this crisis is caused not by the Antichrist in the here and now but by atheism in the long run: public morality cannot be left to the secular authorities, he declares. They are driven only by their own short-term political goals. At the same time, the divisive debate about the Eucharist sidetracks our evangelical clergy into a battle that does not permit them to attend to their first duty, feeding their flock. When thus abandoned, in the long run the mass of people will lose all sense of religion (*ut nihil tandem credat*): "The one hope left is the rod of the Lord to spur us on to return to his path of grace" (January 12, 1538). This rod of God, soon to spur Calvin and international Calvinism, was not a punishment of the end times but a goad to the faithful, to turn them in the direction of a promising future. With John Calvin as its principal architect and preeminent spokesman, this program thoroughly reconceived the nature and mission of Luther's Church Catholic.

The contrast between Luther, the first Catholic, and Calvin, the first Protestant, had much to do with the individual impacts of their respective movements, each of which had a profound influence on the course of events in sixteenth-century Europe. This does not mean that there is no significant continuity between their platforms, even in such contested areas as the Eucharist, or that they were exclusively competitors. Yet the difference in reading the clock of the ages has far-reaching, collateral implications. The discovery that the foundations of the Catholic Church were shaky induced in German Lutheranism a hunger for stability that Calvinism neither sought nor respected. Protection by Luther's Elector, Frederick the Wise, and the stabilizing effects of the Peace of Augsburg in 1555 gave Lutherans a degree of confidence in secular authority that the Reformed refugees never acquired. Besides, Luther encouraged Christians to enjoy the world and its beauty all the more because "tomorrow" is the Day of the Lord. Calvin and international Calvinism, possessed only of a heavenly passport, believed that the time on earth we are granted is for schooling and preparation for life eternal. The Ten Commandments were as a map on a desert trail. Luther, the former monk, had become a true layman while the Reformed laymen, children of Abraham, Isaac, and Jacob, bonding under their abbot, Jesus Christ, joined the oldest order of the true church. This Protestant order was bracing for the coming struggle with the renewed monasticism of Rome for the mind and conscience of Europe.

By the time Calvinist Pilgrims reached the coast of Europe and prepared for a transatlantic crossing, they knew about the rod of the Lord, his will as well as his plan for history. By that time, they were not just a continent but ages away from Luther's end of the world. Their future was in a vast land of destiny. Setting sail, they were swept along by a divine

Inquirer published a review of my *Luther: Man between God and the Devil* (1989) under the headline "The Greatest Anti-Semite of All Times" and chided me for waiting until the second part of the book to treat the theme of Luther and the Jews—and for failing to reach the conclusion so obvious to the reviewer. Nor was the discussion advanced when the German chancellor (who had granted the Adenauer Prize to Ernst Nolte, the court historian of the radical right) awarded the Order of Merit of the German Republic to Daniel Goldhagen, author of *Hitler's Willing Executioners*. By this act the leader of the German government branded with collective guilt all those from whom the grace of a post hoc birth had been withheld. Having myself sallied into this emotional minefield with my book *The Roots of Anti-Semitism* (1984), which took the subject back to the Renaissance and Reformation, I would like to offer the following considerations toward a blueprint for demythologizing this much fabled story.

As a general principle, we can begin by recognizing that wherever Christianity has spread, it has sown the seeds of anti-Semitism, and wherever favorable conditions permit, they spring to life. Anti-Semitism, like a snake, constantly changes its skin. Before Darwin it often appeared as anti-Judaism; in the twentieth century it was more often disguised as anti-Zionism. To understand cases as different as those of Saint Augustine in the fifth century and Pope Pius IX in the late-nineteenth century, therefore, we have to ask different questions, those appropriate to their respective historical periods. For the fifteenth and sixteenth centuries, attitudes toward converted Jews provide a concrete litmus test. The question whether baptism erased the stain of Jewishness became more urgent after the expulsion of Jews from Spain in 1492 led to a growing fear that Marranos were spreading throughout Christian Europe. Results of the test for anti-Semitism do greater damage to the reputation of Desiderius Erasmus than to Martin Luther's (news that must dismay all Erasmus' loyal compatriots as well as the *Philadelphia Inquirer* reviewer, the great Dutch humanist being one of a small number of national icons). Whereas Luther considered converted Jews and Gentiles to be equal members of the one undifferentiated Church, Erasmus did not believe that the water of baptism could reach so deeply. Surgery performed upon any baptized Jew, he declared, "brings forth sixty un-baptized ones." For Erasmus, once a Jew, always a Jew. Johannes Eck, Luther's first German antagonist, in this respect a true Erasmian, assailed Luther in treatise after treatise for favoring the Jews (*Judenvater*) and challenged him to swear off his alleged loyalty to the "Christkillers." So Luther did, and in no uncertain terms, drawing upon and elaborating his medieval Catholic belief that all Jews were enemies of Christ and the Church. Yet, he thought, their hatred was overcome by the Gospel and washed away in the floods of baptism.

If Luther comes off better than Erasmus in the test we have devised for sixteenth-century anti-Semitism, certain other observations count heavily against him. No other medieval opinion maker was as well positioned as the Wittenberg reformer to detoxify the central poison in Christian doctrine, namely, the assumption that through its disobedience Israel had broken the covenant with God and was replaced—indeed displaced— by the Christian church and the new covenant. Luther's discovery of justification by faith through grace alone should have sufficed to establish that God made a name for himself by dealing with human disobedience in his own manner and that he made history not by discarding covenants but by renewing them (Jer. 31:31). Luther made *his* name by discovering that salvation is based on the fidelity of the covenantal God, not on the moral reliability of humankind. Yet Luther was unable to see that the same insight had implications for his severe judgment of Israel. Nor is it enough to justify this failure by saying that Luther was a child of his time, all the while pointing a finger at the more extreme views of such contemporaries as Erasmus and Eck. He who had demanded that the validity of traditional beliefs be tested on the basis of Scripture carries a heavy responsibility for giving his seal of approval to the medieval Catholic hatred of the Jews.

The first stirrings of respect for postbiblical Judaism appear not in the milieu of Luther's Reformation but in the very different world of international Protestantism, which was shaped by that other Reformation of the Refugees. The men and women of this movement learned to question the hoary Augustinian saying that the "Christkillers" ostensibly carry the wrath of God by the very fact that they live lives of instability with no country of their own. In the experience of flight and persecution, the reformed refugees started to read the Scriptures with fresh insight. The Old Testament, restored as an authoritative part of the Scriptures, was recovered as the travel guide for the faithful trekking from land to land without any other papers than a heavenly passport. In the early seventeenth century, Jews for the first time were granted citizens' rights in northern and southern Holland.

If there was an unbroken line from Luther to Hitler it seems that the Nazis themselves did not think so. Under Nazi auspices Luther's anti-Jewish tracts were published in Berlin in 1936 with the reproach that Germany's own Luther scholars had hitherto forsaken their duty by silencing his "authentic voice." Their complaint must have rung truer in Berlin than in Vienna. More than a decade before the Nazis had to remind Germany of Luther's anti-Jewish heritage, Catholic Austria below the Danube was as publicly anti-Semitic as Poland to the east. The correspondence of Walter Löwenthal, an Austrian Jew, from July 1924, recently made accessible, illustrates the climate of thought that had shaped the mind of Hitler and his early followers.

By comparing the growth of anti-Semitism in different countries of Europe in the critical years, 1918–1933, we may conclude that Hitler would have found a more favorable reception for his anti-Jewish platform among large segments of public opinion in France or England, soon to ally against him, than in Germany. In no western country was Jewish assimilation so far advanced as there, even to breaking down the walls of academia. The reversal of the process was as traumatic for a Jew as it would have been for any German. Thus the painfully drawn-out sense of cultural dislocation described by the Jewish historian Arnold Berney, who was forced to renounce his German identity after Martin Heidegger nazified the University of Fribourg (with the support of historians who were to shine again in the Germany of my own day). Thus, too, the perplexity of the Tübingen historian of modern Germany, Hans Rothfels, a Jew wounded in World War I, holder of the Iron Cross, who was almost too late in making his escape to the United States in 1939, two weeks before war broke out. As he put it to me, Rothfels found it inconceivable that "a fanatical Austria could ever conquer my tolerant Germany."

If we are properly to evaluate the thesis of an unbroken link between Luther and Nazidom's willing executioners, we should regard the Third Reich's last decade, 1933–1945, as a separate epoch. Within this period we are well advised to distinguish between the years *before* and *after* the outbreak of the war, as Joachim Fest and Klaus Scholder have been able to show without a trace of German apologetics.[2] As it did in every other parliamentary democracy of the time, the war strengthened national solidarity and weakened the voices of opposition. But even before the war, the Nazi rise to power in 1933 brought a degree of repression surpassing anything in modern experience. This must be taken into account in assessing a people's guilt and responsibility. The new reality of Nazi totalitarianism can best be grasped in the plaint of Jewish refugees who managed to reach the United States: "Our Germany has become one large concentration camp." One of the most profound accounts to come from within wartime Germany, Wolfgang von Buch's *Wir Kindersoldaten*,[3] confirms the accuracy of that lament. Inside that nationwide concentration camp, von Buch, still a boy, saw that dissent was identified with disorder and set in motion a persecuting rage needing no ethnic hatred for its fuel. What started as the legitimation of anti-Semitism in the name of order had become the mask of total terror. That Germany could accept a totalitarian system with complete control over information, law enforcement, and order—an ideal of order that combines security (*Sicherheit*) with service (*Dienst*)—was inconceivable to Hans Rothfels in 1939. But, through whatever combination of circumstances, Germany did accept it, and today we struggle to comprehend its full effects on the realities of daily life.

I do not intend this analysis to serve the cause of exculpating the Germans who were fated to be born too early. Rather I hope to direct attention to the decade of decision between 1925 and 1935, particularly to the responsibility of academic leaders, who enjoyed a status of respect unparalleled in the rest of Europe. Among those leaders Martin Heidegger, Emanuel Hirsch, and others constituted a kind of Nazi think tank that provided Hitler with some of his most effective ideological executioners. Although they are now restored to what may be their rightful glory as scholars, they have forfeited their claim to be regarded as citizens of humanity.

VI

THE CONTROVERSY OVER IMAGES
AT THE TIME OF THE REFORMATION

CRACKS IN THE EDIFICE OF CONTEMPORARY RESEARCH

In the late summer of 1515, Desiderius Erasmus, by then renowned as a humanist and social critic, dramatically encountered an explosive convergence between theoretical and practical reform. Traveling in England with his friend John Colet—on one of those expeditions he later dignified as a *peregrinatio*—they took the road to Canterbury to see the famous cathedral. There both men marveled at the extravagant devotion people lavished on the statue of St. Thomas Becket and at the kisses with which they covered his feet. The reactions of Colet and Erasmus were diametrically opposite. Colet, an Oxford New Testament specialist,[1] regarded this reverence for images as abominable (*indigna*), whereas Erasmus—although agreeing that it was superstition—thought it necessary to be patient until such abuses could be eliminated without commotion (*sine tumultu*). He expressed this deep difference from Colet in a smooth alliterative formula: "in tolendo quam in tollerando" (I see a greater evil in removal than in toleration).[2] Erasmus was much more critical than the modern apologist Eamon Duffy is willing to admit. To him it was super-stition, but he would have been fully in agreement with Duffy's conclu-sion that "Reformation was a stripping away of familiar and beloved observances."[3] The contrasting solutions of Colet (reform by removal) and Erasmus (reform through restraint and reeducation) were not only to divide the Anglican Church but also to shape the course of the conti-nental Reformation as well.

At first glance the Canterbury incident would seem to require only a slight correction to the standard representation of the image controversy in the sixteenth century. Hitherto we have assumed that we should look for its origins in Wittenberg, with most scholars dating it to January 10, 1522, when Augustinian monks first removed images from their monas-tic church, whereupon Andreas Karlstadt energetically recommended their action to the Council and, in his tract *On the Removal of Images,* ele-vated it to the fundamental principle of a comprehensive Reformation. The standard designation "Wittenberger Wirren" (unrest in Wittenberg) suggests that this was a side effect which occurred—not incidentally—during Luther's absence at the Wartburg.

Such an interpretation is supported by a striking passage in the second Invocavit sermon, which Luther delivered on March 10, four days after his hasty return. His use of the metaphor of "sleeping and beer drinking" for the exemplary strategy of waiting while God directs the course of the Reformation is worth quoting at length, in that it has left traces in con-temporary scholarship that, paradoxically, are both too few and too deep:

> In short, I will preach it, teach it, write it, but I will constrain no man by force, for faith must come freely, without compulsion. Take myself as an example. I opposed indulgences and all the papists, but never with force. I simply taught, preached, and wrote God's Word; otherwise I did nothing. And while I slept [cf. Mark 4.26–29], or drank Wittenberg beer with my friends Philip [Melanch-thon] and Amsdorff [Nicholas von Amsdorf (1483–1565)], the Word so greatly weakened the papacy that no prince or emperor ever inflicted such losses upon it. I did nothing; the Word did

everything. Had I wanted to foment trouble, I could have brought great bloodshed upon Germany; indeed I could have started such a game that even the emperor would not have been safe. But what would it have been? Mere fool's play. I did nothing. I let the Word do its work.[4]

In the mass of secondary literature, two prudently argued and meticulously documented contributions stand out, forming a consensus that defines the current state of scholarly opinion. The first is Walter von Loewenich's important analysis of 1980 in which he summarized his conclusion at the beginning of the essay: "For Luther, the question of images had only a secondary significance."[5] To this von Loewenich added two observations, the first, subjective and biographical: "Images no longer had any power for Luther";[6] the second, the indisputable, objective fact that "it [the ban on images in Exod. 20.4] is missing from all of [Luther's] catechetical writings."[7]

Ten years later, in 1990, Ulrich Köpf confirmed von Loewenich's thesis and substantially expanded it by encompassing the entire Reformation in his conclusion: "The image question is not a central theme of Reformation theology."[8] The extent of this inherently elastic meaning of "central" becomes clear with the observation that although in various Reformed confessions of faith a separate section was to be devoted to the question of images, no "independent doctrine" concerning this theme was formulated.[9]

While we still have to go into the assessment of the Reformed movement, the general assent to von Loewenich's thesis is especially significant. What was characterized in 1980 as secondary for Luther is now more precisely understood in terms of the opposition between theory and practice, and, in fact, this assumes the priority of an image-free reform theology which only subsequently set off the icon controversy. "This controversy broke out—first in Wittenberg and Zürich—when the Reformation movement had already found strong popular support and was setting itself the task of translating theological impulses of the Reformation into ecclesiastical practice. Yet, no matter how slight the theological weight of the image question may have been, as soon as it was broached, it powerfully stirred the people whose religious lives it touched. Few themes aroused such surges of passion."[10] We will not go wrong if, behind this opposition between theology and passion, we suspect that other opposition between the quiet of the study and the turbulence of the street, or, as in Luther's contrast, between relaxed beer drinking and violent action, the many variations of which are all contained in his brief Latin formula: *sine vi sed verbo*.

Even if we understand the relation between theory and practice dialectically, however, and if we want to look out from the study into the street to get a true grasp of Luther's reform program, the conclusion that the question of images was of only secondary importance will still remain valid—in any case for Luther himself. However, we will have to relate this thesis to Luther's consideration of the whole Reformation movement in a much more radical way.

With regard to Luther's judgment on images, we are not in the dark. In his report to his confidant Nikolaus Hausmann on the situation he found in Wittenberg, he was unambiguous: "damno imagines." The elimination of images, however, should be brought about by means of a consensus grounded in the faith. As far as the intended action goes, Luther's posture in 1522 appears no different from the position Erasmus had counseled six years earlier—images should be tolerated until they can be removed *sine tumultu*. On March 17, having just arrived from the Wartburg, he summarized his strategy on images in this way: "They would fall of themselves if people were taught and knew that before God symbols are nothing."[11] Yet, taken as a whole, Luther's view of history is just as far removed from Erasmus as from the position of the other reformers.

To clarify this situation we shall proceed by individual steps, starting with Luther. We can then assess the implications of three rather recent conclusions in scholarship.

LUTHER: AN ISSUE ON WHICH THE CHURCH STANDS OR FALLS ("ARTICULUS STANTIS ET CADENTIS ECCLESIAE")

The difference of opinion between Erasmus and Colet in 1515 does not merely show that the Wittenberg unrest came too late to be taken as a chronological point of departure; it also forces us to recognize that already in the ferment preceding the Reformation, in the efforts to transform reform into Reformation, the image question was taken as a fundamental principle by everyone who regarded renewal as a struggle against the externalization of religion. The alternatives of *tollendo* versus *tolerando,* of instant removal versus long-term reeducation, should not mislead us: on the eve of the far-reaching decisions of the 1520s, biblical humanists, not yet divided into hard and fast positions pro or contra Rome, were neither able nor willing to avoid the image question. In this respect, the question was anything but secondary; on the contrary it was unalterably bound up with the issue of church reform.

It is therefore not surprising that, at about the same time as Erasmus' pilgrimage to Canterbury, Martin Luther was referring his Wittenberg students to the immense importance of the image question in his exegesis on Romans. When Paul talked about people who are weak in faith (Rom. 14.1), he was thinking of those who, owing to anxiety or superstition, depend upon outward matters and external laws, since they don't know that "regnum Dei intra vos," the kingdom of God is within you (Matt. 24, 11.24). "In the things which are 'musts' and are matters of necessity, such as believing in Christ, love nevertheless never uses force or undue constraint."[12] This view of inwardness is a liberation from all ceremonies, be they fasts, holy days, ceremonial robes, altar decoration, monks' vows, or images. None of this is any longer required for salvation; such things are to be retained only insofar as they are useful in loving service to one's neighbor.

Luther's answer to the question whether all this, all these venerable ceremonies, was superfluous and therefore *tollendo,* to be removed, is unambiguous: "Absit."[13] Only through the correct proclamation of the Gospel is the conscience set free from fasting and holy days. The same is true for the vow of a monk: "If you think you cannot have salvation in any other way except by becoming a religious, do not even begin. . . . [But] for this reason I believe that it is better to become a monk today than it was at any time in the last two hundred years, because up to this time the monks drew away from the cross and there was a glory in being a religious. But now again it has become displeasing to men, even to those who are good, because of the foolish garb. But this is what it meant to be a religious, that one be hated by the world and regarded as a fool. . . . But now there is no more arrogant class of people than they are, sad to say!"[14]

We have quoted rather extensively here to demonstrate that the image question cannot be seen in isolation. For Luther it is part of a new, all-encompassing way of life, which, in his opinion, naturally—and especially—included the cloistered life. The commentary on Romans is not just a pre-Reformation work. *On Monastic Vows* is based on the same foundation of freedom from ceremonies and, despite all the newly articulated, severe criticism, represents the possibility of an entirely evangelical life as a monk. Thus, in no way does it contain a fundamental rejection of vows: Luther himself did not discard the monk's habit for another three years, in October 1524. Whether in regard to vows or images, the proper stance can be achieved and is determined by that inner freedom that is based on justifying faith.

Although the debate over the dating of the Reformation breakthrough has not yet been settled, we may consider Luther's solution of the question of ceremonies, including the pressing questions of images, vows, and fasting, as definitive proof that he had already arrived at the understanding that Christian freedom was derived from faith. In the 1520s, this would become the general program of the Reformation. However, the same is not true of the principle discussed earlier, "sine vi sed verbo," not by force but by the Word, a phrase quoted frequently but not fully understood. "Not by force but by the Word" did not mean rejection of the sword, nor did it mean a pacifistic solution. While Erasmus and Zwingli both went through a pacifist phase of development, this cannot be claimed for Luther. In 1520 Luther advised that "for the improvement of the Christian estate" superstitious ceremonies should be eliminated by legitimate force. Thus he demands that "the chapels in the countryside and the rural churches" in Wilsznacht, Sternberg, and Trier, in the Grymstal, and even the former Jewish synagogue in Regensburg dedicated to "die Schöne Maria" be razed. It was not merely an attack on images that Luther advocated two years later in his *Kirchenpostille* (1522) but an attack on churches, suggesting that "It would be better to kill all the bishops and annihilate all religious foundations and monasteries than to let a single soul perish, not to mention losing all souls for the sake of those useless idols and dummies."[15]

"Not by force but by the Word" does not mean renunciation of struggle but struggle with different weapons, and indeed with what were still the only effective weapons, those of the Spirit. This "still" deserves to be highlighted since it indicates Luther's narrowing, which separated him from the rapidly growing Protestant movement. It also builds on what we, because of its importance, should call the "second Reformation breakthrough." We can date this second discovery more precisely. During the month of February 1520 Luther studied Valla's attack on the authenticity of the *Donation of Constantine*,[16] which Ulrich von Hutten published seventy years after its completion.[17] With deep pain and an inner commotion such as has not been documented for any of the other Reformers, Luther concluded that there could no longer be any doubt, the pope was the long expected Antichrist. On February 24, 1520, he expressed his dreadful new conviction to George Spalatin: "I am in terrible anguish because I have almost no more doubts that the Pope is truly the Antichrist popular opinion is universally expecting."[18] It is now essential to assess the devil's work correctly as being permitted by God, threatening the Catholic Church at its very center.[19] In a single sentence Luther summarizes the convergence of the first and second Reformation discoveries as a new Reformation strategy in this way: neither intelligence nor powerful weaponry ("prudentia nec armis") is what we need, but prayer and strong faith, with which we can retain Christ on our side ("pro nobis"), whereas if we rely upon our own powers we are finished.[20]

The doctrine of justification as a survival strategy has yet other aspects; the locution "still" also signifies that the decisive struggle would not last long and that the true believers were building a wall of defense against the evil works allowed by God. All these aspects have long been inadequately illuminated in Luther research. For our purposes, however, it is important to understand that von Loewenich's thesis ("for Luther the image question was of only secondary importance") needs to be expanded: that all questions of the implementation of the Reformation that distracted from true faith and inner freedom only led to conflicts that pumped up the Antichrist and fed his rage. Fundamentally, Luther was not so much the first Protestant as the Catholic reformer who knew that he had been called in order to resist the Roman papacy's burglary of the treasury room of the Catholic Church.

Only with the second Reformation discovery does the magnitude of the threat become apparent—that the doctrine of justification is not merely an article on which the church stands but also—literally—on which it falls.

FROM IMAGE TO IDOL: THE ANTICHRIST AS BAAL

While Luther, in his striking beer drinking and sleeping metaphor, was still counting on a changed consciousness as a prerequisite for any action and insisting on waiting for God's intervention, an otherwise unknown Swiss named Uli Kennelbach from Toggenburg had already taken a decisive step further. In the inn at Utznach, he had run his sword through a picture of the crucified Christ together with the Virgin Mother on one side and St. John on the other, while shouting "idols there are worthless and cannot help" ("di götzen nützend nüt da und si möchten nüt gehelfen"). On June 21, 1520, Kennelbach was beheaded for cursing and blasphemy.[21] That the sword was the instrument of his punishment as well as of his crime leads us to suspect that he was a man of some social standing (just two weeks earlier a woman convicted of witchcraft had been burned at the stake, considered a more degrading form of execution), whereas his explanation suggests that this was an act of deliberate protest rather than of loutish drunkenness: he labels the image an "idol." This case reminds us that using the Wittenberg unrest as the standard point of departure too easily leads to the erroneous conclusion that theologians such as Andreas Karlstadt were radical because they rashly transported a new issue, discussed only in academic circles, into the public arena. Long before the Wittenberg unrest, the question of images was a public matter insofar as government had the duty of protecting their sacredness. Nor was it a novelty that images were condemned as idols. Karlstadt rightly defended himself against the accusation that his tract "On the Elimination of Images" ('Von Abtuung der Bilder') incited uprising, since it only expanded upon and explained the Wittenberg Council decree of January 24, 1522, namely, that images must be removed in order to prevent what it called idolatry (*Abgötterei*).

Nonetheless, in this elevation of the reproach from superstition to idolatry we have uncovered an important track which leads to Zwingli and Bullinger and, at mid-century, to France and the Low Countries. With the association of image veneration with the worship of Baal, a split is established in the western church, a split we do not find in the same fashion in Luther. After he espied the Antichrist, his task was to protect the Catholic legacy from its deformation by the Roman papacy. This was a battle within the one Latin medieval church. To the end of his life, Luther understood the struggle over faith in the ongoing Reformation as a wrestling match between the twins in the womb of their mother Rebecca.

The accusation of idolatry takes us in an entirely different direction once it is raised in the name of a newly formed community of faith which, unlike the papal church, is of course threatened, but not possessed, by the Antichrist. This two-church doctrine was fully elaborated as dogma by John Calvin, and accordingly the prohibition of images is firmly established in the various reformed confessions of faith. It was not Karlstadt, as has for so long been maintained,[22] but Ludwig Hätzer (d. 1529) in the period in which he must still be counted a follower of Zwingli,[23] who decisively demonstrated the link between the doctrine of images and of the church. Even in the title of his programmatic tract of 1523, *Ein Urteil Gottes unseres Ehegemahls wie man sich mit allen Götzen und Bildnissen halten soll,* he addresses God as spouse. The degree to which this designation is relevant is then immediately made clear: the ban on images is part of the pact and covenant of God,[24] the divinely drawn boundary line between the papists ("bäpstler") and the chosen people ("das usserwelt volk").[25]

The warm reception and the impact of Hätzer's tract are indicated by his invitation a month after it appeared (September 24, 1523) to keep the minutes of the council disputation that was held at the Zürich town hall on October 26–28. On the first day, dedicated entirely to the image question, Leo Jud referred explicitly to Hätzer's tract. In the December meeting of the council of preachers of the city and province of Zürich which was held to determine how best to preach and provide pastoral care, Zwingli did the same.[26] With a delay in the implementation of this teaching, intended to avoid alienating those who were weak in the faith, Zwingli distanced himself from his own left wing, which Hätzer would soon join. Nevertheless, we have here more than a temporary coalition; indeed, this is the bedrock of the Swiss Reformation, concisely formulated by Zwingli as the "Kingdom of Christ is also external" ("regnum Christi etiam est externum"). Recently Berndt Hamm and Peter Blickle have directed our attention to the political expansion of the concept of liberty, especially as compared to that of Luther:[27] Christian liberty takes on republican features. But even for our subject, the phrase "etiam externum" is relevant, for it demonstrates the central significance of the image controversy.

We can go even one step further: just where the controversy over images intersects with the dispute over the Eucharistic sacrifice, we can see the new point of departure which, thanks to Bullinger and Calvin, was to transform the Reformation into a European movement. The interpretation of "est" (is) as "significat" (signifies), borrowed only two years later from Cornelis Hoen, is already established in Zwingli's rejection of the mass as a sacrifice on the grounds that images are only representations: "Otherwise a painting of a person would also be a person."[28]

In his extensive apology, "Concerning the Origin of the Errors in the Veneration of Saints and Images" (De origine errorum in divorum et simulacrorum cultu, 1529), Heinrich Bullinger reinforces Zwingli's rejection of images for worship, citing Erasmus for this,[29] and rightly emphasizing that this did not diminish his respect for representational art outside the church.[30] But it was not feasible to limit the scope of the image controversy to church decoration. Once images were seen as idols and the veneration of images as idolatry, the debate was caught up with other central issues of faith and piety. Nor was this confined to Zürich. Martin Bucer in his impressive textbook of theological controversies (1534) not only ranked the image question ahead of vows, fasting, and discipline but, just as Bullinger did, related it closely to invocations of the saints and thus directly to justification by faith. The scholarly apparatus in the recently published critical edition of this work, *Defense against the Principles of Catholicism*,[31] readily shows that in the areas of southern Germany and Switzerland the image question is in no way secondary but functions as a central test question in the debate over the boundary between idolatry and piety, between the true and false church.

BACK TO THE STREET: THE IMAGE
CONTROVERSY AS IT WAS ENDURED

In his comprehensive analysis of Greek Orthodoxy, Jaroslav Pelikan comes to the general conclusion that the history of iconoclasm is to be understood as "a religious pretext for rationalizing an essentially political conflict."[32] Such a political grounding might clarify aspects of the Byzantine icon controversy, and it can shed light on iconoclasm as a mass movement in the Netherlands in 1566, but the interpretation is probably too limited for the formative years of the evangelical movement. Thus far, we have given our attention mostly to official statements, theological writings, and council mandates in order to appreciate the importance of the controversy over images and how it related to all other aspects of the struggle over belief. We have further arrived at the conclusion that Zwingli's insistence that the kingdom of God was "also external" raises an important political claim. The perspective of intellectual history, however, should not separate us so far from the grassroots that we negate religious motivation or remove it from consideration on the mistaken notion that it is a pretext.

VII

TOWARD THE RECOVERY
OF THE HISTORICAL CALVIN

> Ne preschez plus la vérité,
> Maistre Michel!
> Contenüe en l'Evangille,
> Il y a trop grand danger
> D'estre mené
> Dans la Conciergerie.
> Lire, lire, lironfa.
> —*Chanson Nouvelle*

CALVIN'S VANISHING ACT

A century ago every serious history of Europe was bound to have a chapter on Calvin and Calvinism. Authors played up the story of heroic Calvinist resistance to the alliance of the Pope, the Catholic King of Spain, and the Most Christian King of France and gave more space to those Calvinist pirates, the Geuzen, or "Sea Beggars," than to the noble family of Guise, Catholic champions in the French Wars of Religion. They followed the spread of Calvinism from the Seven Provinces and the kingdom of Scotland and along an intellectual axis from Heidelberg and eventually to Harvard. It was a truism that the organic center of Calvinism was Geneva, where John Calvin ruled, uncontested.

This interpretation was not the sole property of the now-decried Whig historians. The Saint Bartholomew's Day Massacre of August 24, 1572, was generally treated as a more significant event than the slaughter of the

German peasants in 1525, nearly fifty years earlier. This is true of Calvin's detractors as well as of his admirers. When Stefan Zweig proceeded from *Die Welt von Gestern* to the travail of modern Europe, he cast Calvin as the lofty tyrant who in executing Michael Servetus foreshadowed the terror of Nazi Germany.[1] Indeed, Calvin's condemnation of Servetus and of Sebastian Castellio receives more attention than all the other thousands of sixteenth-century martyrdoms combined.

Calvin's stature, however, has diminished, and to assess what we might call Calvin's vanishing act we shall have to redraw the map of Reformation Europe on a larger scale, for we need first to account for the emergence of international Calvinism. It is not poor scholarship that has denied us access to the historical Calvin, but, among other things, the distortion of perspective induced by certain important scholarly trends. A case in point is the founding of the French journal *Annales d'histoire économique et sociale* in 1929, a signal event in the shift from cultural to economic history and from the focus on personal agency to the search for long-range, underlying, impersonal factors. Yet it should not be overlooked that its founders, Marc Bloch and Lucien Febvre, invited the cultural historian Johan Huizinga to join the first editorial board in what would have been an outstanding triumvirate. Huizinga refused, rejecting the assumption that analysis of long-term developments, however methodologically consistent, would yield processes that would be regarded as historical laws or, as Febvre put it, that the multitude of details would yield general laws (*des lois se dégageront*). Huizinga's response was uncompromising: sheer illusion (*IJdel illusie!*); in the field of history, causality has only a limited validity.[2] In succeeding decades Huizinga's warning went unheeded as the pursuit of long-term process intensified to the point that the demise of biography seemed a foregone conclusion. Why study such historical actors as John Calvin when processes, not individuals, make history?

Yet, though every generation inherits a set of limiting conditions, this does not neutralize individual initiative or foreclose on a variety of free responses. Impersonal material forces are not to be underestimated; they shape the outlines of social history. As the eminent Czech scholar František Graus pointed out, it is a defining characteristic of early modern times that humans were increasingly seen as responsible and therefore culpable for political and economic hardships formerly suffered as acts of God.[3] Calvin's leadership in questioning the status quo and calling attention to the distinction between heaven-sent disaster and the human perpetration of evil had a formative influence on the development of the modern consciousness. It has frequently been noted that God's providence plays an extraordinary role in Calvin's thought. This providence, however, is not the inevitable and necessary process of recent historical thought but the certain expectation of unforeseen and unpredictable consequences. Above all, it provides the rationale for transferring the ills of church and society from the realm of doom and destiny to that of human response to challenge.

Today *Historismus,* or historicism, is a pejorative in-group term used to denote the naive nineteenth-century confidence in discovering the meaning of history through the documents.[4] Yet to this much maligned Historismus we owe the landslide of critical editions that set the modern standard for medieval, Renaissance, and Reformation studies: such works of painstaking scholarship as the *Monumenta Germaniae Historica, Corpus Reformatorum, Bulletin de la Société de l'Histoire du Protestantisme Français,* and the *Corpus Catholicorum.*

The twentieth century's issue-driven rejection of this mighty achievement has produced a stark historical narrowing. In sixteenth-century studies, Reformation history was reduced first to the life and work of Martin Luther and then, since mid-century, to the young Luther and his Reformation breakthrough. The initially promising investigations of the printing, preaching, and politics of the City Reformation became stuck in the 1520s and 1530s. Reformation historians, possessed by the misguided notion of a "Lutherische Engführung,"[5] the tunneling toward Luther, no longer seem interested in following the German story as far as the division of the Hapsburg empire, the effects of the Schmalkaldic War, and the abdication of Emperor Charles V. The failure to encompass these epoch-making events into the Reformation narrative helps explain the startling conclusion reached by Thomas A. Brady, Jr., in his reconstruction of the politics of the Reformation in Germany: "The decisive force in making Luther's movement into the German Reformation was not his message's content."[6] It is exactly the parochial study of church history that engenders such marginalization of the impact of theology.

Because they are usually treated as an appendix to German Reformation history, Calvin studies have suffered a like atrophy. The much hailed Calvin renaissance of the 1930s was the result of an intensive theological debate between Karl Barth and Emil Brunner over Calvin's anthropology. After World War II this was joined and amplified by Otto Weber and Ernst Wolf in their search for the reformed roots of the resistance against Hitler.[7] When the learned Gottfried W. Locher opened the first Calvin Research Congress on September 16, 1974, he addressed the participants as fellow believers sharing a vision of continuing Calvin's Reformation by following a research program geared toward the theology of Calvin.[8]

The conference volumes produced over the next twenty years show that little has changed; admiring disciples are still investigating the theological issues in the faith that Calvin's revelations continue to be timely. In his important study of Calvin, William J. Bouwsma renewed the quest for the historical Calvin by ignoring the icon of the Doctor Ecclesiae and looking for a man who was inconsistent, had doubts, felt pain and pleasure and, above all, anguish.[9] In deploring the hegemony of theology in Calvin studies, I do not mean to deny that the decisive force in Calvin's foundation of the French Reformation is to be found in his "message's content," to use Brady's term. At the same time, only by following the iconoclastic course taken by Bouwsma will we recover Calvin's actual role in the reception of the Reformation in France. As we shall see, the social and political history of Calvinism has been significantly advanced by the work of William Monter, Robert Kingdon, Francis Higman, Henry Heller, Bernard Roussel, Harro Höpfl, and Philip Benedict.[10] Yet Huguenot research will not be able to profit from Calvin studies as long as the chasm between Calvin's thought and Calvin's influence continues to be widened by historians of theology who set their research agenda by the standard of its contemporary relevance and its connection with contemporary spiritual trends.

Ironically, the very riches of the Geneva archives prove to be a barrier as well as a bonanza. The surviving records of the city council, the Compagnie des Pasteurs, and the Consistoire contain detailed information about the ebb and flow of Calvin's faction, the unsettling effects of an endless inflow of refugees, and the Consistory's unflagging efforts to establish some form of controls over Genevans' behavior. Naturally, historians go where the sources are, but in this case the incremental advances in knowledge hinder a broader, more balanced assessment of Calvin's actual place and function. By concentrating on the local archives we get a much better grasp of actual conditions and daily life, yet this only further consolidates the already fixed idea that to say Calvin is to say Geneva.

Geneva was never Calvin's foremost concern. When he first took up his station there in July 1536, he served as lector and right-hand man of the French reformer Guillaume Farel. Thrown out by the city council two years later, Calvin decided he would never return. He changed his mind in September 1541, only because he was made to see that with Geneva so close to France it could become a convenient staging area from which he could introduce the Reformation to his beloved homeland.

Calvin did not accept citizenship in Geneva until 1559, five years before his death. To this and other evidence that Geneva never occupied first place in his thoughts, biographers have paid little attention. Thanks to the research of Charlotte C. Wells, however, we can now discern what it would have meant for Calvin in terms of rights, duties, and loyalties to make his exile official by giving up French citizenship.[11] In that same year of his naturalization, the Genevan Academy was established to take Lausanne's place in training missionaries for the rapidly emerging French Reformed churches. Calvin wanted Geneva to carry through its Reformation, of course, but primarily to serve as a model—and if the Reformation failed there, as a scandalous model—for the Kingdom of Christ in France and Europe. In brief, Calvin the city reformer is not sufficiently understood without giving due place to Calvin the territorial reformer who exploited the Genevan connection for his Reformation of the Refugees in France and Europe at large.

Among the factors responsible for the fading of the historical Calvin confessionalization has played a significant part. This version of confessionalization hails from Bielefeld and Fribourg and is now firmly established in German historiography. One of its chief proponents, Heinz Schilling, is an early modern historian with a far wider range than his reputation usually admits.[12] Possessing a firm grasp on the social, political, and cultural history of the young Dutch Republic, he has made a major contribution to our understanding of civic Calvinism, the impact of Calvinism on the Netherlands and northern Germany.[13] Together with Wolfgang Reinhard, he has advanced the confessionalization thesis to characterize the parallel shift from church to state control in the Lutheran, Catholic, and Reformed territories of the late sixteenth- and seventeenth-century Empire.[14] This form of big history has a number of advantages, not the least of which is the interconfessional approach that can integrate related fields of interest long divided into religious, social, and political history. But the concentration on a single theme can have the effect of a spotlight casting deep shadows over the surrounding area.[15] For one thing, although efforts to test the European-wide applicability of the confessionalization theory have been made, its origin and design are firmly grounded in German soil and Imperial developments that came after the Reformation. The characterization of Calvinism as the "Second Reformation" is particularly misleading since this term applies only to a limited number of territories in Germany.[16] For the majority of Europe, Calvinism spelled the *first* advent of the Reformation. Outside Europe it was responsible for a transition from religious to social and political ideas that challenged the establishment.

As Martin Heckel has shown, the Peace of Augsburg of 1555 legalized the fiction of the one, undivided church, a territorial *itio in partes,* each part with a limited form of religious self-determination.[17] This legal solution was fully in keeping with Luther's "Catholic" conviction that reformed and unreformed Christians continue to be attached to one another in the body of the church, vying for their birthright, like the twins in Rebecca's womb. Where Calvinism appears in Europe as the first Reformation, it demands not only a withdrawal from Roman obedience, but also the establishment of independent local congregations charged to ban the "Nicodemites," who do not wish to join the organized, visible church. Henceforth, two clearly separated churches are vying for the same birthright.

A further drawback of the confessionalization thesis is that it includes the dubious assumption of inevitability.[18] The religious concept of divine destiny is here secularized, but its potential for explaining Germany's reconstruction and state building after the disaster of the Thirty Years' War is limited. Early Calvinism, in the century between 1550 and 1650, confronts the assumption of inevitability by displaying a network of short-term processes constantly interrupted and dislodged by unforeseen events. Calvinism's war-torn path was marked by battles which by definition are uncertain in outcome.

Good historians are the guardians of contingency. They are aware that it is difficult to understand what actually did happen if they do not also ponder what might have happened.[19] For example, if the reformist cardinal Reginald Pole had not lost the papacy by one vote in the 1549 election, there would have been no Julius III to pave the way for what we might call the curial Counter Reformation.[20] Again, a victory for the Spanish Armada in 1588 would have overturned the precarious Elizabethan settlement and materially affected the balance of power in Europe. We know now that Spanish naval tactics were not suited for the stormy weather and, perhaps even more important, that the Spanish ships were undergunned in comparison to those of the English.[21] Such explanations are more convincing than either the religious myth of God's direct intervention or, in the case of the Spanish failure in the Low Countries, the secular reference to the continental pirates' Dutch courage. The point is, however, and all extant sources confirm it, that these outcomes were close calls.

The victory of an absolute Catholic monarchy in France between the late sixteenth and late seventeenth centuries is yet another example of the uncertainties of history. The ascendancy to the throne of the Huguenot Henry of Navarre in 1589 was itself unlikely, and it was followed by a series of unpredictable contingencies. In the summer of 1590, the newly crowned Henry IV initiated a military campaign, winning victories at Arques and Ivry, which nearly gained him access to Paris, where the anti-Huguenot leadership "had unleashed a reign of terror."[22] On August 30 the Parisians were expecting the victorious monarch to enter the city; instead Henry decided to withdraw to cover his lines of communication.[23] By March 22, 1594, when he at last entered Paris, the king had returned to the Catholic fold, and at Nantes, four years later, in a further act of national consolidation, he granted limited toleration to his former coreligionists. Louis XIV's revocation of the Edict of Nantes in 1685 might well seem to have been a necessary event in the inevitable progress toward absolutism in France, but the events leading up to the edict and then to its revocation were neither necessary nor inevitable. The phenomenon of French absolutism can no more easily be harmonized with the process of confessionalization than confessionalization can be invoked to explain the rise and near victory of the Huguenots.

Religion, not the philosophy of history, is the chief cause for the recent scholarly neglect of Calvin, at least that part of contemporary religion we refer to as its spirit of ecumenicism. Intolerance of confessional polemics muffles the sounds of past battles. The unacceptable connotations of the term *Counter Reformation* have led to its banishment as a separate entry in *The Oxford Encyclopedia of the Reformation*.[24] The three Counter Reformation pillars—the Inquisition, the Jesuit order, and the Council of Trent—are undergoing remodeling. The Inquisition is being transformed into an administrative institution with a protomodern respect for due process. The Jesuits are portrayed as enthusiastic heirs of the educational ideals of Renaissance humanism and spiritually rejuvenated global missionaries. Only those decrees of the Council of Trent that initiated the Catholic Reformation are deemed worthy of mention. Scholars who question any or all of these revisionist trends as apologetic devices are dismissed as Whig historians, nineteenth-century-style spokesmen for the myth that parliamentary democracy and social emancipation had to be wrested from the hands of an aggressive, empire-building papacy.

Whatever else may be wrong in this progressivist sentiment, it neglects the reality of the Counter Reformation as the program of the conservative Rome-led coalition which early Calvinism had to confront and with which it competed for hegemony in postmedieval Europe.[25] To be sure, in 1580 the Jesuit Luca Pinelli could still pay a personal visit to Theodore Beza at his house in Geneva, but as Scott Manetsch has shown in his extensive analysis of Beza's European-wide correspondence, reports arriving in Geneva from the persecuted Reformed churches in France toward the end of the sixteenth century leave no doubt as to the fierce competition between the early Calvinists and the new Catholic orders, especially the Jesuits.[26] The main contested fronts were education and the dissemination of information. Well before the Jesuits gained access to Versailles as confessors to Louis XIII and XIV, they supported the Catholic League's Counter Reformation platform, and the French Jesuit Provincial was their agent and fund-raiser at the court of Philip II.

The competition between Jesuits and Calvinists in the marketplace of ideas was so fierce that we are surprised when we find that they agreed in their criticism of medieval episcopacy and the mendicant orders. Nevertheless, as Dale Van Kley observes, while they were both dedicated to the honor and glory of God, "for the Jesuits, glory and honor did not remain confined to the heavens but rather cascaded downward on to the heads of kings and noblemen, making the social hierarchy a reflection of the Divine."[27] The drawing together of heaven and earth was even more pronounced than he describes. Even before the Jesuits became the pillars of royal absolutism, they had been in the vanguard of the conservative establishment battling for the recatholicization of Europe. In France this meant a head-to-head contest with Calvinism.

Luther's Reformation did not unfold in the same circumstances of competition and for that reason is more readily understood than Calvin's. When Luther returned from the Wartburg and confronted his own radical, revolutionary wing in March 1522, he explained his nonviolent program in these almost forgotten words: "Our battle is not with the pope or a bishop but with the devil."[28] Calvin made no such distinction between human and diabolic power; he confronted the devil in the rule of popes and bishops and their *suppôts*, or hit men. If it is Whig history to regard the Inquisition, Jesuits, and Council of Trent as the tripod of the conservative, backward-oriented Roman Catholic counteroffensive, then John Calvin himself was the first Whig historian. Whatever we may think of Calvin's formulation and however we may think the concept of Counter Reformation needs more precise definition, we cannot understand John Calvin's world by overlooking the first and denying the second.

VIII

TOWARD A NEW MAP OF
REFORMATION EUROPE

Nous prions donc le Roi du Ciel
    Par sa bonté
Qu'il nous envoye sa lumière
Et qu'il nous escrive au coeur
    Par la douceur
Le contenu en l'evangille.
Lire, lire, lironfa.
          —*Chanson Nouvelle*

The myth of the ideological and structural weakness of the late medieval church, propagated in ecumenical unison by Protestant and Catholic historians alike, has long led us to ask the wrong question. The puzzle is not why and where the Reformation failed, but where and why it succeeded. Heavily weighted against change were such institutions as the benefice system and the system of precedent in canon and secular law, the first much maligned and perhaps wasteful but powerful in resources and functional; the second boasting the authority of centuries of brilliant Roman and ecclesiastical jurisprudence. A pervasive conservativism, moreover, regarded most innovation as upsetting a God-established order. In retrospect, it is clear that apart from the old dream of true reform initiated by an angelic papacy there were two novel, systemic, and realistic options for the self-reform of late medieval Christendom. One was the conciliar program as pursued by the Councils of Constance and Basel. In his *Foundations of the Conciliar Theory,* Brian Tierney uncovered the traditional, canonistic roots of the seemingly revolutionary decree *Haec Sancta,* which declared the supremacy of the council above all other levels of church authority. As Tierney puts it, "all conciliarists were papalists."[1] Even more important, a decreasing number of papalists were conciliarists. Fears in the Curia of the explosive potential of conciliarism made for a twenty-five-year hiatus between the Edict of Worms and the beginning of the Council of Trent. This proved to be the window of opportunity for the Protestant Reformation. Hungry for a settlement that would not come, reforming energy passed from a frustrated Lutheranism in Germany to a dynamic, pan-European Reformation.

A second possible avenue to the reconstruction of late medieval Christendom was by way of conciliarism. Although the effort to enforce *Haec Sancta* at the Council of Basel failed, Basel did provide the matrix for the rise of the *ecclesia Gallicana.* The full story of the emancipation of the eldest daughter of Rome has not yet been told.[2] The emergence of a Gallican church on French soil nationalized papal jurisdiction. Without questioning the spiritual authority of the see of Peter, the Gallican liberties nullified the papal claim to the plenitude of power. In the Concordat of Bologna of 1516 the papacy granted the French king extensive power over the Gallican church; but while Gallicanism was centralized, it was by no means terminated. With the support of Marguerite d'Alençon, the king's sister and later queen of Navarre, a mixture of Gallicanism and biblical humanism produced a climate favorable to the spread of the Reformation and helped it survive the ill-fated Affair of the Placards of 1534.[3] Calvin was to assail as Nicodemites those who continued to adhere to the platform of the Gallican church, but there can be no doubt that throughout the Wars of Religion Gallican independence from Rome favored the search for a *via media.* In the English kingdom there were no parallel developments for another twenty years, at which time the king's Great Matter led to the establishment of the *ecclesia Anglicana.* The monstrous ego of Henry VIII may have colored his treatment of Catherine of Aragon and Thomas More, but there were important dynastic issues at stake.[4]

A similar drive toward ecclesiastical territorialization resulted in the emergence of the *ecclesia Teutonica*. With the consensus of all imperial estates, including the prince bishops and the emperor's brother Ferdinand, the summons to the founding session in Speyer on November 11, 1524, was ready to be dispatched when the emperor in Spain vetoed it. The act had momentous consequences because while Charles V went on to promote his own Hapsburg design for reform in head and members he failed to get his agenda accepted by the Council of Trent.[5] Having rejected the emperor's plan to put limitations on the papal plenitude of power, the council turned to the reform of resident episcopates. This was a more modest achievement, but it was arguably the council's greatest. The story of the ensuing Catholic Reformation is also the story of the Counter Reformation. Under the leadership of Philip II and along the path from "Madrid to Purgatory," the Tridentine Reformation was complemented by an escalating military offensive whose successes in France would be matched by losses in the Low Countries.[6]

A familiarity with late medieval Christendom's papal, conciliar, and national platforms of systemic reform is indispensable for investigating the conditions which made possible that least likely of all outcomes, a nonsystemic reformation. The most difficult task of such a reformation was to establish an acceptable Catholicism without the papacy. An ecclesiastical council might have been able to do this, or alternatively the laity might have taken the initiative. Had Luther presented himself as a strict conciliarist, or had he been prepared to ride the strong wave of anticlericalism, he would have been able to retain the loyalty of many more of his early supporters. Instead, the priesthood of all believers, his most radical innovation, and its concomitant doctrine of justification by faith alone did not eliminate an ordained priesthood; on the contrary, they depended upon pope, bishop, or priest to sustain the faithful in their battle with the devil through preaching the Word, celebrating the Eucharist, and hearing (private) confession.

The survival of Luther's Reformation was due, in the first place, to the so-called "reformation of the princes." As Manfred Schulze has shown, the reformation of the princes was not the dismal end product of the Protestant Reformation but rather the late medieval incubator that provided the conditions in which the fledgling Reformation movement came to maturity.[7] In the century before the Reformation, the papacy, pre-occupied with the extension of the papal states and the threat of radical conciliarism, had increasingly granted territorial princes, particularly in the Empire, privileges of ecclesiastical oversight and reform. The Saxon province of the Augustinian Observants had already become a major instrument of such a princely reformation well before it provided Luther with his first audience. The precarious security Frederick the Wise provided for Luther after the promulgation of the Edict of Worms owed far less to the personal piety of this thoroughly late medieval ruler than to his long-established electoral reform policy. There is in my mind no doubt that without this princely protection, Luther's voice would have been silenced and the ensuing Reformation movement nipped in the bud.

A background of earlier princely reforming efforts was a necessary but not a sufficient condition to determine the outcome of Luther's rebellion. Luther also shaped the conditions in which his Reformation went forward. Returning posthaste from the Wartburg to Wittenberg in March 1522, Luther for the first time confronted the communal movement that had accelerated the tempo of reform and, under the leadership of Karlstadt, legitimized iconoclasm. In a week-long series of sermons, he preached the gospel of patience, warning against riot and revolt (*Treue Vermahnung*). At this time Luther was able to control the situation, but three years later the spiritual allies of Karlstadt mobilized the peasants, serving as chaplains and articulating their platform—a platform condemned by Luther in no uncertain terms. During a series of clashes at Mühlhausen and in the ruthless retaliation that followed, some seventy thousand peasants were killed, almost as many as were slaughtered in 1572 during the Saint Bartholomew's Day Massacre.

In an incisive epitaph for the Peasants' Revolt, Peter Blickle was able to invoke a number of eminent historians for the thesis that 1525 "saw a turning point in the Reformation." The Reformation is said (not always with a sense of disappointment) to have lost "much of its vitality."[8] Occasionally a modern perspective dominates, linking the ruthless repression of the peasants with a "typical" German lack of *Zivilcourage,* matched by an overdose of civil obedience (*Obrigkeitsgehorsamu*).[9] Without questioning such intriguing efforts to use the past to criticize the present, there should be little doubt that if Luther had sided with the Wittenberg

IX

THE CUTTING EDGE
The Reformation of the Refugees

Prenez en patience,
Vous serviteurs de Dieu,
Jettans vostre espérance
En nostre doux Sauveur.
C'est le seul médiateur,
Ayant toute puissance;
C'est le seul médiateur,
Rendons luy tout honneur.
— *Chanson Nouvelle*

The survival of Calvinism raises the same question we had of Lutheranism: namely, how do we explain the fact that the Reformation did not fail? Luther gained precious time by exploiting the Augsburg Interim to appeal to universities, the emperor, and a future council. Calvin had no such breathing space. With the university and the royal court already moving against evangelical dissenters, he was forced to flee Paris and seek refuge in Switzerland. Even before he was fully established in Geneva, he was taking up his pen to write the "Antidote" against the decrees of the Council of Trent.

Above all, however, Calvin had to contend with the widespread disenchantment resulting from the perceived failings of German Lutheranism. In his 1543 manifesto on the need for reformation, *De necessitate reformandae Ecclesiae*, he listed four critical problems in the German situation: theological discord; a failure to improve the quality of Christian life; the slackening of popular religious observance owing to the abolition of fasting, pilgrimages, and spiritual exercises; and finally, the expropriation of church property by greedy princes intent on filling their own pockets.[1] Calvin unhesitatingly admits that the success of a true reformation would be a miracle on the order of the resurrection of the dead.[2] "Yet, ours is not the task to assess the chances of success," but to pray and sweat. "Ours is the task to preach the Gospel, let the chips fall wherever they may, and face the consequences."[3]

Confronting his own activist wing in March 1522, Luther had expressed the same view, but with a significant variation: "I have attacked the papacy by preaching the word of God. This word has done the job while I slept and drank Wittenberg beer 'with my Philip and Amsdorff.' "[4] Though Calvin would never have counseled drinking beer, he shared Luther's view that the success of the Reformation could not be the fruit of human ingenuity. At the same time, Calvin failed to find the evidence of a great awakening on German soil: not just Luther with his Philip and Amsdorf, but the whole of Lutheranism had fallen asleep. For twenty years emissaries had beseeched German Protestant princes to support the persecuted Huguenots, begging for soldiers and money, but to no avail. German Protestantism, content with the Peace of Augsburg and preoccupied with preserving the balance of power in the Empire, was ill prepared to be the bold ally Calvin realized he needed in the battle for Europe's soul.

To help us understand the dynamics of Calvin's Reformation, we need to draw a map that shows more than the original German axis between Wittenberg, Schmalkald, and Innsbruck, one that will also include the Spanish Trail from Madrid to Paris and Antwerp. The geopolitical scope of Calvin's Reformation can best be understood by tracing its course from Geneva via Paris and Antwerp to the newly emerging provinces, Zeeland and Holland. Looking in vain for support from a weary Lutheranism content with its settlements after years of struggles, French Calvinism was no match for the Spanish flow of money and troops. It was sufficiently resilient, however, to forestall a second armada against England and to bring the Netherlands victoriously out of eighty years of warfare.

What we have sketched here is not an inevitable process but the tumultuous accumulation of small skirmishes and local battles, a crowded picture in which we must try to discern the elements of Calvin's platform that allowed the Reformation of the Refugees to survive as "churches under the Cross" against the heavy odds of a rejuvenated and aggressive Catholicism. To ask the same question from a different perspective: what were the strengths of Calvinism that made it possible for the Reformation to survive its German beginnings and take root elsewhere in Europe? To be sure, some of the central features of Calvinism might have been expected to have the opposite effect, militating against a wide reception. As I argued earlier, Calvin's stark message of total human depravity, his divisive doctrine of predestination, and his uncompromising moralism might have been the death warrant for the nonsystemic reformation if they had exploded in violence and iconoclasm in the Empire.

"When one constitutes a society and gives laws for it, it must be taken for granted that all men are evil, and that they always will give vent to the evil will that is rooted in their minds whenever opportunity arises." This quotation would seem to document Calvin's radical understanding of sin and support the widespread conviction that Calvin's anthropology was profoundly pessimistic. It would, if it were Calvin's, but the passage is from Machiavelli's *Discorsi* (book 1, chapter 3), written in 1527. I hope I may be forgiven for this unacademic deception on the plea that it serves to expose a deep-seated prejudice. The somber view of the power of evil, seemingly typical of Calvinist pessimism, proves to be the fundamental axiom of Machiavelli's notorious realism. Actually, reversing the viewpoints of the two men is more than a rhetorical strategem; from the perspective of modern political theory, Machiavelli is the pessimist, who has less confidence in the ruled than in the ruler. Calvin, on the other hand, combines a biblical realism about the force of evil with a strikingly optimistic view of the possibility for private and public improvement and sanctification. His view of the world as the "Theater of God's Glory"[5] is an optimistic call for action on the basis of a radical assessment of *human* institutions, equally dysfunctional in the emerging absolute state, in the church, and in popular religion. It has not been sufficiently understood that as part of Calvin's platform, depravity spells a call to arms, not despair of human endeavor.

Understandably, Calvin's doctrine of predestination has also been viewed as an obstacle to the success of his Reformation. Philip Benedict acutely captures predestination's repellant aspect: "Moral rigor shades over easily into self-righteousness, and the elect are rarely loved when they let the remainder of the community know that it is damned."[6] While statistics provide Benedict with an underpinning for most of his fine book on Rouen during the Wars of Religion, he bases this particular statement on common sense. Unfortunately this includes a common misunderstanding of Calvin's doctrine of predestination. There is no evidence in Calvin's own writings or in the reactions of his readers that the doctrine of predestination was either intended or received in this divisive way.

If we moderns find it difficult to grasp the dynamics of predestination, we owe it principally to the historians of theology who have made it part of a speculative system using Calvin's *Institutes,* a theological handbook, as their main authority. On the other hand, it is a historian of theology, Willem van 't Spijker, who observed that this doctrine, as puzzling in the sixteenth century as it is today, was born out of experience;[7] and we may add, in Calvin's case, the experience of exile. Even the secondary differences that divided Martin Bucer and Calvin were related to their different social experiences. Bucer, the city reformer, could not avoid the question of why some in Strasbourg accepted the Gospel and others did not. Like Saint Augustine, who had similar experiences in Hippo, Bucer concluded that it was God's predestination that explained why the eyes of some are opened while others are closed. Calvin accepted Bucer's Augustinian interpretation, but with a difference that can be attributed to his having lived through the transition from the City Reformation to the Reformation of the Refugees.

The Calvinist doctrine of predestination is the mighty bulwark of the Christian faithful against the fear that they will be unable to hold out against the pressure of persecution. Election is the Gospel's encouragement to those who have faith, not a message of doom for those who lack it. In particular, it responds to the anguish that Calvin already felt in the early wave of persecution, which spread through Paris on the eve of his escape to Switzerland fearing that torture would force him to betray the other members of his underground cell.[8] Rather than providing grounds for arrogance, predestination offers all true Christians the hope that even under extreme duress they will persevere to the end.[9] Later, when the refugees had become settlers and citizens, they developed the scriptural insights fostered by this experience into a systematic theology that lost touch with its initial purpose and hardened its doctrinal crust. It was then that election came to be regarded as a civil right.

Finally, we turn to that disruptive matter of revolt and iconoclasm that had nearly aborted Luther's Reformation. No doubt, Calvin would have been sympathetic to Karlstadt's activism in 1522.[10] Still, Calvin's "war against the idols" is easily misunderstood. Carlos Eire, who so precisely inventoried the piety of Philip II in the face of death and purgatory,[11] was misled by earlier Calvin scholarship to assume that Calvin fought against images on the Platonist assumption of God's absolute transcendence.[12] Actually, Calvin did not attack idols because God transcends the world of time and space, but on the contrary, because God is omnipresent in every detail of reality and in every act of history.[13] Calvin criticized popular religion for making images into idols because of the perceived implicit lack of confidence in God's presence in all matters of daily life.

This same issue brings us back to the vulnerability of the nonsystemic reformation. The outbreak of iconoclasm in France and the Netherlands heavily compromised the Huguenot movement. It was essential, therefore, for Calvin to do everything in his power to restrain his followers from *tumultus*, riots and the use of force in occupying churches and breaking images. When the cause of the Reformation and the very survival of the Huguenot movement seemed jeopardized, he went so far as to break with his own left wing, even distancing himself from his old comrade-in-arms Guillaume Farel.[14]

While the systemic reformation was our point of departure, iconoclasm marks the proper point of conclusion for it shows us how the dynamics of a theological program may be influenced and transformed by social and political factors. The rise of iconoclasm marks the point where the original message was translated, transferred, and absorbed in a suspense-filled web of processes of both *longue* and *brève durée*.[15] But unless we first re-create the original message in its historical context and as experience gave it shape, we cannot properly understand either the beginning of the Reformation in Germany or its Calvinist completion.

X

CALVIN'S LEGACY
Its Greatness and Limitations

W hat follows is a settling of accounts with the Reformed fathers and especially with their predecessor, John Calvin. By settling accounts I mean drawing up the balance sheets, a process of both addition and subtraction, of a simultaneous pondering and weighing, an exercise that calls for both granite and grit. It is not intended exclusively for a closed academic circle but as a public appraisal of Calvin's aims and meaning—of what he gave the Western world, did for it and to it. To come close to this goal within a small space, I have opted for two points of entry. In the first place, I have not been willing to write down a single sentence or dared to render a single verdict without listening afresh and giving the floor to Calvin's opponents and adversaries. Although this may seem self-evident, it is not so within the circle of the leading interpreters of Calvin. In this connection I have not aimed at the academic pseudo-virtue of neutrality; my concern, rather, was to have the adversaries show me where the points of stress and sensitivity can be found.

In the mirror of their reactions to Calvin—which range from resistance to outright abhorrence—the themes of theocracy, predestination, discipline (the Reformed way of life!), and biblicism are clearly visible. These themes must be addressed here, however briefly. From Ami Perrin, Calvin's contemporary and political opponent in Geneva, to his twentieth-century accuser Stefan Zweig, continuing protest has been sounded against a kind of religious terrorism associated with these themes in a variety of ways.

I shall devote special attention to the Calvin scholar Allard Pierson. Although he has never been acknowledged as such, Pierson, who died in 1896, was the counterpart of Abraham Kuyper, the great critic of liberal Protestantism in the Netherlands. Pierson sought to warn the thinking public against what he experienced as the cold grip of Calvin, the man who threatened all the cultural and ethical values of an erudite humanism. This Erasmian admirer of classical antiquity, an authority on the phenomenon of religion, equally at home in the history of Rome and of the Reformation, deliberately bade farewell to what would later be dubbed, tongue in cheek, "clerics' country."

Since we will encounter him again and again as an interpreter of Calvin, Pierson needs to be introduced. He was the spokesman of a cultural segment of the Netherlands, although since World War II his voice has been reduced to a hoarse whisper by forces quite different from those generated by Calvin. In the winter of 1885–1886, just as Abraham Kuyper was mounting his campaign against liberal Protestantism, Pierson gave a series of lectures in Amsterdam. In these lectures, now virtually unknown, he marked off his social and cultural distance from both Kuyper's "little people" and Calvin's ordinary believers, saying that "a democracy that equalizes everybody and everything may politically be the inescapable demand of the hour; however with regard to art, science, and religion, that is, with regard to all our spiritual goods, a sense of self-worth and aristocratic awareness is a great and indispensable driving force. In this domain we regard as high that of which one can and must say with Goethe: 'it is not for the uneducated' (es is nicht für den Pöbel da)."[1]

Certainly, Pierson's aristocratic view of culture may not be construed at the expense of his social concern. On the contrary he regarded learning as the driving force of the breakthrough of human dignity and hence of the emancipation of a genuine society from the bonds of rank and class. Even in his conclusion there are echoes of the voice of Calvin: there is in this world such an "overwhelming accumulation of physical and moral misery," he said, that "human life can have no other demonstrable purpose" than to join in working for the diminution of this misery.[2] Accordingly, the issue here is not simply one of being for or against Calvin. In comparing Kuyper and Pierson, these two Dutch pioneering thinkers of the nineteenth century who outside the borders of their own country are known only to a few, we confront a fundamental problem and a conflict international in scope. Whereas Calvin managed to unite in his person both humanism and Reformation, that is, a respect for both classical letters and the words of Scripture, the erudite classical tradition which passed from Erasmus through Hugo Grotius to Allard Pierson shows the tensions to which that combination was subject from the very beginning. The recently discovered and expertly edited work of Grotius' youth, *Meletius,* of 1611,[3] would today bear the title "Ecumenical Catechism." Amid the ungodly wars of religion and with an appeal to classical antiquity, Grotius watered down the controversial ingredients of the Christian faith, presenting an anodyne version of it that had to be palatable to all parties. By comparison with this tradition of conciliatory irenicism, Calvin, insisting on such provocative issues as the opposition between free will and predestination, can only appear as a grim headbasher.

My second point of entry leads directly to what I regard as the heart of the matter. Traditional Calvin scholarship rightly focuses on what the reformer said and wrote. Modern social historiography has a keener eye for what *motivated* Calvin, for the matrix of circumstances from within which he spoke and for the audience he addressed. Predestination is an excellent example of a teaching which, however well and extensively documented with precise quotations, cannot be grasped unless one has an eye for its social and psychological roots. This apparently abstract doctrine was a matter of existential faith for the exiles who, far from home, in a language arising from their experience of banishment, "traveled through the wilderness." Even as they went "behind the pillar of fire," they clung to the providential guidance of God.

It is this existential context I shall examine. My starting point is Calvin's fundamental experience, the experience in which and from within which he read Scripture: "And we know that it is a hard lot when one is driven far away from his own country."[4] It is fitting for us to close this introduction with the prayer of Calvin's which gives expression to "heavenly guidance" and reproduces the vital context of what is scarcely intelligible today as the teaching of predestination:[5]

Prayer

Since You promised us rest nowhere but in Your heavenly kingdom, so grant, almighty God, that on our earthly pilgrimage we may consent not to have an abiding city but to be driven here and there, and despite all that still call upon You with a quiet spirit. Permit us to carry on our warfare, which You have designed to train and to test us, that we may be firm and steadfast in this warfare until at last we arrive at that rest which has been obtained for us by the blood of Your only-begotten Son. Amen.

A CHRONOLOGY OF SOME IMPORTANT EVENTS IN THE LIFE OF CALVIN[6]

July 10, 1509	Born at Noyon.
Until 1523	Pupil at the Collège des Capettes at Noyon.
1523–1528	Student at the Collège de la Marche and the Collège of Montaigu at Paris. Obtains master's degree in the liberal arts.
1528–1531	Law student at Orléans and Bourges. Obtains a licentiate in law.
May 26, 1531	Calvin's father dies. Calvin at Noyon.
Summer 1531– Fall 1533	Studies, with interruptions, with the "royal lectors" at Paris.
1532	*Commentary on Seneca's "De clementia."* Humanist.
Nov. 1, 1533	Nicolas Cop delivers speech at Paris. Calvin flees from the city.
	First to Noyon; brief stay at Paris; then to du Tillet at Claix by Angoulême.

May 4, 1534   At Noyon gives up his ecclesiastical benefices. His conversion must have taken place earlier.

1534   Wanderings: Paris, Angoulême. Together with du Tillet, off to Orléans and Poitiers. Affair of the Placards (October 17); heavy persecutions. With du Tillet, flees abroad: via Metz to Strasbourg.

1535   Arrival at Basel (January). Writes the *Institutes* with a dedication to King Francis I.

1536   To Ferrara (February). The *Institutes* appear at Basel (March). Via Costa (April) and Basel he goes to Paris. Plans to go to Strasbourg; has to detour over Geneva; while there Farel adjures him to stay (July). Lector at Saint Pierre. Religious colloquy at Lausanne (October).

1537   *Articles for the Organization of the Church* presented January 17, followed by a *Confession of Faith* and a *Catechism* accepted by the Council (April). Opposition in Geneva.

1538   Conflict with Council over liturgy and discipline. Farel and Calvin banished (April) to Berne and Zürich. Stay at Basel. Called to Strasbourg: pastor of the French refugee congregation and lector at the academy (September).

1539   Second, greatly expanded, edition of the *Institutes*. Also *Commentary on Romans* and *Reply to Sadoleto*. Conference at Frankfurt.

1540   Religious Colloquy at Hagenau (July). Marriage to Idelette de Bure at Strasbourg (August). Colloquy at Worms (October 1540–January 1541).

1541   Called back to Geneva. Religious Colloquy at Regensburg (February–June).
       Arrival at Geneva (September 13). Preacher and teacher at Saint Pierre. *Ecclesiastical Ordinances* accepted (November 20). *Little Treatise on the Lord's Supper*.

1542 Birth of a son (July 28), who dies shortly afterward. *Forms for Prayers and Spiritual Songs. Commentary on Jude.*

1543 *Defense of the Doctrine of the Bondage and Freedom of the Will*, against Pighius. New edition of the *Institutes*. Treatise on relics. *Humble Exhortation to Charles V*. Resignation of Castellio.

1544 *Articles of the University of Paris—with Antidote.*

1545 Witch trials of Peney. Aid to the Waldensians. *Catechism. Against the Sect of the Libertines. Commentary on I and II Peter.*

1546 *Commentary on I Corinthians.*

1547 *Commentary on II Corinthians. Acts of the Council of Trent with Antidote.* Tumult in the Council (December).

1548 *Commentaries* on various epistles of Paul.

1549 Death of Idelette (March 29). Negotiations with Bullinger at Zürich. *Consensus Tigurinus. Commentary on Hebrews.*

1550 *Commentary on Thessalonians* and *James*, Tractate *Concerning Scandals.*

1552 *Defense of the Doctrine of Election*, against Pighius. *Commentaries* on Isaiah and Acts.

1553 Trial of Michael Servetus. Servetus burned at the stake (October 27). *Commentary on the Gospel of John.*

1554 *Defense of Faith in the Trinity. Commentary on Genesis.*

1555 Libertines defeated in elections (January). *Defense of the Doctrine of the Sacraments*, against Westphal. *Commentary on the Harmony of the Gospels.*

1556 Journey to Strasbourg and Frankfurt. Physical problems worsen.

1557 *Commentary on the Psalms.*

1558 *Slanders of a Windbag*, against Castellio.

1559 *Outline for the French Confession of Faith*. Opening of the academy (June 5). Final edition of the *Institutes*. Receives Genevan citizenship.

THE "CATHOLIC" CHURCH FATHER:
THE WHOLE TRUTH FOR THE WHOLE WORLD

In Search of Calvin

Around our subject it has become quiet. True, Calvin's legacy still plays a stubborn role in the books of foreign historians who rack their brains over the rise and character of the Netherlands, bent on explaining the strange Dutch mixture of industry and narrow-mindedness. This legacy is also embarrassing to scholars in the Netherlands who look into the mirror of South Africa, rarely with honesty, and abjure their own past.

Twice in recent history our theme was hot, so to speak—fifty years ago and fifty years before that. Fifty years ago theological interest was focused on Calvin's legacy when the great Swiss theologian Karl Barth dared appeal to the Genevan church father in support of his fierce crusade against the religiosity of the nineteenth century. This was part of Barth's spirited defense of the absolute passivity of humans in receiving divine revelation: "straight down from above" and totally without any "point of contact." Away from the dust and smoke of those impassioned salvos, with the cool perspective of today's historical distance, the terminology and even the effort itself are meaningless to the uninitiated. Accordingly, there is a chasm between the historical Calvin and a Calvinism which seeks to make the Genevan church father relevant by wresting words from him which he never uttered—at least not in the way they are used. Nor could he have so uttered them.

Calvin knew his Cicero, Vergil, Tacitus, and Quintillian by heart.[7] He was a biblical humanist who found in Plato and Cicero a view of human-kind and of the purpose of human life which, in his own words, light up

on behalf of pristine Calvinism, faithful to Calvin's great legacy. We cannot, however, refrain from asking whether this was a correct view, especially since Abraham Kuyper, in his famous cadences, urges the question on our attention: "Call to mind that only by Calvinism did the psalm of liberty find its way from the troubled conscience to the lips; that Calvinism captured and guaranteed to us our constitutional civil rights, and that simultaneously there went out from Western Europe that mighty movement which promoted the revival of science and art, opened new avenues to commerce and trade, beatified domestic and social life, exalted the middle classes to positions of honor, caused philanthropy to abound and, more than all this, elevated, purified, and ennobled moral life by puritanic seriousness; and then judge for yourselves whether it will do to banish any longer this God-given Calvinism to the archives of history and whether it is so much of a dream to conceive that Calvinism has yet a blessing to bring and a bright hope to unveil for the future."[9]

For a long time now the good grounds for Kuyper's Doleantie have been called in question by alternately listening to and borrowing arguments from Hoedemaker, Noordmans, Haitjema, and—if we really knew the ropes—from Arnold A. van Ruler. But thanks to the introversion of the church press we have for decades muzzled the most sagacious and materially the most radical critic, Allard Pierson, who five years before the Doleantie had already demonstrated, in his study on John Calvin in 1881, why it would in fact be a blessing for the world were Calvin and his Calvinism to be forever relegated to the archives of history. In their evaluation of the Reformed Church of their days and hence of contemporary Calvinism in the Netherlands, Kuyper and Pierson, two men at the intellectual, religious, and cultural antipodes, were to a surprising extent in agreement. Wrote Pierson on the eve of the Doleantie: "The Reformed Church, in which for some thirty or forty years we have been nurtured, was the Remonstrant church without the name. At that time our Reformed orthodoxy was disguised Remonstrantism."[10] In the following years Kuyper was to repeat the same thing in a variety of ways. Pierson does not, as is the custom these days, attribute secularization to industrialization and the alienation of the laboring masses. His diagnosis was no different from that of Kuyper, although Pierson concluded that this secularization was at the same time a liberation: "Liberal theology broke down dogma; the *Reveil* broke down the church.[11] Is it any wonder that a significant segment of the present generation is permanently estranged from Christianity . . . ? People are increasingly open about their break with the church. I cannot help but rejoice in this spirit, persuaded as I am that our moral life, as we ought to understand it, has nothing to expect any more from any church communion or any doctrine of God."[12]

Precisely because we wish not only to unearth Calvinism's greatness but also to ferret out its limitations, we wish to pay particular attention to Pierson's fierce reaction to Calvin and his legacy. The great debates of fifty and a hundred years ago have not led to a clear resolution. Whether we are discussing cruise missiles, political party affiliation, or ecumenical ventures, in ever changing form and in however subterranean a way they are present among us now. Still, around the core issues which are our central theme, things have gotten quiet, so quiet that for the historian there is now a real chance to get to work. He or she can now exploit the apparent truce to enter into reckless proximity to sacred cows and, where necessary, to slay them.

The key to Calvin's enormous oeuvre (which after twenty years of constant exposure still yields fresh surprises to me) is the Genevan reformer himself, growing up amid the particular circumstances of his time, mediating lived-through and thought-through truths, forming people, founding institutions, and developing a Protestant culture such as could be found nowhere outside his sphere of influence. My method or, more modestly, my procedure, is to ask repeatedly what part of Calvin has been preserved in the history of Calvinism and how this is to be judged.

Calvin: An Inside Look

There are authors who in their ability to communicate directly come and sit beside you, as it were. Some, like Luther, are naturally talented in this. Others have to learn that art, by discovering that the written word can only reach and possibly persuade the reader by addressing not only his intellect but, through and with the intellect, the entire person. Only in this way is the reader touched. Humanism rediscovered the programmatic significance of rhetoric, and in this regard Calvin was a humanist through and through. In contrast with the scholastic method, the rhetorical art did not aim only to reach the intellect of the listener; its goal was to reach, indeed to move, the listener in his or her totality, in heart as well as mind.

In France in the early part of the sixteenth century, humanism was largely the sustaining worldview of jurists, just as it had been in Italy a century earlier. Calvin, like so many other well-educated preachers of his time, came to theology from the study of law. His style was and remained rhetorical, a style he learned at the feet, so to speak, of Cicero, who in his great orations expounded the right and wrong of his causes and those of his adversaries—the right of his own, to be sure, and the wrong of his adversaries'—before the jury of his audience and readers. This is also the source of Calvin's aggressive tone, which frequently repels us today, as in the caustic language of the *Institutes*. That mighty book is an eminently rhetorical document, not to be read without a thorough knowledge of the rules of rhetoric. It is a running indictment, like that of a prosecutor in a courtroom. The *Institutes* is intended to move people, to persuade by argument and evidence, and therefore the witnesses and sources have to speak for themselves; the author himself may not even make an appearance. In this respect Calvin's mode of writing and thinking is totally different from that of Martin Luther, whom Calvin so greatly respected. In all of his writings Luther wears his heart on his sleeve. So open is he that the historian finds it much easier to get inside him.

It is not my discovery that Calvin was reserved in his style of communication; he was thoroughly aware of it himself. His reserve challenges us to delve more deeply, and here reflection upon his own succinct judgment proves rewarding. "De me non libenter loquor"—I am not eager to speak of myself.[13] From here a line can be drawn to Calvin's personality, to Calvin's profession, and above all to the long-sought-after center of his theology.

Concerning personality and profession, we can be brief. Calvin is not easy to know because he was introverted to the point of being shy, withdrawn, and extremely reserved. It is no coincidence that while Calvin was critical of the classical authors, the ethics of the Stoa come off particularly well in his writings, although to the Stoic ideal of self-possession he expressly adds the virtue of *misericordia,* or compassion. Self-possession, especially in the sense of self-sufficiency, means that a person is free from external influences. Calvin escapes the limitation this implies when he says that the Christian Stoic must add emotional involvement. This is particularly clear when Calvin expresses it in his mother tongue, in letters, and especially in sermons, making it as clear as he can that the genuine Stoic who tries to steel himself against the outside world is more a child of Satan than of Christ. To this emotional armor the Christian must add *misericordia*. Calvin sums this up in a word which could indeed be found in the French language before his time but only later becomes common parlance. The word is *nonchalant,* and when he uses it, it has not yet become trite, as it is today.[14] A Christian may not be nonchalant toward his fellow human beings. That would be on the same level with poking fun in relation to God; it would be indifferent, *nonchaleur,* to have no warmth, to be unconcerned about others. Calvin is different; he is concerned and as such lives an encumbered life: enriched, to be sure, but clearly burdened by his deep and extensive God knowledge.

The line I have drawn from Calvin's self-confessed reserve to his personality can also be drawn to his profession as lector. From his first post in Geneva to the end of his life Calvin was and remained a scholar. His *Institutes,* from its second edition, was intended as a textbook for future preachers. He himself regarded his *Catechism* as his main work. It is a genuine textbook for life, that is, a life in the school of the Holy Spirit. Even his sermons are scientific treatises and didactic discourses. Of Luther one can say that in the lecture hall he was still the preacher, whereas even when Calvin was in the pulpit he was still the lector, the executor and amanuensis of a high and holy cause.

Even in his letters Calvin was reserved about himself. In his Bible commentaries he disappears almost totally behind his colorful depiction of God's actions in history. Only five times in his hundreds of sermons did he introduce himself as speaker, citing his own experiences and reflections. One of these references has until now, so far as I can tell, escaped the attention of scholars. This is the statement that in the entire Bible his favorite book is Paul's Second Epistle to Timothy, and it will be rewarding to examine carefully the main themes of that epistle and the commentary on it.[15]

The third line to be drawn from the psychologically charged little sentence "De me non libenter loquor" runs to the center of Calvin's theology and therefore requires our special attention. Here the interpretive scratches we make on Calvin's theology must not be allowed to blur its actual contours. Precisely Calvin's modesty tempts us to cast off all restraint and urgently, aggressively—immodestly—to raise the question concerning the greatness and limitations of the Genevan reformer, so we must proceed with caution.

The historical context of that brief little sentence ("I am not eager to speak of myself") is as follows: in 1539 Calvin had to reply to the challenge issued by Cardinal Sadoleto, who called the renegade church of Geneva back to the mother church with the brief sentence "sentirene cum universa ecclesia"—are you not then prepared to believe and to agree with the world church of all places and all times?[16] When Calvin once more summarized Sadoleto's long attack, he said it differently but just as tersely. What you are really saying, Sadoleto, is this: "You Protestants have apostatized from the church because you have seceded from its fellowship."[17] Secession, accordingly, equals apostasy. It is important to note that Calvin does not argue against or reject this equation: for him also secession was apostasy or, in any case, decline, *ruina ecclesiae,* the collapse of the church. However, with these words he was describing the medieval church which had increasingly become the papal church, an instrument of power in which the real marks of the real church were obscured and suppressed. The true Church of Christ, the Catholic Church, though it can be found in the medieval church, is no longer identical with it.

Countering Sadoleto Calvin asks, "Are not the soldiers who again raise up the standard of the king while all others flee from their posts and run from the enemy, are not precisely these the more faithful to the King?"[18] This rhetorical question indicates that adherence to the Word and Sacrament is simultaneously adherence to the true Catholic Church and enables Calvin to draw a clear line of demarcation between constructive endeavor and decline. Preceding this striking image there is a personal confession, the famous story of Calvin's conversion. Despite the fact that he so clearly introduced it with the remark "Of myself I am not really willing to speak," the story would always be understood as describing his personal religious conversion. This was quite clearly not his intention; when he spoke of conversion he meant the discovery of the true catholicity of the church. He is not describing here his personal experiences and sentiments, not the personal search and hunger for a gracious God described by Luther. Rather, Calvin shows how through the word and work of the Reformers of the first generation he learned increasingly to test the church of his time by the standard of the Church of the Gospel. It was precisely his respect for the church—*ecclesiae reverentia,* as he calls it[19]—which had restrained him, until he discovered that the unity of the church of all times and places is to be found in the church which "should begin with Thee, O God, and end in Thee."[20]

As Rudolf Otto and, after him, Otto Weber have demonstrated, Calvin was no independent, but unblushingly high church.[21] The church is not constituted by individual believers but by the office which represents Christ, whether that be the consistory, or in later times the synod or even a bishop, a possibility for which Calvin expressly leaves room. It is the Christ-representing office which works through preaching and the ministry of the Word in baptism and the Lord's Supper. The church Calvin discovered is not the invisible church but the visible church of all times and all places which begins its pilgrimage through history in God's election and ends it in the feast around the throne of the Lamb. With the aid of Calvin's favorite book of the Bible, the Second Epistle to Timothy, we will have to lay bare the problems this entails. But one thing is already clear: though he is not eager to speak about himself, Calvin loves to speak about the fellowship of all believers, the Church.

Telltale Expressions

We must summon our courage to take still another step toward an inside view of Calvin. To this very day the 99 percent of Calvin interpreters who are theologians continue to search for the system in his work, for his "doctrine," as they call it. In my attempt to recover the historical Calvin, however, I have to spy out what opens up the system or does not click with it. In Calvin's Bible commentaries I look for that which changes the direction of the text or which cannot be explained either from the text or from the exegetical tradition. Accordingly, I am partial to the obiter dicta, remarks that do not directly or by logical necessity arise from the context. Here I listen for the voice of Calvin, trying to get on the inside track. In all the genres of his work, from letters to sermons, I attempt to sniff out original or favored word usage—that which is peculiarly Calvinian. We already encountered one striking word which has been unremarked in four hundred years of system research, the word *nonchalant,* meaning, literally, "without heat" or "without warmth," "heartless toward God and humankind." It gained currency in France as a result of the rise of the baroque salon culture and consequently also through the culture of the Counter Reformation. Next it acquired the more shallow meaning of being devoid of style, until among the countercultural types of our day the word again has achieved a positive flavor. With regard to the church Calvin had three such strikingly favored expressions, and it is most important to note their mutual relationship.

No medieval theologian, no author from the late Middle Ages, no other reformer of the sixteenth century uses the word *secret* as often or as enthusiastically as Calvin. Both in the French word *secret* and the Latin *arcanum,* Calvin is always referring to the *arcana operatio,* the secret operation of God. Satan's opposition is not called secret but surreptitious (Latin: *furtim, clanculum,* or *in occultu*).[22] The resistance of the devil is a caricature of God's operation and as such a mirror, and an important commentary to us. We will have to return to it.

Before we do so, however, let us consider Calvin's understanding of God's work, his modus operandi. God always creates, governs, and preserves in the same way—secretly, that is invisibly, unless one has the spectacles of Scripture, the eyes of faith. God does this in three concentric circles, as it were. The largest of these circles encompasses the whole creation; nothing grows, no breeze blows, no horse whinnies without God's secret power. No human being can see this, nor can any natural scientist discover it, nor even the historian, without being given the eyes to see it. The whole of nature, the entire cosmos, is pervaded by the power of God, who by this general providence (*providentia generalis*) upholds and maintains it. This is not pantheism: here, and here alone, the often abused word *theocracy* is appropriate. God, by his *arcana operatio,* his secret operation, reigns in the entire cosmos.

In the second circle, the same domain but with a smaller radius, God rules over humankind with his special providence (*providentia specialis*): for every human life God has a plan, but by his secret operation weaves it into his plan for the whole of history. This idea is familiar to us from the expression "Man proposes, God disposes." In his common grace God sends rain on the just and on the unjust; in the things that grow and blossom he rules as theocrat over a creation incapable of self-government. This is how he deals with nature—and in part humans participate in nature—which Calvin sometimes calls God's body. But pivotal to the second circle is generic humankind in the unity of body and spirit. There God does not rule theocratically but operates through his *pneuma*, his spirit. In this sphere God rules by influencing—as I would interpret his French and Latin word usage. God takes pride—here we glimpse something of his glory—in winning people by his spirit, as his voluntary cooperators, who spontaneously join in working as participants in his secret government. It is precisely thus, by the secrecy of his operation, that he protects their spontaneity. Someday it will all be over with that arcana operatio—that is at the feast around the Lamb. There every knee shall bow, including Satan's. Accordingly, that will be the end of cooperation with God, for then the great Sabbath begins in which all the saints will rest from their labors on a day of feasting that will never end.

We still have to talk about the third and innermost circle, the *providentia specialissima,* God's care for his church. But already, in retrospect, it is clear how far in our sense of life we have drifted in a direction away from Calvin, how vast a distance we need to traverse to be able to read and understand Calvin again. Whereas Calvin feels, speaks, and thinks in the framework of God's theocracy, we think in terms of natural laws that are successively puzzled out by Nobel prize-winners so that gradually there is no room left for an uncharted or unchartable secret operation. Calvin also knows and acknowledges such construal of natural laws, but he lives too intimately with the Scriptures not to know of God's freedom to govern and act within and also outside of that framework (*intra sed etiam extra*)—from natural catastrophe to the cross, from the burning bush to the resurrection. Until recently the average person still knew the meaning of the two words of the apostle James, for which the Latin is *Deo volente.* But today that person fills in his or her agenda without this reservation, making appointments for a future viewed statistically as certain. We are dealing here with more than the loss of sacred words, for it is precisely in God's nontheocratic way of associating with and enlisting his creatures that room is created for prayer. By prayer God is persuaded and so it took place.[23] It is by his arcana operatio that God's spirit upholds and maintains the church. It would seem that on this subject Calvin is very optimistic, because another of his stock expressions is "magis magisque in diem"—daily it grows. He can use it with reference to the growth in sanctity of individual believers but he regularly connects it just as clearly, since in the Middle Ages that leap from the individual to the church had already been rehearsed exegetically, to the church. They grow every day, the individual believer as well as the church of God which advances through all lands and times. That seems very optimistic, but along with the growth of the church the adversarial power of the devil also increases. Consequently God has to surround the church with the special care which is sometimes called his faithfulness and sometimes his covenant. In both cases we are dealing with God's secret government, but differently from the way it operates in nature and history. For in that faithfulness to the covenant, God bound himself to be rod and staff (*adminicula*) for the guidance of the church through history and finally also through the valley of the shadow of death. For having linked his power to the Word and Sacrament, his word never returns to him empty. That is the promise of preaching. His baptism is a sign and ensign even through death; and in the Supper of the Lord, says Calvin, speaking in French, he links the figure with *la chose* and *l'effet*, the signs of bread and wine with Christ himself, for that is the food we need. The Consensus Tigurinus of 1549 is a historically understandable but theologically regrettable political concession made under the pressure of extreme Lutherans, a concession to Zürich which Calvin clearly corrected later although he never found a hearing in the Netherlands on this central point.[24] Accordingly, the secret power of God communicates the presence of Christ and makes us into companions at table with the disciples and the men of Emmaus. This is Calvin's concern in the innermost circle.

Still another favorite expression of Calvin's belongs in this context: "meditatio vitae futurae." In contrast to the other loaded expressions, this is often cited in the Calvin literature and is usually translated as "meditation on the future life." It is an aspect of Calvin that fills moderns with revulsion, as though it were a call to consider the pilgrimage of this life as of little importance in the seductive light of the life to come. It seems to invalidate the political preaching of the church and to call on believers to another, author after author writes that Calvin added discipline as a third. But in the *Institutes* Calvin clearly says that the true Catholic Church can be recognized, seen, and felt wherever the ministry of the Word and the administration of the sacraments can be found, and these without doubt (*indubitanter*) will not fail to have effect.[26]

Neither discipline nor the so-called Genevan or Reformed way of life is a mark of the church. In all the French, German, English, and Dutch translations of Calvin that I have been able to check, one important sentence has been fatally misread, not because of a flawed knowledge of Latin but because of a deep-rooted, mistaken view of Calvin which led to distortion. Calvin points out that since Geneva joined the Reformation, the Gospel is freely preached there, so that a better form of the church has come into being (*melioram formam*), one which, as all the interpreters correctly say, also included external discipline.[27] However, in that connection an important little word has dropped out. Calvin himself says that in Geneva a *slightly* better form of the church has come into being: "paulo melioram ecclesiae formam." Discipline is important, but it does not make all the difference and it certainly does not constitute the line of demarcation between Jerusalem and Babylon.

Now we are ready to summarize: Calvin is not eager to speak of himself. For that reason we hear very little about his conversion. His theme is not his own *conversion* but the big *conversio,* the reformation of the church. Accordingly, he does not wish to emphasize his own way-wardness before, or his intense remorse in, conversion; rather he would describe the history of the church, the history of the great reformation under the hidden government (*arcana operatio*) of God.

Later Calvin succumbed to the pressure, pressure that came from gnesio-Calvinists on the right and Anabaptists on the left, to aspire to create a church that was visibly holy, to bring together in good Puritanical style only those who were genuinely born again and so to individualize the church as a fellowship of visible saints. If Calvin's discovery of the church is the center of his legacy, this has implications for an ecumenicism that knows how to resist the appeal of visibility. Whether, by linking the church to election, Calvin himself laid an even more perilous foundation is a question we shall consider later.

I wish to close by quoting Allard Pierson, that greatest and deepest of

Calvin despisers with whom I began. A hundred years ago he described Calvin's clinging to the Catholic Church and commented, "Evident here is a conservative spirit. He does not want to abolish the authority of the church; he does not even want to detract from it."[28] Indeed, the reformer of Geneva is conservative, but conservative in the sense of a restorer who works to rebuild the ruins of the church on the old foundation. In that important sense the medieval church is the mother church of the Reformation. Calvin does not want to do away with the authority of the church, as though it concerned something temporary and mercenary. Nor does he want to fail to do it justice. On the contrary he wants to restore the church's honor and authority without falling into Protestant triumphalism: we are only a little bit better (*paulo melior*), he says. The terrible truth is that we can do a great deal of damage to the church, make it almost unrecognizable, deforming it into the *ruina ecclesiae*. But thanks be to God: He does not forsake the work his hands have begun.

CALVIN'S BLINDERS

One can distribute judgments on greatness and limitations in such a way that the Genevan reformer emerges as the greatest rediscoverer of the Gospel in stark contrast to later Calvinism as mere decline and watered-down religion. That certainly was my implication in sketching Calvin's discovery of the true catholicity of the church, an institution which becomes visible in and around office, Word, and Sacrament. I opposed this view to the late-Calvinistic tendency to make the church visible in discipline and the quality of its life and—for our own time, one has to add—to make it audible in its political witness. This is a perverted Calvinism insofar as it expects from the world a discipline (*censura morum!*) which, according to Calvin, can only be the fruit of faith.

It may be, however, that we should look for the limitations of Calvin's greatness not in the area of interface between the reformer and his heirs but rather in his own beliefs, thought, and action. In that case, our verdict may turn out to be the very opposite: Calvin's children and grandchildren may very well criticize and correct the reformer or even aspects of the Reformed confessions and still—or precisely for that reason!—be entitled to claim his legacy, to be considered Calvinists. Indeed, more in the spirit of Calvin, they may be seen as Reformed, as long as his Christocentric church order, with its whole range of offices from bishop to elder, is maintained (in order—in Calvin's words—to drive all tyranny from the church) and as long as Holy Scripture as the Word of God is the guideline for the church's teaching. It is sound reformational thinking to consider how in the centuries since the Reformation, the Reformed church may have arrived at a fuller and more catholic (in the truer sense of that word) faith, for all its fidelity to Calvin. This could have resulted from social changes and scientific discoveries in its cosmology and in its study of the Bible. Here we can point to four sensitive areas in which the descendants of the Genevan reformer have outgrown him without leaving him behind.

That statement is less arrogant than it sounds. Calvin himself knew how to express his respect for the church fathers and doctors of all the ages. The true Calvinist owes his critical distance to Calvin. Moreover, Calvin could not have spoken for the church of all times and places definitively—that is, with finality—because in many respects he lived and thought as a historically conditioned, hence as a historically limited, person. I advance four such limiting factors, although I comment fully on only one of them.

For the sake of clarity, however, I must first urge one more introductory caution: to speak of a historical limiting factor is to suggest not only blinders but also keenness and clarity of insight. This is comparable to the keener hearing of blind people and to the precise observation made possible by a microscope at the expense of broader horizons. These factors, thus defined, lie in the areas of psychology, philosophy, law, and politics.

Psychogram: Growth and Undergrowth

The first factor is Calvin's psychogram, the peculiar vortex of complexes and animation, of desires and drives in a person which were in the past viewed as inexplicable temperament and today are seen as the product of genetic disposition, character, environment, and upbringing. Although one can say little with any certainty about Calvin's hereditary bent, it does have to be maintained as an X factor in the mystery of his life, if for no other reason than to recall the historian to modesty.

In contrast to our relatively abundant information about Luther's early life, we do not know the key experiences of Calvin's youth—how, for instance, he responded to the love and punishment of his mother or father. His libido does not appear to have been strongly developed; in any case, as regards the joy of sexuality Calvin is less explicit than Luther. Yet it is remarkable that, whereas Augustine views concupiscence as the great driving force behind all sins, when Calvin comments on biblical passages referring to moral excesses, with surprising frequency he warns the reader not to think, at least not in the first place, of lust and sex. As for what can be said about his character, I have already sketched as much of it as we needed for gaining entry into his theology. While he says but little about his father in his own brief *vita*, he unburdens himself of his resentment by reporting that his father pulled him out of his theological studies and forced him to study law because it offered a better prospect of a good and promising career. Calvin judges himself to be quick-tempered, but this judgment may very well reflect his high view of the Stoic ideal of self-control; in any case it occurs only later, when he suffers from stomach and gallbladder troubles. We do not know, however, what enabled Farel to make such an overwhelming impression on Calvin that in 1536 he could throw him totally off course and win him for the ministry in Geneva by luring him away from the delightfully free occupation of the professional humanist.

What was the personal component in his clash with Servetus, with whom he was so intensely annoyed long before Servetus came to Geneva, but especially when he sat in jail awaiting sentence? What explains his spontaneous and lifelong love for Martin Luther, the father figure of Wittenberg, or his breathtaking identification with Augustine of Hippo? Finally, why is the Second Epistle to Timothy more rewarding to him than any other book of the Bible? Who would presume to say that it is only the theological factors which explain things and not also those other mysterious emotions which other generations may not be obliged to share!

The Medieval Calvin

While Calvin's psychogram cannot be adequately documented and, given the current state of psychohistory, must remain an X factor not to be further defined with any certainty, the second factor is even more mysterious because it has not as yet been observed at all. I have in mind that second formative period in Calvin's adolescence when, as a fourteen-year-old boy, he began his ten years of university study, spending 1523 through1528 at the Parisian Collège de la Marche, then at the Collège Montaigu.

Rabelais and Erasmus also had gone through the ascetically rigorous education mill of Montaigu. And before Calvin left Paris as master in the liberal arts to begin his study of law in Orléans, he might still have encountered in Montaigu's quarters Ignatius of Loyola, who began his study of theology there in February 1528. Erasmus and Rabelais, Calvin and Ignatius: Montaigu became the rigging station for ships that would sail very different courses. None of the four was ever grateful to the school for it. The genius of Rotterdam once recalled the harshness of its training and how in Montaigu he was so helplessly exposed to the drumfire of Scotism that he fell asleep in the classroom. We have only recently begun to discover how much Erasmus, apparently while asleep, must have absorbed, for a great many of his arguments—not the least in his polemics with Luther concerning the freedom of the will—find their parallel in the great Duns Scotus.

The same influence is traceable in John Calvin. It is impossible to grasp his view of predestination, justification, and sanctification as a coherent whole if one does not see how strongly Calvin depends on Scotistic premises for his arguments. This parallel has eluded all Calvin scholars with the exception of François Wendel, the great Calvin authority of Strasbourg. It seems that Calvin specialists not only believed they could do with even less knowledge of the Middle Ages than was needed for Luther and Erasmus but also failed to appreciate how catholic Calvin was, viewing him too exclusively as the humanistic interpreter of the Bible and too little as one engaged in dialogue with the patres and doctores of the confessing church of all ages.

Just as Calvin himself said that we can discern the hand of God in creation only through the spectacles of Scripture, so we can say that on the essential and critical points in his theology he read Holy Scripture through Scotistic glasses. This is not a criticism—certainly I do not intend it so—for it is a great advantage over the closed system of Protestant orthodoxy. It does mean, however, that the claim of members of the Synod of Dordt that the Canons could be based directly, squarely, and verbatim on the works of Calvin was untenable, if for no other reason than that the Reformed fathers of Dordt had long since trampled those Scotistic glasses beneath their feet.

The Italian medievalist Umberto Eco, known worldwide for his philosophical whodunit *The Name of the Rose*, has inimitably pictured the significance of Thomas Aquinas in words which in turn enable me to sketch the personal profiles of Scotus and Calvin in just a few sentences. In his encomium on the great scientific breakthrough which the entire Christian world owes to Thomas Aquinas, Eco points to the reconciliation between Aristotle and Christianity which Thomas managed to effect and to which he gave such high status.[29] Thomas succeeded in this by making God, the Creator of heaven and earth, into the first cause and life principle of all that exists so that—and here I quote Eco—"if God were to decide to cut off the electricity—which Thomas calls 'participation'— there would be a cosmic blackout." As Eco further explains, this means that all that exists proceeds from the being of God, "which is full of love and spends its days not doing its fingernails but supplying energy to the universe."[30]

What moves Eco to great admiration of Thomas was the very ground for Duns Scotus' most important criticism. The God of Christian revelation, says Scotus, is not a power but a person. He is not the source of the energy of his creation, which as a kind of Aristotelian cause keeps the world machine in operation; he is the God and Father of Jesus Christ, who directs and governs the world as nature and history in all of its movements: *Deus est gubernator*. The course of the history of the individual and of humankind does not, in automatic organic fashion, flow from God's being but proceeds from God's counsel—his eternal counsel. There the great decisions are made concerning election and acceptance, about the beginning and end of the history of salvation, decrees which center in the fundamental decision of the incarnation, the coming of Jesus Christ as the first of the elect.

Whereas Duns Scotus still had to be careful to safeguard the moral freedom of humans because the remains of Thomas' energy imagery still played a role in his thinking, in Calvin the presence and rule of God are perhaps even more directly evident. God is directly active and present in every event. But for both Calvin and Scotus, the fundamental structure of this world was not—to say it with the wonderful crispness and clarity of the Latin—the *ordo* which flows from God's being but *ordinatio,* a decision to set in order; not energy but the energy policy that proceeds from God's will, yes, from his eternal counsel.

However philosophers and theologians may find this lamentable, God has conducted his deliberations behind closed doors. Not even the most gifted metaphysician or systematic theologian can pass through. There they must stop before the mystery of God. On account of the *decretum horribile,* the doctrine of reprobation, Calvin was sometimes accused of knowing too much about God and of not respecting the boundary line between the hidden God and the revealed God. The contrary is true. Thomas (and Eco!) knows infinitely more about God's doings than Calvin. Both Scotus and Calvin are very careful to insure that theology will stay in the vestibule outside of God's council chamber. Dordt cleared the way for those who would attempt to pry open the door to God's chamber and analyze God's being as this was done before Duns Scotus by Thomas Aquinas. Then Calvinism found its way back to the God "who spends his days . . . supplying energy to the universe."

Here is a painful April Fool's joke: some fifty years after the fall of Den Briel people could rightly sing: "On the first of April Gomarus lost his bril [glasses]."[31] Shortly after those glasses were removed and trampled, we observe the peculiar phenomenon that the more Calvinistic thought and Reformed orthodoxy succeeded in bugging God's secret council chamber, the more the devout had to protect themselves by means of what gradually became the only two words of Latin the average Calvinist still knew: *Deo volente,* the Latin form of the old saying "Man proposes, God disposes." Where faith and experience, or theology and piety, become estranged from each other, accidents are bound to happen in theology, and in the Reformed tradition, which seeks so strongly to build upon that conjunction, those accidents are full-fledged disasters. Such a disaster occurs when the expression *Deo volente* or the saying "Man proposes, God disposes" are connected with an omnipotent God apart from his revelation, hence connected with the great Energy Supplier, and disconnected from the council chamber in which decisions are made about the salvation of human beings. The clear result is that we end up far removed from Calvin, for in him world government and the individual guidance of believers were based on the faithfulness of God—not on the omnipotence but on the faithfulness of him who does not forsake the work of his hands. Accordingly, the second limiting factor is a philosophical structure which modernity has unconsciously abandoned.

Calvin between Democracy and Tyranny

The third determining, and therefore limiting, factor arises not from the fields of psychology and philosophy but from law, and in a very particular historical form. Especially in the *Ordonnances Ecclesiastiques* of 1541 and the *Institutes* (beginning in the second edition, 1539) Calvin developed a series of biblical principles for the ordering of church and city which very clearly mirror the Genevan situation and were by no means discovered in isolation from that world. Thus, with the consent of the reader, and stated in a provocative formula, *sola scriptura civitata inspirata:* Holy Scripture alone but as interpreted in the light of experience in the city.

A good example of such combined play between political experience and biblical exegesis can be found in the new office of deacon. In the past twenty-five years the revolt against a one-sided theological-historical evaluation of the sixteenth century and the opening up of its social-historical dimension has made us much more aware of the fact that in 1536 Calvin came to a city in which the forerunner of the deacon (French, *procureur;* in Strasbourg, *the Pfleger*) had long had a central function in hospital care.[32] Calvin described the Scriptural data concerning the diaconate as though he were reading them from the Bible, but in a number of specific instances he lifted them straight from the practice of Geneva. Beginning in the fourteenth century, what has been called the movement of urban emancipation spread from Italy to the north. In the cities increasing church criticism was transformed into action. On a principle today known as "welfare" or the social "safety net," city governments made themselves responsible for the common good. Such social outreach expressed itself in a series of measures all placed under the rubric of "reformation." Typically, the bishop was driven from the city, church jurisdiction was urbanized, schools for the city's youth were founded, hospitals were placed under the supervision of the city council, and preachers were called without the consent of the bishop. And these were preachers of a solid classical training who were able to interpret the Bible on the basis of their knowledge of Hebrew and Greek.

Calvin knew these city communities well. Born and bred in Noyon, as an anonymous refugee in 1535 he had found shelter in Basel, where a year later he produced the first edition of the *Institutio*. In addition to his intensive contacts with Zürich he spent three years in Strasbourg, from Easter 1538, when he was forced to leave Geneva, until September 1541. Under the leadership of Bucer and Capito, the Reformation had been able to establish a solid beachhead in Strasbourg because, as in all these city republics, the priesthood of believers and good works—now no longer owing to God but owed to one's neighbor—were readily and happily united with late-medieval city ideology. But whereas the diaconate could serve as a symbol for everything Calvin found in and was able to take over from the pre-Reformation city community, there is an important line of fracture in his reformation. Calvin was familiar with the development of social welfare in the cities, but he rejected it to the degree that he was concerned to distinguish the civic community from the church community. His purpose was to put discipline, *censura morum,* in ecclesiastical hands. Thus when the mayor of Geneva wanted to attend a church gathering as a consistory member, he had to leave his mayoral staff of office outside the door. Calvin insisted on a distinction between magistracy and consistory.

But now the other side of the coin. The opposition party in Geneva—which Calvin was able to eliminate as a significant factor only after 1555—is characterized in the Calvin literature as "libertine," a simple repetition of Calvin's own negative judgment. In fact the libertines were the party of the urban freedoms, and they were obliged to see in Calvin the reincarnation of the medieval bishop from whom so many had gone to so much trouble to liberate themselves. It seems to have escaped Calvin scholars that the city register of August 9, 1535, records that Amy Perrin, the leader of the urban party who would be Calvin's powerful opponent until 1555, was summoned to appear before the Little Council to answer for an outbreak of iconoclasm the previous day. That was a year before Calvin's arrival. Perrin courageously admitted his responsibility but stated that he could not have acted otherwise because the images were contrary to the will of God ("contre la parole de Dieu").[33] From this Perrin does not appear terribly libertine, at least not in Calvin's negative sense of the word. Further, if we remember how as a result of Calvin's powers of attraction first hundreds and soon thousands of refugees from France streamed into Geneva, we can well understand that Perrin's party greatly feared losing its identity. The Geneva census showed that around 1550 there were some 10,300 people in the city. From 1550 to 1564, the year of Calvin's death, we must figure with a growth of about 7,000 immigrants, mostly from France and Italy. In addition to its fear of being overrun, the urban party must have had ideological misgivings lest the commonwealth be shaped and governed from within a church organization not really urban. In that quarter Calvin was viewed as an agent of reaction who would push Geneva back into the dark times of medieval papal bondage.

In the literature the libertines are dismissed as carousers and guzzlers, people who did not shrink from violating any marriage bed. But this urban party was not protesting the repressive antiliberal ordinances against drinking, blasphemy, card playing, and excessive luxury, the things moderns associate with Calvin's Geneva. Those ordinances were already on the books of city councils in the late Middle Ages, and in Geneva after the breakthrough of reformation in 1535 they could simply have been appropriated. Rather, the Perrinists complained that in Geneva, in contrast to Zürich, oversight to enforce compliance with these ordinances would be part of the consistory's responsibility and would not fall under the jurisdiction of the mayor and the Council of Two Hundred. In this respect the Perrinists were more modern than Calvin.

Calvin's vision of the one kingdom of Christ, daily enlarged through the expanding Reformation by the restoration of God's honor in church and politics, is currently in high esteem. This is understandable in the light of German Protestantism's failure to oppose Hitler during World War II. However, the shadow side of this vision, and by implication the limitations of the greatness of Calvin's legacy, must also be viewed with maximum clarity.

Where law and gospel are no longer kept distinct, where public morality and church ethics are made binding in a single code of law, there the replacement of medieval canon law by a Reformed biblical code makes little or no difference in the degree of tolerance practiced toward dissidents. Let me formulate this somewhat more technically for those familiar with the terminology. The problem is not the third use of the law as rule of gratitude, but the telescoping of the third use into the first, the law as the standard for the social order. Where the demands of faith and civil obligation are no longer distinguished, biblical law turns into tyranny. In its initial revolutionary phase this view of biblical law gave Calvinism the necessary thrust to conquer a place for itself in France, the Netherlands, Scotland, and large parts of the United States. In all these areas world Protestantism succeeded in avoiding the weakness of Lutheranism insofar as the latter declared the Gospel a matter of the heart and totally left public life to the authority of the secular state.

Although in the conclusion of Book 4 of the *Institutes* Calvin may ever so subtly have distinguished the church community from the civic community, in practice he did not entrust the political well-being of the city to the civic community. He did not believe it was in good hands there. In practice the unitary outlook of the Reformed in matters of morals and mores, which was based on a consensus between church and state, was not a form of renewal but of restoration—by no means an opening to modern times. For, with Calvin, although one can work in ecumenical relations, one cannot build a state.

The Reformation of the Refugees

The fourth determining, and hence limiting, factor of Calvin's Reformation is that with him a new phase in Reformation history begins, the phase of the Reformation of the Refugees. When I said that with Calvin one cannot build a state, I had in mind a state in which Calvinism has gained a majority. But wherever Calvinism loses its leadership role or is forced into coalition or opposition, it proves to be extremely fruitful for the promotion of political democracy and social responsibility for the economically less fortunate. The foundations for this were laid in the period of the great persecutions, roughly in the sixteenth and seventeenth centuries, when by silent prayer and loud agitation the persecuted churches had been forced to insist on being heard in church and city.

In support of my contention I cite the case of the Dutch refugees in London in 1561. As I worked through the consistory records of the refugee church it struck me how well the congregation functioned as subculture under the alien jurisdiction of the wise bishop of London, Edmund Grindall, who later became archbishop of Canterbury (d. 1583). There was of course no question—thank God!—of the refugees exercising control over London, but they did introduce, exercise, and develop democratic rules for the internal decision-making process. A brief example chosen at random may illustrate the important and healing ways in which church discipline—often depicted as tyranny by people who speak of "social control"—functions in such a semi-uprooted community. On August 6, 1560, the consistory received a complaint about the weaver Anton Maddan. This father of five children, the youngest two of whom were born in London, would not let his family attend church and for four days shamelessly abused them with a stick or whip. After being visited by two elders, however, Maddan promised improvement.[34] I take back nothing of what I said earlier about the danger of discipline viewed as a mark of the church. But here we encounter that other side: discipline as protection against that uprootedness which affords so much opportunity for the exercise of brute force and tyranny in all forms, that therapeutic discipline which aims to protect not the sanctity of the church but the socially less advantaged—and all this carried out under democratic rules.

This Reformation of the Refugees exhibits its own characteristics. Accordingly, I have at times denominated it the third Reformation. After the Reformation of Luther, who in spirit and organization proceeded from a base in the monastery but addressed himself to the territory and the kingdom, comes the second Reformation, that of the cities, Strasbourg, Zürich, Nuremberg, and numerous others where inside the walls the city became the laboratory for thinking through and applying the religious, social, and political implications of reformation.[35]

The third Reformation began after the defeat of the Protestant princes in 1548 and 1549, when the cities that had opened their gates to the Reformation were violently recatholicized and Protestant citizens had to either adapt or flee. This expulsion through the city gates—thirty years before the Massacre of Saint Bartholomew's Day and 140 years before the revocation of the Edict of Nantes—caused a metamorphosis of Protestantism. Ideas arose which, when Calvinism again gained a firm footing in the Netherlands, the Palatinate, Scotland, and the United States, would no longer be understood; hence they were misconstrued. This is the historic context of the development of the dogma of election and predestination. In succeeding ages this would be the characteristic dogma of Calvinism, but in modern times it would be rejected with so much annoyance that Calvinists who still cling to this dogma are as scarce as hens' teeth. Since I am persuaded that here in the repudiation of election we are dealing not with a limitation in the theology of Calvin but with a limitation of modern Calvinism and modern Christianity, I want to make the issue of predestination the main theme of what follows. Before we proceed to this issue, however, I need to make a historical and theological clarification.

Historically, Calvin is a transitional figure between the second and the third Reformation. As Bucer was in Strasbourg, Oecolampadius in Basel, and Zwingli in Zürich, so Calvin was the city reformer in Geneva. But the resistance he encountered there between 1536 and 1538, the first two years of his ministry, can be explained only partly by the excessive haste with which he attempted to push his program of city reform. In part it was due to the Genevans' reaction and opposition to him as a stranger from the outside. In those three rich years before he returned to Geneva in 1541, there to remain until his death, he served as pastor to the church of the French refugees under Bucer in Strasbourg and caught a vision of the church of Christ in the diaspora.

In this ecumenical age we are fond of speaking of *Calvinus Oecumenicus*. Though that is well founded, it is not well focused. Calvin discovered the ecumenical church at his conversion, the Catholic Church of all places and all times. But in Strasbourg he discovered a new mark of the church (*nota ecclesiae*): the authentic church of Christ, like the people of the Jews, is persecuted and dispersed. He addressed his first theological work, the little *Institutio* of 1536, to the king of France in defense of fellow believers in the kingdom. By this act he basically broke out of the limits of the cities. But increasingly through his pastorate in Strasbourg, his founding of the academy in Geneva for the purpose of training pastors in the diaspora, and his wide international correspondence he became the leader of the third Reformation. Besides, in his local (Genevan) preaching he always had in view the growth of the Reformation in all of Europe—and in his words that meant the growth of the kingdom of God. For that reason he liked to conclude his sermons with the brief prayer: "May this grace be bestowed upon all peoples of the earth." This entirely new political and social context—which will disappear and be forgotten in the later, national phase of world Calvinism—produced new theological accents, because in light of the experience of the diaspora the Gospel was read with new eyes.

To avoid artificially and therefore dangerously isolating the problem of predestination, I wish to point out two such new accents, one concerned with the relationship to the Jews and one with the interpretation of history. As to the first: the City Reformation was anti-Jewish and, at the risk of seeming anachronistic, anti-Semitic. Luther and Zwingli shared Augustine's conviction, not doubting the truth of the so-called *argumentum augustinianum,* that the diaspora of postbiblical Judaism was publicly and historically documented proof that God's wrath rested on the Jewish people. Since Jews had no *patria,* which in the language of the day meant they had neither homeland nor ancestral city, the dispersion itself had been convincing proof of guilt. However, now that Protestants had to leave their patria and flee for their lives before emperor and king, they had to let go of this argument. In a totally new way the parallel between God's dispersed people of the old covenant and those of the new was brought home to them. When at the end of the century in the Netherlands commercial relations with Spain and the economic interest of the East Indian Company made this desirable, Jews could obtain Dutch citizenship, and economic interest no longer had to contend with an age-old, seemingly forever irrefutable, theological argument, the argumentum augustinianum. While in 1520 all theologians regarded the diaspora as *the* evidence of Jewish guilt, fifty years later this argument had completely disappeared from the anti-Jewish arsenal of Calvinism.

A second theological shift takes us even closer to the mystery of predestination. The doctrine of providence played a large role in the City Reformation: as people within the city walls conformed their lives to the will of God not only was the Gospel proclaimed but social distress was alleviated. One could refer to the Christian city of Zürich, which lived under God's providence, that is, under God's blessing and hence under his protective care.

It is difficult now to imagine the shock occasioned by the death of Zwingli at Kappel in 1531. Added to personal grief over the loss of the great reformer was the startling realization that the history of God's kingdom is not a history of undeviating success. The pain of that defeat of Zürich, as a result of which permanent limits were set to the Reformation in Switzerland, is comparable in its impact only to the experience of Marburg little more than a year before (1529). There learned theologians, all of them intent upon thinking and judging matters on the basis of Holy Scripture, were still unable to extend to each other a fraternal hand of fellowship and to arrive at agreement in such a central issue as the Lord's Supper. This double shock taught the young reformational movement a lesson which exorcised its early triumphalism. Thus Marburg and Zwingli's death constituted a preparation for 1548, the date of the beginning of the great flight, the diaspora which was to become characteristic of European Calvinism. The church-in-flight discovered the comfort of providence and election. That is evident from Calvin's heartfelt cry, "We have no other place of refuge than his providence."[36]

It is these historical experiences and the theological assimilation of them which provide the context within which the doctrine of predestination has to be located and understood. By the time the Canons of Dordt were written, this context had changed. Nor would it any longer be known when in modern theology Calvin's doctrine of predestination was sidelined in Barthian fashion, or suppressed with an air of importance, or condemned in the name of missions and apostolate.

If we are to draw correctly the line of demarcation between the greatness and limitations in Calvin's legacy, we should unhesitatingly begin by acknowledging his greatness. The limitations emerge when election is no longer the confession of the church-in-the-diaspora which, with only one patria left, cries out: "We have no other place of refuge but his providence." The doctrine of election becomes not merely a limitation but an abomination when it is uprooted and displaced in its turn, torn from its biblical context in the pilgrimage of the church on its journey from the burning bush to the final feast around the throne of the Lamb.

CALVIN: HONORED, FORGOTTEN, MALIGNED

Calvin's Shadow

In 1891 the great Allard Pierson concluded the third volume of his *Studiën over Johannes Kalvijn*, studies one could properly describe as an indictment, with an appraisal of the still young Free University in Amsterdam. First he praised "the sacrificial spirit of burgher and farmer," the mentality of which he described as follows: "It elevates the spiritual level of our people; for its part it is the salt of our nation."[37] However, Pierson then shrewdly proceeded to plunge in the sharp knife of his analysis: with Calvin as one's guide one cannot build a university which aims to unite faith and science, wisdom and virtue. For Calvin is "a political man, a calculating man" who from a moral point of view is not entitled to a place amid "the cloud of witnesses who support and help us in our weaknesses."[38] With the aid of his shallow knowledge of Hebrew and Greek, Calvin lifted a series of truths from Holy Scripture which he then unreservedly identified with the truth of God and of Christ. Can such a person be the mentor of the Free University? Pierson concluded by answering his own question: "It seems to me that religion in all of its dimensions has become a hindrance to the desired development of the human spirit." That which is genuine in religion must remain, i.e., "all that can pass into an ethics that is independent of all religion." But then it is imperative that authentic religion "prove its own indispensability; that, like wisdom in the Gospel, it is justified by her children."[39]

Although Pierson had already resigned his ministry in 1865 and preached his farewell to his last congregation, in that final leave-taking of church and orthodoxy one can still feel the fire of a Reveil in whose warmth, thanks to his sparkling mother, Ida Pierson-Oyens, he had basked. To this heartfelt impatience he gave expression in one of Holland's oldest protest songs:

> I hate the mindset which imprisons,
> Not letting eagle spirits soar;
> And fearfully holds down in safe environs
> That which best lives where breakers roar.[40]

The act of settling accounts with Calvin constitutes the final chord of this same protest song. Allard Pierson, the Erasmus of Amsterdam, turned his back on the church; still, one cannot avoid sensing in every line that this secession is an authentic Doleantie, a movement of aggrieved protest. We are, however, dealing here with far more than a chapter from the cultural and ecclesiastical history of the Netherlands. Pierson's projected fourth volume, unwritten by the time of his death in 1896, was to have been devoted to the subject of election and to Michael Servetus. With this we touch upon the two themes which have led to the international isolation of Calvinism and which so clearly mark its limitations that even among its heirs defenders have become as rare as the Word of the Lord in the time of the young Samuel (1 Sam. 3:1).

Allard Pierson, who took aim at the windowpanes of the Free University, was actually shooting at John Calvin. And if his volley is no longer remembered it is not because those shots were unimportant but because the marksman himself has been largely forgotten. Pierson made official the divorce between humanism and Reformation, held over and held up for so many centuries within Calvinism. The fracture line between faith and learning he made definite, or at least he declared it final. Abraham Kuyper, strikingly characterized by Jan Romein as "the bell ringer of the little people" (*kleine luyden*),[41] eulogized the victory procession and blessed the progress of Calvinism through Western history, but this eulogy sounds in our ears like a typical product of nineteenth-century optimism and of kleine luyden triumphalism. At the end of the twentieth century Calvin's heirs stand looking about them in bewilderment, if not with empty pockets, nevertheless turning them inside out in search of hard coin.

The simplest way to shield Calvin would be to make so much of the weaknesses of the Free University that everyone could see that Pierson's shots—fired in the fading light of the late nineteenth century—were bound to miss. But this way of escape is unhistorical; there is too much kinship between the parties for one to take that road. The radical humanists, the ethicists, and the theologians of the national Dutch Reformed Church all belong to one and the same original source to the degree that they all drank deeply from the stream of tradition which goes back via the so-called *Nadere Reformation*[42] and the Reformation to the late Middle Ages, and formed an initial recognizable vortex in the *Devotio Moderna*.

The power of this tradition clearly shows up when Pierson so strongly interprets the truth in personal terms. In Donatist fashion, he thinks he can discredit Calvin as faith witness on the ground of his human defects, a striking parallel to Kuyper's concentration on regeneration as the condition for God's truth in baptism and for human truth in genuine science. Both men battle for the old Dutch cause of actual faith experience versus the formal obligation of faith, for the self-actualization of the individual against the pressures of the community. But Pierson's renunciation of Calvinism as a malignant tumor in the spiritual and intellectual history of Europe is an international issue which resonated far beyond Dutch borders.

The Case of Servetus: The Damage and Disgrace

In 1936, in a barely concealed allegory on Adolf Hitler and the rise of national socialism, Stefan Zweig published a book on Sebastian Castellio, the courageous defender of Michael Servetus. He called the book *Castellio gegen Calvin,* with the significant subtitle *Oder ein Gewissen gegen die Gewalt* (Conscience versus Power). Zweig gives us a very different image of Calvin from that depicted by Kuyper a quarter of a century earlier. Upon closer scrutiny of the book we discern the lineaments of the Calvin of Allard Pierson. Fortunately, says Zweig, Calvin, aided by his agents Theodore Beza and John Knox, could not hold back the vital élan of tolerance: "What sobriety, what monotony, what dreadful greyness would have descended upon Europe! Hostile to beauty, happiness, life itself—how these zealots raged. . . . Happily, Europe did not allow itself to be disciplined, puritanized, 'Genevesed': as against all attempts made to imprison the world in a single system, so also this time the will to life, which ever desires renewal, asserted its irresistible countering energies."[43]

I am impatient to pass by all the well-intentioned and sometimes partially plausible attempts of Calvin biographers to lessen or to make psychologically and politically comprehensible the responsibility of the reformer for the legal proceedings against Michael Servetus, who was executed on October 23, 1553. Relatively cautious but still characteristic of this apologetic school are the words of Wilhelm Neuser: "To this day the name of Calvin stands for the odium of intolerance. Wrong! The sixteenth century was full of such heresy trials."[44]

Calvin has two faces. One is directed toward the Reformation of the Cities within whose walls the kingdom of God must be realized. The other is directed toward the Reformation of the Refugees. In this context, although its intent was against Calvin, the subtitle of Stefan Zweig's book, *Conscience versus Power*, is eminently applicable in a positive sense. Here the influence of Geneva serves as a ferment mediated by the underground system of the dispersed, persecuted churches. In creating this system they again made religion a matter of conscious faith, choice, and sacrifice, and so plowed up the unitary culture of the Middle Ages, worked it over, and brought under cultivation long-hidden layers of it, at least for as long as hegemony was not yet or no longer within reach.

But the situation inside the city boundaries was that the unitary culture was confirmed and even fortified. The words of Paul, taken from Calvin's favorite Bible book, the Second Epistle to Timothy, lead directly to the trial of Servetus. In 1550, three years before the trial, Calvin commented on 2 Tim. 2:16–18 (Avoid such godless chatter. . . . Their talk will eat its way like gangrene): "Unless counteracted as quickly as possible it will spread to adjoining parts. . . . Once [false doctrines] are allowed in they spread till they completely destroy the church. Since the contagion is so destructive we must attack it early and not wait till it has gathered strength, for then there will be no time to give assistance." This is precisely how "the dreadful extinction of the Gospel among the Papists came about because, through the ignorance or sloth of the pastors, corruptions prevailed for a long time without hindrance and gradually destroyed the purity of doctrine. If we allow people who are contriving the ruin of the whole church to remain concealed, we only give them an opportunity to do harm. Can it be right that, in order to spare one, a hundred or a thousand should perish through my silence?"[45]

There are two points here we must not overlook. First, for Calvin the truth is not self-evident—not so self-evident that it cannot evaporate or become distorted unless it receives care and protection. Just as ordinary believers must know what they themselves believe and not be content with an implicit faith which defers to the parish priest for real faith-knowledge, and just as parents must introduce their children into the doctrine of salvation, so pastors and teachers must lead their congregations into the truth of the Gospel: for "such is the propensity of men to vanity that there is no absurdity so monstrous that the ears of some will not be open to hear it."[46]

The second point to note is the concept of office held by all the reformers.[47] The office of pastor does not arise from the priesthood of all believers but has been posed by God over against the congregation in the ministry of Word and Sacrament. Accordingly, in the Final Judgment pastors will be called to render an account of the spiritual well-being of the sheep entrusted to their care.

Given the above considerations, we may not lull our consciences to sleep by such arguments as "Servetus was a pain in the neck; by his provocative trip to Geneva he himself sought out a confrontation with Calvin," or by the political argument that Calvin had to deal with a libertine majority in the city council opposed to his radical Reformation. In accordance with Calvin's own explanation of Holy Scripture, Servetus was surgically removed from the Christian body as a cancerous tumor, in order to avoid its spreading to the rest of the body and to prevent the ruination of the church which had led to medieval catholicism.

The notion that we are heading in the right direction when we interpret the Servetus case on the basis of principle—not in terms of psychology or political tactics—is refreshingly confirmed by the newly reconstructed records of the trial of the jurist Anne du Bourg, an impressive martyr of the Reformation. Six years after the Servetus case in Geneva, du Bourg, jurist, member of parliament, and staunch Huguenot, was arrested after making a courageous speech in the parliament of Paris. A few months later, in December 1559, the thirty-nine-year-old du Bourg was burned at the stake.[48] The detailed transcripts of the interrogations, carried on day after day and week after week, are by themselves breathtaking, but everything culminates in the conclusion: "Stop, stop, your burnings; turn back to the Lord."[49] This cry cannot be turned, à la Stefan Zweig, against Calvin, because du Bourg, himself a jurist, expressly acknowledged that the government is a divine institution ordained by God to protect the good and to punish evildoers. By contrast with Castellio, Coornhert, and many later Erasmians, his answer to the question of the Inquisitor, whether heretics were to be punished, was fully in the affirmative. They are to be turned in, and in serious cases such as blasphemy they are to be given the death penalty. But the question who is a heretic has to be answered on the basis of Holy Scripture.[50] By way of this notable piece of existential jurisprudence we have reached precisely that transition from medieval canon law to the modern privatization of matters of faith which is typical of the Geneva of Calvin and Servetus.

Du Bourg's impassioned cry "Stop, stop your burnings" could not prevent the bloodbath of Saint Bartholomew's Day on August 24, 1572, in Paris, nor the misery of the refugees following the revocation of the Edict of Nantes in 1685. But along with the refugees this appeal did spread through all of Europe and united itself with the voice of the *philosophes* of the Enlightenment into what today we have learned to respect as indispensable human rights. Now it is of the greatest importance to hold on to the fact that this appeal of the Parisian martyr and faithful pupil of John Calvin was coupled with the express exclusion from all tolerance of Anabaptists and Servetists—the reference is to the asocial Baptists and the anti-Trinitarians of the school of Michael Servetus. At a time in which the term *religion* still stood literally for "bond" and "ligature," Servetus' dogged public denial of the Trinity, to Calvin a malignant tumor, constituted a threat both to the horizontal and vertical structures of society—and that right down to its foundation.

To us moderns, du Bourg's cry of "stop, stop," combined with the simultaneous elimination of Servetus, is an unheard-of inconsistency and even an example of moral dishonesty—that is, until we have learned to translate the thought categories of the sixteenth century into our own vocabulary.[51] As long as blasphemy was considered a social disease, Servetus had to be viewed as subversive. Although Michael Servetus and Anne du Bourg fought on opposing fronts, they stood shoulder to shoulder in the battle for religious toleration, two mileposts on the one road which led to a curb on the totalitarian antidemocratic spirit of medieval Christianity. The price which had to be paid for this benefit was as necessary as it was high: the separation of church and state and the privatization of the faith. Paradoxically, Calvinism's contribution to the modern state and today's social order had to be wrested from Calvinism and only came to fruition after it failed in its attempt to seize power. Only then, but then truly with a vengeance, it became a pillar of democracy and toleration. This, at least as far as the sector of public life is concerned, defines the limits of the greatness of Calvin's legacy.

It was not the triumph of the Kingdom of God in Geneva, but a bloody series of defeats of persecuted churches, which gave Europe a road to the future. Christianity in general, and Calvinism in particular, again become a virulent danger, however, when its adherents, perplexed by the problems of modernity, become nostalgic for the fleshpots of Egypt, that is, for the establishment by force of the visible Kingdom of God. Where Calvinistic politics and theology want to be more than a witness mediated by an individual's own life and sacrificial spirit, there they have crossed the fatal boundary line between influence and coercive power, and we can smell again the first wisps of the smoke rising from the stake. The old saying that city air is the air of liberty does not apply to that kind of Calvinistic city-state.

Election: Faith on Its Way to Tomorrow

Turning from the public face of Calvinism to its heart and center, we encounter the doctrine of predestination—more accurately, of election, for predestination concerns the series of executive decrees which follows election. However, I will adapt myself to the looser word usage of modern theology: the doctrine of predestination is an internationally recognized limitation of Calvinism—which is reason to view it as an obsolete Christian tradition, one with which it no longer pays to enter into dialogue. Nationally too, Remonstrantism has won out and the pithy Canons of Dordt barely resonate among the handful of people who still know the confessions.[52] The doctrine of predestination, once a precious heirloom, now shows up only here and there at theological discount markets.

Earlier we pointed out that the teaching of predestination acquired special meaning in the third phase of the Reformation, the Reformation of the Refugees. This phase originated after 1548, when the Reformation of the Cities was halted and changed into the Reformation of the Refugees. For those who had no permanent place of residence, not even a fixed stone on which to lay their heads, neither a valid passport nor a residence permit, predestination became their identity card. Called *providentia specialissima* by Calvin, this doctrine was experienced in a special way as "being led by God's hand," trusting "his plan for history," and protected "under his wise guidance." These key expressions became code words belonging to faith and experience in the diaspora, to *life* in the dispersion, in the search for *survival* amid a triumphant Counter Reformation.

This is not to say that the doctrine of election is not biblical. Neither do I mean to say that Calvin designed it exclusively for his followers. Nor was the doctrine unknown to theology before him. Augustine and Thomas, Duns Scotus and Zwingli, all knew it and decoded it for individual believers. But it was the third Reformation which opened up the sustaining power of the doctrine for the entire church down to its biblical roots. Thus in its passage through history the church keeps discovering ever new treasures in the kerygma of Holy Scripture. That is also the reason why we need the unity of the church of all times and places: to gather up these experiences of faith, to test them, and to hold them in readiness for an uncertain future, even in times when they are not rated high and not much in demand.

Although almost all of European Protestantism, including that of the diaspora, was represented at the Synod of Dordt, I cannot find there much evidence of that great trek under the guidance of the hand of God. Especially the Dutch spokesmen, having established residence in the United Provinces, had long been in possession of a new passport and a new homeland. But what that trek really meant jumps out from every page of *The Diary of Jean Migault Concerning the Religious Persecution under Louis XIV*, which my Utrecht-Leiden colleague Posthumus Meyjes issued in a concisely annotated Dutch edition.[53] There they are again, the predestinarian roots of religious experience as one finds them already in abundance in Calvin. Systematic theologians, in their learned treatises which are generally based solely on Calvin's *Institutio*, tend to ignore them, abstracting the rich tradition of faith from the living context of our common history and so drying it up. Following the revocation of the Edict of Nantes in 1685, when the great flight reached tidal wave proportions which only some 150,000 Huguenots survived, Jean Migault, the author of the diary, finally fell victim to so much pressure, persecution, and terror that he, schoolmaster and notary public from the district of Poitou, caved in. In La Rochelle, formerly a safe Reformed haven, Jean was arrested and put in prison until he was prepared to renounce the religion *prétendue reformée*, "the religion which claims to be reformed." Upon his arrival in the Netherlands, as he looked back at the moment of his arrest, he wrote to his children: "Only then did I begin to see that all the days that I was on the run had been given me by God to prepare me to endure imprisonment. It had been a long time since I had last thought of it and even now I still believed that I would be able to stand up under it. But, unfortunate person that I was, how could I ever properly describe my own weakness. I had not sufficiently placed my destiny in the hands of the Eternal One and trusted too much in my own strength, which in a single moment proved to have gone up in smoke."[54]

The prison authorities calculatedly allowed just enough visitation to make Jean aware how urgently his children, scattered and in hiding, needed him until finally, beaten to a pulp, he became unfaithful. "It would soon become clear that I had not sufficiently trusted in the Providence of God, because four days later (day of misfortune!) I let the authorities know I wanted to leave prison. I did not realize that I would be casting myself into a new dungeon, rather, into an abyss in which I would have been buried and consumed forever had not God in his mercy overlooked my sin. . . . In his abundant grace he has granted me the joy and comfort of knowing that nine of you can listen to his Word in complete freedom."[55]

In the course of his eight-year flight, before he reached freedom in Den Briel on May 18, 1688, the simple schoolmaster Migault lost five of his children and, one week after she gave birth to her fourteenth child, his wife. Migault's account of his experience furnishes us a better point of entry to the seemingly so repugnant doctrine of predestination than the thousands of theological treatises which have been written on this subject. Indeed, it is a better point of entry than Calvin's *Institutes*, which on this issue too is a cookbook, not a dinner; a textbook, not a book to live by.

We do find this existential point of entry in Calvin's commentary on Paul's Second Epistle to Timothy, to him Paul's testament of faith. Calvin concludes his commentary with these words: "God grants us not only the beginning of salvation as though he had left its continuation to our free wills; rather, the perseverance of believers is rooted in the grace of God and his eternal election, not in their own strength. Paul, in ascribing to God the work of leading us into His kingdom, openly asserts that we are ruled by God's hand during the whole course of our life, until with all our warfare finished we obtain the victory."[56] That is Calvin's explanation of the words of Paul: "The Lord will rescue me from every evil and save me for his heavenly kingdom. To him be the glory for ever and ever. Amen" (2 Tim. 4:18).

"Save," says Paul; "in God's hand," says Calvin, for the elect are untouchables, invulnerable, outside of danger: the Lord has taken us into his care, his tutelage.[57] Thus the schoolmaster Migault landed safely in Den Briel. But it is precisely this safety—to Migault the protection of civic toleration, to later generations peace and order, and to us the security of the safety net—which blocks existential access to Calvin's biblical doctrine of predestination and leads to one of the most appalling misunderstandings in church and theology. It is as though the doctrine of election peaked when it subtracted reprobation, the *decretum horribile,* and rashly sought to penetrate God's eternal counsel.

Paradoxically, the external prosperity of the Golden Age and the progressive features which the political, social, and religious life of the Christian West have gradually begun to exhibit have led to the drying up of this sparkling fountain of religious experience. Election, the biblical doctrine of God's faithfulness and overpowering grace, which was rediscovered in time of distress and persecution, as a result of being coupled with the shibboleth of the doctrine of reprobation, became a plaything for theologians and a rock of offense to believers. To all who with a sigh of relief chucked out the memory of Den Briel and gave up on the preachers' republic, the precious asset of the social safety net seemed to offer more security than the misleading myth of God's majesty and gave preference to justice from the cradle to the grave.

Today we are more conscious than previous generations that the security of the Golden Age is forever past. Thus we are not just engaging in the historical analysis of an old debate but dealing with the recognition of the structures of the existence of refugees in our own time. We are also rediscovering one of the catholic treasures of faith preserved in the Calvinistic tradition, but one which, as a result of our embarrassed silence, is in danger of being lost.

That which was hushed up belongs to the being (*esse*) of the church, not just to its well-being (*bene esse*), and is to be characterized as one of the fundamental articles of the church, an article by which it stands or falls (*articulus stantis et cadentis ecclesiae*). That may perhaps become clear from the three aspects, or better, the three beams of light, which shine so brightly in Calvin's view of election.

Election as Witness

First of all there is the doctrine of election as Calvin found it in the formulations of Holy Scripture and the tradition of the church. Just as in the case of Paul, Augustine, the older Thomas Aquinas, and—cautiously interpretive—Duns Scotus, but above all in Luther and the city reformers, the doctrine of election serves to fend off all forms of Pelagianism which teach that at some stage, whether early or late, humans are responsible for their own salvation.

Calvin correctly refers to the golden chain of Rom. 8:30: "And those whom he predestined he also called; and those whom he called he also justified; and those whom he justified he also glorified." This golden chain locates the initiative, the beginning, and the carrying out of the salvation of all believers in what Calvin calls the gracious eternal counsel of God.[58]

In his commentary on Ephesians Calvin refers tersely to chapter 2, verses 8–10: "For by grace you have been saved through faith; and this is not your own doing, it is the gift of God—not because of works, lest any man should boast. For we are his workmanship, created in Christ Jesus for good works, which God prepared beforehand, that we should walk in them." About this Calvin says: "For he treated of election and of free calling so as to reach the conclusion that they obtained salvation by faith alone." Nor is this merely a marginal comment of Paul's: "in these three phrases he embraces the substance of his long argument in the Epistles to the Romans and to the Galatians, that righteousness comes to us from the mercy of God alone."[59] In clear opposition to the Tridentine doctrine of justification of 1546, and at the same time in accord with modern impulses in Roman Catholic exegesis, Calvin crisply concludes with a few words—cutting off the misunderstanding that God is no more than the starting motor of our good works: "[Our works] were drawn out of His treasures in which they had long before been laid up."[60]

Election as the Church's Foundation

Whereas the first aspect of election constitutes the *cantus firmus* of the Reformation in which the three melodies of faith, grace, and Scripture (*sola fide, sola gratia, sola scriptura*) are united into a symphony—nowadays with promising ecumenical resonance—with the second aspect, matters become more perilous. Here election has a double face, one that looks toward both the Counter Reformation and the Nadere Reformation.[61] At this point I must remind the reader of the theme of my first discussion, where I dealt with Calvin as the discoverer of the church and with *reformatio* as return to the true catholicity of the church. Calvin illumines the second aspect of election most briefly and succinctly in his exegesis of 2 Tim. 2:19: "But God's firm foundation stands, bearing this seal: 'The Lord knows those who are his.'" Human fickleness or unfaithfulness, says Calvin, cannot "prevent God from preserving His Church to the end." Accordingly, in election we are dealing not only and not even in the first place with the individual believer and his solitary journey to eternal blessedness but with the foundation of the church which, because God holds on to his own, will not be overcome by the gates of hell: *Portae inferorum non praevalebunt.*[62] God preserves his church to the end.[63]

Calvin, in distinction from Luther, believed that the last days mentioned in 2 Tim. 3:1 ("understand this, that in the last days there will come times of stress") do not specifically refer to the time of the Reformation. To Calvin those stressful times cover the entire history of the church, so that the apostle also has in mind his own time: "Already immediately at the first preaching of the Gospel the church began to suffer under such prophets of untruth."[64] From the beginning there is the great division between those who remain true to the Gospel and those who fall away. Thus Calvin thinks fundamentally from within the church and does not, as is the case in the later treatises on predestination, speculate about people who never come into contact with the Gospel or belong to other religions. The shadow side of election concerns the ecclesiastical opposition; non-Christians are to the end potentially the "workers of the eleventh hour."

The church is the Catholic Church of all times and places in which believers will ever be persecuted by enemies in the church's bosom who "wish to be reckoned among the members of the church."[65] The true church will always be subject to persecution by banishment, imprisonment, and flight, for the moment a genuine believer confesses his faith in Christ that believer evokes the fury of all pseudo-Christians. Why does God permit this? Answer: "God wants to train and so to strengthen his Church."

Clearly, in the cultural climate of external safety and privilege which characterizes the Golden Age in the Netherlands, this second aspect of election was bound increasingly to fall into oblivion. Specifically in the Nadere Reformation "banishment, prison, or sudden flight"[66] were interiorized, psychologized, and especially individualized, and Calvin's view of the persecuted church of Christ of all times and places was lost. It is as if Calvin foresaw the dangers which his heirs would incur when he underscored Paul's teaching that the Lord "knows and seals his own." This means, says Calvin, that "we are not to judge according to our own opinion whether the number of the elect is great or small. For what God has sealed He intends to be as it were a closed book to us: also, if it belongs to God *to know who are His*, it is not surprising that often a great number of them are unknown to us and that we should make mistakes as to who they are."[67]

Election as Consolation

With this we have arrived at the third aspect. The doctrine of election, far from being speculation about billions of earthlings, is addressed to the children of God and refers them to their place in the Catholic Church of all ages, thus making them participants in the treasures of salvation prepared for them before all times in God's treasure house. This aspect concerns God's primordial caring act of election as consolation, and that in a double sense. There is first of all the consolation believers desperately need when they realize how weak they are in facing the temptations of the world. They must know that "in spite of this great weakness of the flesh the elect are nevertheless not in danger, for they do not stand in their own strength but are founded on God."[68] To be grounded in God is to be grounded "in Christ, the Lord of the Church," as every member of the body is united with the head; that head is Christ and that body is his church. In Christ we have been chosen in love; in Christ, who is not only the "first-born of the dead" but also the beloved Son and the first to be elected. Accordingly, he is the only mirror in which we discern our election. Hence that election in Christ is not a discovery made first of all by Karl Barth but one made by the reformer of Geneva. Otto Weber pointedly remarks: "Barth doubts this, but he does not know Calvin well enough and he does not like him."[69]

"He who calls is faithful" and "He will not forsake the works of his hands": these two texts are the two supporting pillars of election. By means of election as the expression of the faithfulness of God who overcomes all salvation anxiety Calvin takes a position against the whole medieval tradition and also against Augustine when he, the great *doctor gratiae*, makes the gift of perseverance (*donum perseverantiae*) an uncertain extra gift of grace which has to be added at the end of the road of salvation but about which you can never be completely certain. We are here touching upon a sensitive point, namely the certainty of faith on the basis of election, an issue as yet not dealt with in modern ecumenical dialogue. In its Decree on Justification the Council of Trent clearly pronounced itself against the Reformation discovery of the teaching of the assurance of salvation. It rejected this teaching as the "vain confidence" of heretics.[70] Nor did the Second Vatican Council alter a jot or tittle of its unbiblical condemnation. Indeed, the assurance of salvation was to have far-reaching consequences for religious practice surrounding indulgences, the confessional, and Low Mass.

No one has formulated this point more clearly and crisply than Jürgen Moltmann, who in 1959 pointed out dimensions in Calvin which in retrospect prove to have been the foundation for his later theology of hope: "[Calvin's] doctrine of election remains open to misunderstandings as long as people do not see how it serves to exhibit the faithfulness of God and the perseverance of faith."[71] It will ever be misunderstood if one does not hear in it these basic themes.

We have to point out still another dimension of the comfort inherent in the doctrine of election. Just when the refugees learned to read the Bible anew and when, politically and socially uprooted, they had to learn to walk through Europe and through history with their hand in God's hand, so amid persecution and apostasy they also drew courage from the doctrine of eternal election. How essential this was every time even the pillars of an underground church came crashing down! Thus we read— again, of course, in Calvin's commentary on his favorite Bible book— how deeply a church was affected and could be scandalized when a member of great reputation could no longer stand up under the terror of persecution. Then faith needed a deeper foothold. "This is Paul's concern here . . . when he points out that men's fickleness and unfaithfulness cannot prevent God from preserving His Church to the end. . . . The number with which God is satisfied remains untouched."[72]

In the quiet study of a nineteenth-century thinker, even one so alert as Allard Pierson, that sentence alone must have completely discredited the reformer: "How can one judge so lightly concerning the apostasy of people?!" The problem was that Allard Pierson, along with the Reformed adversaries he most passionately opposed, held a belief in cultural progress which separated all of them from the third Reformation, the reformation of the persecuted refugees. On the long road of the diaspora— from Strasbourg and Geneva to Heidelberg and Dordt, to Leiden and Utrecht, to Secession and Doleantie—the horizon changed from persecution to progress. A deep gap was opened, not only as a result of the Enlightenment or the French Revolution but also as a result of the missionary export of a European-Christian civilization, or the establishment of Christian schools and universities in one's own country.

Calvin, on the other hand, spelled out Scripture in the light of the persecution of the church and addressed his letters, commentaries, and sermons to the afflicted churches. Their members, eyes darkened by blood and tears, could not see a thing of God's omnipotence and faithfulness and, against all the evidence of their senses, clung only to that one Word: the Lord knows those who are his; he will not forsake the work of his hands. *Outside of this context Calvin's doctrine of election is not only abhorrent but also ungodly. But within this horizon of experience it is a precious experiential asset* which churches subject to persecution can only dispense with to their great detriment and which we, for as long as we may live under the protective canopy of our democratic rights, must keep alive and pass on to prepare ourselves and our children for the things which are coming.

For, as Calvin rightly warned, the cross and persecution belong to the true church, even though there are times without persecution. "Thus, although all are not faced with the same attacks and not involved in the same battles, they have a common warfare to wage."[73]

Calvin's Biblicism

As we look back upon the road we have traveled, a road on which we have searched, making every effort not to disguise the facts, it seems that regarding the limitations of Calvin's legacy we have cautiously and cleverly stolen past one horrible abyss. That is what Pierson called Calvin's "deification of the Scriptures."[74] And who will deny that from Calvin there is a line which runs through Reformed orthodoxy to the present, a line of thought that has to be categorized as biblicistic and in that sense as fundamentalistic? It is also the reason why modern Bible research with its historical-critical method has been able to hit the Reformed family of believers harder than it has affected the rest of the world church. Both Greek and Russian orthodoxy could retreat to the ecumenical councils of the ancient church; since 1870 Roman Catholicism could fall back on the infallible teaching office of the pope, extended in our own day to embrace also the ordinary teaching office of the church; and Lutheranism had the loaded guideline *Was Christum treibet,* the witness to Christ as standard for the evaluation of the "layers of revelation" in Scripture, long before source analysis announced its own arrival.

Calvinism had the most unfavorable starting point imaginable. Calvin himself said that Holy Scripture was dictated by the Holy Spirit and that "we owe to the Scripture the same reverence as we owe to God, since it has its only source in Him and has nothing of human origin mixed with it."[75] In these formulations a clearly biblicistic line is present, one we can follow via Assen and the speaking serpent in Paradise to our own day.[76] In America the modern peddlers of indulgences, the Protestant prairie television preachers, have demonstrated how lucrative the Bible, biblicistically interpreted, can be. Of the Reformation and of Calvin there is not much left in them—except for their boasting over Holy Scriptures. Am I not right?

As a jurist Calvin became a humanist, and as a humanistic jurist he became a reformer. It was especially in French jurisprudence that the humanistic avant-garde, following the model of the human "testament," had developed its program of source studies. Inherent in this program was the idea that in interpreting a testament one had to go back to the will of the testator and not rely on autonomous interpretations after his death. This testament, having been formulated by the testator, has the same authority as its formulator. For Calvin that is the decisive point: one does not toy with Scripture! It has authority, divine authority, because God himself is the testator. The word *dictate* derives therefore from the imagery of the death chamber and the diligent notary public who may not add or subtract anything on his or her own.

In later Calvinism, when this historical background has been forgotten and Calvin's profession is no longer known, Holy Scripture becomes a divine law book which has been dictated verbatim. Not only does it come from God but must—literally—be accorded the same adoration. That is precisely how it reads in the German translation of Calvin's commentary on Timothy: "Das ist das erste, dass wir der Schrift dieselbe Verehrung entgegenbringen wie Gott."[77]

Still, if as Calvin says the Scriptures constitute God's infallible law book which when randomly opened on the table yields divine words, why then does he state so emphatically that the majesty of God which is displayed everywhere in Scripture can only be seen by the elect?[78]

The answer to this question comes from Calvin himself. There is one key sentence which seems to me to have so far been overlooked in the Calvin literature and in any case has been lost in the Reformed tradition. I am citing from Calvin's interpretation of 2 Tim. 3:15. First Paul: "the sacred writings which are able to instruct you for salvation through faith in Christ Jesus." Now Calvin: "What if somebody is interested only in curious speculations? What if he adheres only to the letter of the Law and does not seek Christ? What if he perverts the natural meaning with interpretations alien to it? He has good reason to recall us to the faith of Christ which is the center and sum of Scripture. For what immediately follows also depends on [this] faith" ("ad fidem Christi revocat, tanquam ad scopum adque adeo summam. Nam et ex ea dependent quae mox sequuntur").[79] Everything that now follows, everything Calvin is about to say further about Scripture, depends on these central sentences: Christ is the sum of the Scriptures. Look at Luther's German leitmotif "Was Christum treibet" in Calvin's Latin!

But there is more: faith in Christ is the center and heart of the Bible which can only be grasped by the elect. For their eyes have been opened by the Holy Spirit: *a spiritu sancto illuminati*.[80] Luther called all believers *sancti* (saints). Calvin addressed all believers as *electi*. Today we moderns absolutely run stuck in Calvin if we do not consistently translate his "elect" back to "believers." Conversely, Calvin is convinced that we will run stuck in the church and in the world, in our ecumenical relations and our own experience, in inner distress and external persecution, if we do not learn again to see in believers elect people. For God will test his church, his elect, his beloved church, and "no one shall snatch them out of my hand" (John 10:28).

Calvinists are not fixated on Calvin as Thomists are on Thomas or Scotists on Duns Scotus. Nor are they like Lutherans focused on their spiritual father; they are "Reformed" and know themselves to have been led back by Calvin into the deep channel of the true Christian tradition. I once asked Arnold A. van Ruler, whom I regard as one of the most creative theologians of this century, a man who loved to speak of "operating in predestinarian fashion" and of the "saving event of regeneration," how he dealt with H. F. Kohlbrugge, that greatest of Reformed alternatives to Abraham Kuyper. His laconic answer was: "Kohlbrugge is like a hot bath; it is very healthy to take it but one must not stay in it too long!" If I am not mistaken, every true Calvinist would be willing to apply the very same imagery to John Calvin—although I would recommend a somewhat lengthier sauna. However, once, thanks to Calvin, they have discovered the way of the church through all times and places, those persons will know themselves to be surrounded by the cloud of elect witnesses among whom the reformer of Geneva is a forceful, resonant, and authentically biblical voice.

On February 16, 1546, two days before he died in Eisleben, Luther wrote a note which he signed with the famous words: "We are beggars—that is the truth" (Wir sind Bettler. Hoc est verum [= amen]). The paramount reason why this copious witness to the Gospel saw himself as a beggar comes out in the following sentence: "Let no one think he understands Holy Scripture well enough if he has not served the church for a hundred years alongside such prophets as Elijah and Elisha, and alongside John the Baptist, Christ, and the Apostles."[81] I do not hesitate to add to this list: and alongside John Calvin, who served hundreds of churches as the *pastor pastorum* of the refugees in the diaspora and encouraged beggars on the secret, veiled, but not uncertain road of election.

In the light of Calvin no joint ecumenical venture can have any meaning unless it follows the path on which the church has been set in love before all eternity. On this path we today need to travel farther as believers who know themselves elect and consequently not threatened by fear of ruin and persecution, of apostasy and distress. These beggars are as happy as kings. I know of no better way to conclude these Calvin discussions, therefore, than with the words "We are beggars. Nous sommes des gueux. Hoc est verum. We are destitute. And that is the truth."

ABBREVIATIONS

Some sources will hereafter be cited by the following abbreviations:

ARG   *Archiv für Reformationsgeschichte*

ARH   *Archive for Reformation History*

ASD   *Opera omnia Desiderii Erasmi Roterodami,* ed. J. H. Wanzink, L-E. Halkin, C. Reedijk, and C. M. Bruehl, 9 vols. in 29. Amsterdam: North-Holland Publishing Co., 1969–1996

AWA   *Archiv zur Weimarer Ausgabe der Werke Martin Luthers,* vol. 2, *D. Martin Luther operationes in psalmos, 1519–1521,* pt. 2, *Psalm 1 bis 10 Vulgata,* ed. Gerhard Hammer and Manfred Biersack. Cologne: Böhlau Verlag, 1981

CO   *Ioannis Calvini opera quae supersunt omnia,* ed. Wilhelm Baum, Edward Cunitz, and Eduard Reuss, vols. 29–87. Braunschweig: *Corpus Reformatorum,* 1863–1900; repr. 1964

CR   *Corpus Reformatorum*

LW   *Luther's Works* (American ed.), ed. Jaroslav Pelikan et al., 56 vols. St. Louis: Concordia Publishers, 1955–1986

OS   *Joannis Calvini opera selecta,* ed. Peter Barth and Wilhelm Niesel, 5 vols. Munich: C. Kaiser, 1926–1952

SHCT   Studies in the History of Christian Thought, 101 vols. Leiden: Brill, 1963–2002

SMRT   Studies in Medieval and Reformation Thought, 84 vols. Leiden: Brill, 1966–2003

TRE   *Theologische Realenzyklopädie,* ed. Gerhard Krause, Gerhard Müller, and Horst Robert Balz, 31 vols. Berlin: de Gruyter, 1977–2000

WAD   *Martin Luthers Werke: Kritische Gesamtausgabe Abteilung*
      Werke [Writings], ed. D. Knaake et al., 61 vols. Weimar:
      H. Böhlaus Nachfolger, 1883–

WABr *D. Martin Luthers Werke: Kritische Gesamtausgabe,*
      Briefwechsel [Letters], ed. O. Clemen et al., 18 vols. Weimar:
      H. Böhlaus Nachfolger, 1930–1985

WAT   *D. Martin Luthers Werke: Kritische Gesamtausgabe, Tischreden*
      [Table Talk], ed. E. Kroker, 6 vols. Weimar: H. Böhlaus
      Nachfolger, 1912–1921; repr. 2000

ZW   *Huldreich Zwinglis Sämmtliche Werke,* ed. Emil Egil et al.,
      14 vols. in 18. Zürich: Theologische Verlag, 1908; repr. 1982

NOTES

CHAPTER I: THE GATHERING STORM

1. Leopold von Ranke, *Deutsche Geschichte im Zeitalter der Reformation* (Leipzig: Duncker und Humblot, 1881). Bernd Moeller, "Das Berühmtwerden Luthers," *Zeitschrift für historische Forschung* 15 (1988), 65–92; reprint, *Die dänische Reformation vor ihrem internationalen Hintergrund,* ed. Leif Grane and Kai Hørby, Forschungen zur Kirchen- und Dogmengeschichte 46 (Göttingen: Vandenhoeck und Ruprecht, 1990), 187–210.
2. Karl Holl, *Gesammelte Aufsätze zur Kirchengeschichte,* 3 vols. (Tübingen: J. C. B. Mohr, 1923–1963); id., *Die Rechtfertigungslehre im Licht der Geschichte des Protestantismus,* 2d ed. (Tübingen: J. C. B. Mohr, 1922).
3. Werner Elert, *Morphologie des Luthertums,* 2 vols. (Munich: Beck, 1931, 1958). I discuss the work of Emanuel Hirsch in further detail in chap. 3.
4. Berndt Hamm, "Werner Elert als Kriegstheologe: Zugleich ein Beitrag zur Diskussion 'Luthertum und Nationalsozialismus,'" *Kirchliche Zeitgeschichte* 11, no. 2 (1998); id., *Frömmigkeitstheologie am Anfang des 16. Jahrhunderts: Studien zu Johannes von Paltz und seinem Umkreis* (Tübingen: Mohr, 1982).
5. Joseph Lortz, *Die Reformation in Deutschland,* 2 vols. (Fribourg: Herder, 1939).
6. Mack P. Holt, "Putting Religion Back into the Wars of Religion," *French Historical Studies* 18, no. 2 (1993), 524–551. See Henry Heller's response, "Putting History Back into the Religious Wars: A Reply to Mack P. Holt," *French Historical Studies* 19, no. 3 (1996), 853–861. Mack P. Holt, "Religion, Historical Method, and Historical Forces: A Rejoinder," *French Historical Studies* 19, no. 3 (1996), 863–873.
7. Bernd Moeller, *Reichsstadt und Reformation,* Schriften des Vereins für Reformationsgeschichte 180 (Gütersloh: Gütersloher Verlagshaus, 1962; reprint, Berlin: Evangelische Verlagsanstalt, 1987).

8. Thomas A. Brady, Jr., *Turning Swiss: Cities and Empire, 1450–1550* (Cambridge: Cambridge University Press, 1985); id., *Ruling Class, Regime and Reformation at Strasbourg, 1520–1550,* SMRT 22 (Leiden: E. J. Brill, 1978).

9. Heinz Schilling, *Die neue Zeit: Vom Christenheitseuropa zum Europa der Staaten: 1250 bis 1750* (Berlin: Siedler Verlag, 1999).

10. See my "The Devil and the Devious Historian: Reaching for the Roots of Modernity," in *Koninklijke Nederlandse Akademie van Wetenschappen/ Heineken Lectures, 1996* (Amsterdam: Edita Koninklijke Nederlandse Akademie van Wetenschappen, 1997), 33–44.

11. Richard Marius, *Martin Luther: The Christian between God and Death* (Cambridge: Belknap Press of Harvard University Press, 1999).

12. Thomas A. Brady, Jr., Heiko A. Oberman, and James D. Tracy, eds., *Handbook of European History, 1400–1600: Late Middle Ages, Renaissance, and Reformation,* 2 vols. (Leiden: E. J. Brill, 1994), esp. vol. 1, xiii–xxii, 665–670.

13. *Fasciculus Morum: A Fourteenth-Century Preacher's Handbook,* ed. and trans. Siegfried Wenzel (University Park, Pa.: Pennsylvania State University Press, 1989), 608, lines 105–107.

14. See my *Harvest of Medieval Theology: Gabriel Biel and Late Medieval Nominalism* (Cambridge: Harvard University Press, 1963; reprint, Durham, N.C.: Labyrinth Press, 1983); id., *Forerunners of the Reformation: The Shape of Late Medieval Thought Illustrated by Key Documents* (New York: Holt, Rinehart, and Winston, 1966; reprint, Philadelphia: Fortress Press, 1981).

15. See my presentation on the occasion of the Fiftieth Anniversary Meeting of the Medieval Academy of America in Cambridge, Mass., on April 18, 1975: "Fourteenth-Century Religious Thought: A Premature Profile," in *The Dawn of the Reformation: Essays in Late Medieval and Early Reformation Thought* (Edinburgh: T. and T. Clark, 1986), 1–17. Originally published in *Speculum* 53 (1978), 80–93.

16. Siegfried Wenzel has pointed out that "the medieval plague experience left a surprisingly small and unremarkable imprint on the artistic consciousness and imagination in England." "Pestilence and Middle English Literature: Friar John Grimestone's Poems on Death," in *The Black Death: The Impact of the Fourteenth-Century Plague,* ed. Daniel Williman (Binghamton, N.Y.: Center for Medieval and Early Renaissance Studies, 1982), 148.

17. Jan de Vries, "Population," in Brady, Oberman, and Tracy, *Handbook of European History,* vol. 1, 21.

18. Bartolomé Yun, "Economic Cycles and Structural Changes," in Brady, Oberman, and Tracy, *Handbook of European History*, vol. 1, 131.

19. Three lectures delivered by David Herlihy at the University of Maine in 1985, posthumously published as *The Black Death and the Transformation of the West*, ed. Samuel K. Cohn, Jr. (Cambridge: Harvard University Press, 1997).

20. Ibid., 51.

21. Ibid., 72.

22. Compare the assumptions in the encyclical "Fides et Ratio" (1999).

23. See my *Contra vanam curiositatem: Ein Kapitel der Theologie zwischen Seelenwinkel und Weltall*, Theologische Studien 113 (Zürich: Theologischer Verlag, 1974).

24. Norman Kretzmann, Anthony John Patrick Kenny, and Jan Pinborg, eds., *The Cambridge History of Later Medieval Philosophy: From the Rediscovery of Aristotle to the Disintegration of Scholasticism, 1100–1600* (Cambridge: Cambridge University Press, 1982; reprint, Cambridge: Cambridge University Press, 1997).

25. Of John Emery Murdoch's numerous works, see *Late Medieval and Early Modern Corpuscular Matter Theories*, Medieval and Early Modern Science 1 (Leiden and Boston: E. J. Brill, 2001); William J. Courtenay, *Covenant and Causality in Medieval Thought: Studies in Philosophy, Theology, and Economic Practice* (London: Variorum Reprints, 1984).

26. See my article "Wessel Gansfort: Magister Contradictionis," in *Wessel Gansfort, 1419–1489, and Northern Humanism*, ed. Fokke Akkerman, Gerda C. Huisman, and Arie Johan Vanderjagt (Leiden: E. J. Brill, 1993), 97–121.

27. Brian Tierney, *Foundations of the Conciliar Theory: The Contribution of the Medieval Canonists from Gratian to the Great Schism*, Cambridge Studies in Medieval Life and Thought 4 (Cambridge: Cambridge University Press, 1955); Francis Oakley, *Natural Law, Conciliarism, and Consent in the Late Middle Ages: Studies in Ecclesiastical and Intellectual History* (London: Variorium, 1984); Antony Black, *Council and Commune: The Conciliar Movement and the Fifteenth-Century Heritage* (London: Burnes and Oates, 1979).

28. See Brian Tierney's extensive new preface to his *Foundations of the Conciliar Theory: The Contribution of the Medieval Canonists from Gratian to the Great Schism*, rev. ed. (Leiden: E. J. Brill, 1998); and the revealing postscript to his *Origins of Papal Infallibility, 1150–1350: A Study on the Concepts of*

Infallibility, Sovereignty, and Tradition in the Middle Ages, 2d ed., SHCT 6 (Leiden: E. J. Brill, 1988).

29. Hans Küng, *Structures of the Church* (New York: Crossroad, 1982).

30. Bernard Chevalier, "France from Charles VII to Henry IV," in Brady, Oberman, and Tracy, *Handbook of European History,* vol. 1, 369–401.

31. See Jean Calvin, *Three French Treatises,* ed. Francis M. Higman (London: Athlone Press, 1970), 23–25.

32. See the critical evaluation of Geoffrey Elton's contribution by Patrick Collinson, "Geoffrey Rudolph Elton, 1921–1994," in *Proceedings of the British Academy: 1996 Lectures and Memoirs,* vol. 94 (Oxford: Oxford University Press, 1997).

33. R. R. Post, *The Modern Devotion: Confrontation with Reformation and Humanism,* SMRT 3 (Leiden: E. J. Brill, 1968). Willem Lourdaux, *Petri Trudonensis: Catalogus Scriptorum Windeshemensium* (Leuven: Leuven University Press, 1968).

34. John Van Engen, "The Virtues, the Brothers, and the Schools: A Text from the Brothers of the Common Life," *Revue Bénédictine* 98 (1988), 178–217; id., "A Brabantine Perspective on the Origins of the Modern Devotion: The First Book of Petrus Impens's *Compendium Decursus Temporum Monasterii Christifere Bethleemitice Puerpere,*" in *Serta Devota: In memoriam Guillelmi Lourdaux,* ed. Werner Verbeke et al., *Mediaevalia Lovaniensia,* Series 1, Studia 20 (Leuven: University Press Leuven, 1992), 3–78.

35. Kaspar Elm, "Die Bruderschaft von dem Gemeinsamen Leben: Eine Geistliche Lebensform zwischen Kloster und Welt, Mittelalter und Neuzeit," in *Geert Grote und Moderne Devotie: Voordrachten Gehouden het Geert Grote Congres, Nijmegen, 27–29 September 1984,* ed. J. Andriessen, Petty Bange, and Antonius Gerardus Wieler, *Ons geestelijk erf* 59 (1985), 470–496; id., "Verfall und Erneuerung des Ordenswesens im Spätmittelalter: Forschungen und Forschungsaufgaben," in *Untersuchungen zu Kloster und Stift,* Veröffentlichungen des Max-Planck-Instituts für Geschichte 68 (Göttingen: Vandenhoeck und Ruprecht, 1980), 188–238. Elm has succinctly summarized his findings in his contribution to TRE, s.v. "Orden," vol. 25 (1995), esp. 323, 11–38.

36. See my "Die Gelehrten, die Verkehrten: Popular Response to Learned Culture in the Renaissance and Reformation," in *Religion and Culture in the Renaissance and Reformation,* ed. Steven E. Ozment, Sixteenth Century Essays and Studies 11 (Kirksville, Mo.: Sixteenth Century Journal Publishers, 1989), 43–62.

37. Augustin Renaudet, *Humanisme et Renaissance: Dante, Pétrarque, Stan-*

donck, Érasme, Lefèvre d'Étaples, Marguerite de Navarre, Rabelais, Guichar-din, Giordano Bruno, Travaux d'Humanisme et Renaissance 30 (Geneva: Librarie Droz, 1958), 119; cf. his earlier magnificent work, *Préréforme et humanisme à Paris pendant les premières guerres d'Italie, 1494–1517,* Biblio-thèque de l'Institut Français de Florence 1 (Paris: E. Champion, 1916; reprint, Paris: Librairie d'Argences, 1953).

38. Heinrich Bullinger, *Diarium (Annales vitae) der Jahre 1504–1574,* ed. Emil Egli (Basel: Basler Buch- und Antiquariatshandlung vormals Adolf Geer-ing, 1904), 3; as quoted by John Van Engen, in *Revue Bénédictine* (1988), 193 n. 39.

39. George Huppert, *After the Black Death: A Social History of Early Modern Europe* (Bloomington, Ind.: Indiana University Press, 1986), 150–151.

40. Kaspar Elm, *Vitasfratrum: Beiträge zur Geschichte der Eremiten- und Men-dikantenorden des zwölften und dreizehnten Jahrhunderts* (Werl: Dietrich-Coelde-Verlag, 1994), 297–337. The subtitle of this Festschrift is mislead-ing but in keeping with Elm's usual modesty in claiming too little rather than too much.

41. Ibid., 325.

42. Jeremy Cohen, *The Friars and the Jews: The Evolution of Medieval Anti-Judaism* (Ithaca, N.Y.: Cornell University Press, 1982).

43. Quoted by Elm, *Vitasfratrum,* 513.

44. Robert J. Bast, *Honor Your Fathers: Catechisms and the Emergence of a Patriarchal Ideology in Germany, 1400–1600,* SMRT 63 (Leiden: E. J. Brill, 1997).

45. Peter A. Dykema, *Conflicting Expectations: Parish Priests in Late Medieval Germany,* SMRT (Leiden: E. J. Brill, forthcoming).

46. *On the Eve of the Reformation: Letters of Obscure Men,* trans. Francis Griffin Stokes (New York: Harper and Row, 1964).

CHAPTER II: LUTHER AND THE VIA MODERNA

Epigraph: "Bonaventura is the best of the scholastic doctors," ca. 1530–1535. WAT, 1.330, 1, no. 683.

1. Edward P. Mahoney, "Metaphysical Foundations of the Hierarchy of Being According to Some Late Medieval and Renaissance Philosophers," in *Phi-losophies of Existence: Ancient and Medieval,* ed. Parviz Morewedge (New York: Fordham University Press, 1982), 165–257.

2. See my *Harvest of Medieval Theology: Gabriel Biel and Late Medieval Nomi-nalism* (Cambridge: Harvard University Press, 1963; reprint, Durham, N.C.: Labyrinth Press, 1983). Cf. id., *Masters of the Reformation: The Emer-*

gence of a New Intellectual Climate in Europe, trans. Dennis Martin (Cambridge: Cambridge University Press, 1981); and id., "*Via Antiqua* and *Via Moderna:* Late Medieval Prolegomena to Early Reformation Thought," *Journal of the History of Ideas* 48 (1987), 23–40.

3. "Primo grammatica videamus, verum ea Theologica." *Operationes in psalmos,* Ps. 1:1 (1519); WA, 5.27, 8; AWA, 2.29, 4. In his favorite book, the *Commentary on Galatians* (1531/35), Luther points to this theological grammar as the fundamental key for opening the Scriptures: whenever you read in Scripture about the great deeds of arch-fathers, prophets, and kings—how they resurrected the dead and conquered countries—always be mindful to interpret these and similar passages "secundam novam et Theologicam Grammaticam." WA 40 1.418, 21–24.

4. "Fidei oculis et auribus opus est, ut haec verba spiritus ['Beatus vir qui non abiit in consilio impiorum / et in via peccatorum non stetit, / in cathedra derisorum non sedit,' Ps. 1:1] spiritus audias et eorum rem videas. Homo enim non potest ea intelligere." WA 5.31, 11 f. = AWA 2.37, 5 f.

5. *Disputatio de homine,* Theses 4 and 5 (1536); WA 39 1.175, 9–13. Luther's critique of Aristotle concerns the disregard of that fundamental nominalist *axioma,* the demarcation line between the realms of reason and faith. Provided that this distinction is respected, Aristotle is not merely useful but indeed to be respected. In a Latin sermon probably preached to the Wittenberg *confratres* on Christmas Day, 1514, Luther formulates this subtle balance beautifully: "Pulchra haec Philosophia, sed a paucis intellecta, altissimae Theologiae utilis est." WA 1.29, 27 f. The "pagan" Aristotle of Thomas and the via antiqua is targeted in the observation that this apt application of Aristotle in the service of theology only applies "si non ut ipse voluit, sed melius intelligitur et applicatur." WA 1.28, 20 f.

6. "Acta Iohannis Pauli PP. 2. Litterae Encyclicae cunctis catholicae Ecclesiae episcopis de necessitudinis natura inter fidem et rationem," *Acta Apostolicae Sedis* 91 (1999), 5–88, 40 f., September 14, 1998.

7. As in Etienne Gilson, *History of Christian Philosophy in the Middle Ages* (New York: Random House, 1955), esp. 489–500. Cf. Armand A. Maurer CSB: "In comparison with the thirteenth century, the fourteenth was a period of disunion and disintegration." *Medieval Philosophy,* vol. 2 of *A History of Philosophy,* ed. Etienne Gilson, 2d ed., 2 vols. (Toronto: Pontifical Institute of Medieval Studies, 1982), 265. It should be noted, however, that Gilson's student and successor Paul Vignaux, along with Philotheus Boehner OFM, laid the groundwork for a complete reevaluation of the significance of nominalism. See Vignaux, *Luther: Commentateur des Sentences*

(livre 1, *distinction* 17*),* Études de Philosophie Médiévale 21 (Paris: J. Vrin, 1935); and Boehner, *Collected Articles on Ockham,* ed. E. M. Buytaert, Philosophy Series 12 (St. Bonaventure, N.Y.: Franciscan Institute, 1958). Jürgen Miethke unfolded the political, legal, and social implications of Occam's thought beginning with his *Ockhams Weg zur Sozialphilosophie* (Berlin: Walter de Gruyter, 1969). The theological implications of the Franciscan view of church and sacraments are traced by Berndt Hamm, who explored the foundation of this theology of piety in his *Frömmigkeits-theologie am Anfang des 16. Jahrhundert: Studiën zu Johannes von Paltz und Seinem Umkreis,* Beiträge zur historischen Theologie 65 (Tübingen: J. C. B. Mohr, 1982) and *Promissio, Pactum, Ordinatio: Freiheit und Selbstbindung Gottes in der scholastischen Gnadenlehre,* Beiträge zur historischen Theologie 54 (Tübingen: J. C. B. Mohr, 1977). For an introduction to Hamm's concept of the "theology of piety," see his "Normative Centering in the Fifteenth and Sixteenth Centuries," trans. John M. Frymire, *Journal of Early Modern History* 3 (1999), 307–354, esp. 325–330 and 307–309.

8. Heinrich Denifle OP died just two weeks after completing the preface to his *Quellenbelege: Die Abendländischen Schriftausleger bis Luther über Justitia Dei (Rom. 1,17) und Justificatio,* vol. 1 of *Ergänzungen zu Denifles Luther und Luthertum* (Mainz: F. Kirchheim, 1905); see esp. p. xx. In Joseph Lortz's obituary of February 27, 1975, in the *Frankfurter Allgemeine Zeitung* (no. 49, p. 21), Karl Otmar Freiherr von Aretin not only notes the remarkable influence of his two-volume *Die Reformation in Deutschland* (1939–1940), but also calls attention to the fact that Lortz was the cofounder of the "brown" organization "Kreuz und Hakenkreuz." Richard Marius looked in vain for evidence that Lortz ever withdrew from the Nazi party: "Lortz claimed, after the war, that he had dropped out of the party in 1936, but there is no evidence that he did. His dossier in the files of the party, captured intact by the American Army at the end of the war, makes no mention of any resignation." *Luther* (Philadelphia: Lippincott, 1974), 246–248, 247. It may not exculpate but perhaps explain Lortz's "national" interpretation of Luther that as a born outsider (Luxembourg) he tried to be "plus royaliste que le Führer." The cult of Luther as "Person der Weltgeschichte" was so widespread among "brown" Protestant scholars that this accolade might easily seem ecumenical from a later perspective: for Lortz, the reformer belonged to a uniquely German heroic tradition climaxing in Adolf Hitler. Such explicit reference to the political stance of a scholar sharply deviates from the deep silence usually observed. The line from the later, postwar Hermann Heimpel to Bernd Moeller alerts us to the fact that

the indicated "cult" more generally, though by no means necessarily, displayed Nazi tendencies but was quite typical of national aspirations informing Reformation scholarship.

9. In a rare, revealing World War II pamphlet, Joseph Lortz published theses about the Reformation in order "to further the ecumenical dialogue." One of his typical statements is: "Nicht voll katholisch ist z.B. was nicht ein existentielles Verhältnis hat (1.) zur Wahrheit, (2.) zur Gnade, an beiden fehlt es dem nominalistischen Okhamismus." *Die Reformation: Thesen als Handreichung bei ökumenischen Gesprächen* (Meitingen bei Augsburg: Kyrios-Verlag für christliches Geistesgut, 1940; reprint, n.d. [1946]), 7. Cf. "Nur ein Geist, der von Grund auf an das unreale Denken (ja Hinwegdenken) des anscheinend so empirischen Nominalismus gewöhnt war, konnte in der Imputationstheorie allein eine genügende Darstellung der Rechtfertigung sehen." Ibid., 21. Cf. "an der Trennung [ist] . . . die Mangelhaftigkeit katholischer Theologie des 15/16. Jahrhunderts Mitschuld." Ibid., 27. Cf. "Der Vater der Reformation, Martin Luther, wuchs . . . unabsichtlich [!] aus der römischen Kirche heraus. Die damalige Theologie des okhamistischen Nomimalismus war an dieser Entwicklung entscheidend mitbeteiligt." Ibid., 2 f. Cf. "Luther . . . ist nicht 'Hörer' [der Schrift] im Vollsinn des Wortes . . . er gibt vielmehr aus der Bibel eine persönlich bedingte Auswahl." Ibid., 6.

10. Cf. the characteristically well-documented, evenhanded essay by Hubert Jedin, *Kardinal Caesar Baronius: Der Anfang der katholischen Kirchengeschichtsschreibung im 16. Jahrhundert,* Katholisches Leben und Kirchenreform im Zeitalter der Glaubensspaltung 38 (Münster: Aschendorff, 1978), with the passionately confessional Remigius Bäumer, *Johannes Cochlaeus, 1479–1552: Leben und Werk im Dienst der katholischen Reform,* Katholisches Leben und Kirchenreform im Zeitalter der Glaubensspaltung 40 (Münster: Aschendorff, 1980). For Iserloh, see the Lortzean identification of late medieval nominalism with "dogmatic unclarity": "Angesichts der dogmatischen Unklarheit der Zeit war es Ecks Verdienst, in Klarheit, ja Unerbittlichkeit aufgewiesen zu haben, daß Luther nicht Reform, sondern Revolution bedeutete." Erwin Iserloh, *Johannes Eck, 1486–1543: Scholastiker, Humanist, Kontroverstheologe,* Katholisches Leben und Kirchenreform im Zeitalter der Glaubensspaltung 41 (Münster: Aschendorff, 1981), 80.

11. "Wieder eine andere Funktion als historisches Leitbild erhielt Luther. Die Erinnerung an ihn setzte die staatstragende protestantische Kirche, deren Oberhaupt der Kaiser war, in heroisch-tiefsinnige Beleuchtung. Zugleich

hob die Luther-Beschwörung den Gegensatz zur weniger gründlichen, weniger religiösen romanischen Welt hervor, besonders zu Frankreich, aber auch zu Italien. Schließlich schien nach 1918 Luthers Schmähung der Vernunft und seine anknüpfungs- und vermittlungsfeindliche Gnadenlehre dazu dienlich, Zusammenbruchserfahrungen des Kriegsendes und das Ende des Staatsprotestantismus zu verarbeiten." Kurt Flasch, *Die geistige Mobilmachung: Die deutschen Intellektuellen und der Erste Weltkrieg: Ein versuch* (Berlin: Alexander Fest Verlag, 2000), 71.

12. Hans Blumenberg, *Die Legitimität der Neuzeit* (Frankfurt: Suhrkamp, 1966); English ed., *The Legitimacy of the Modern Age,* trans. Robert M. Wallace (Cambridge: MIT Press, 1983). See the revised edition of parts 1 and 2 in *Säkularisierung und Selbstbehauptung,* Suhrkamp Taschenbuch Wissenschaft 19 (Frankfurt: Suhrkamp, 1974). Rudolph Lorenz, *Die unvollendete Befreiung vom Nominalismus: Martin Luther und die Grenzen hermeneutischer Theologie bei Gerhard Ebeling* (Gütersloh: Gütersloher Verlagshaus Mohn, 1973). See the response by Gerhard Ebeling in his *Lutherstudien,* vol. 2, *Disputatio de homine* (Tübingen: Mohr Siebeck, 1971), pt. 3, 392 n. 389; id., "Luther and the Beginning of the Modern Age," in *Luther and the Dawn of the Modern Era: Papers for the Fourth International Congress for Luther Research,* ed. Heiko A. Oberman, SHCT 8 (Leiden: E. J. Brill, 1974), 11–39.

13. The best-documented critique of Blumenberg has been offered by Karl-Heinz zur Mühlen, who not only presents a well-balanced description of Luther's understanding of the limits of reason but also succeeds in pursuing the discussion of Blumenberg into the domain of modern philosophy and theology. See zur Mühlen, *Reformatorische Vernunftkritik und neuzeitliches Denken dargestellt am Werk M. Luthers und Fr. Gogartens,* Beiträge zur historischen Theologie 59 (Tübingen: J. C. B. Mohr, 1980).

14. Such reductionism is becoming rare. Wilfrid Werbeck at least adds the unexplained but more appropriate term "late-Franciscan" to his characterization of Biel's "ockhamistisch-spätfranziskanisch bestimmter Theologie." See "Gabriel Biel als spätmittelalterlicher Theologie," in *Gabriel Biel und die Brüder vom gemeinsamen Leben,* ed. Ulrich Köpf and Sönke Lorenz, Contubernium 47 (Stuttgart: Franz Steiner Verlag, 1998), 25–34, 34.

15. Eberhard Jüngel, "Quae supra nos, nihil ad nos: Eine Kurzformel der Lehre vom verborgenen Gott—im Anschluss an Luther interpretiert," in *Entsprechungen: Gott-Wahrheit-Mensch: Theologische Erörterungen,* Beiträge zur evangelischen Theologie 88 (Munich: Chr. Kaiser, 1980), 202–251; 229.

16. Eberhard Jüngel, *Gottes Sein ist im Werden: Verantwortliche Rede vom Sein Gottes bei Karl Barth: Eine Paraphrase* (Tübingen: Mohr, 1965; 4th ed., Tübingen: Mohr Siebeck, 1986). This highly original essay, which, with the inchoative connotation of "im Werden," promises to reflect the Franciscan paradigm, neutralizes this intention by speculatively pursuing "Entsprechungen" in an untranslatable language so far removed from "natural signs" as to constitute the "schärfste Kritik" of the via moderna. Notwithstanding his attention to precise historical documentation in context, Wolfgang Maaser's substantial Habilitationsschrift has a similar speculative tendency. *Die schöpferische Kraft des Wortes: Die Bedeutung der Rhetorik für Luthers Schöpfungs- und Ethikverständnis,* Neukirchener theologische Dissertationen und Habilitationen 22 (Neukirchen-Vluyn: Neukirchener Verlag, 1999). *N'en de'plaise* his sympathy for Jüngel's conclusions, Maaser grants Luther's proximity to the via moderna—within limits. Ibid., 216–218, 217.

17. "Fortasse fuerim attentior et fortasse linguarum opibus instructior, certe quam Aquinas, qui latine tantum novit." Desiderius Erasmus, *Novum Instrumentum* (Basel, 1516; reprint, Stuttgart-Bad Cannstatt: Fromman-Holzboog, 1990) *Apologia,* fo. bbb 8^r.

18. For the covenant interpretation in modern Exodus scholarship, see Werner H. Schmidt, *Exodus, Sinai und Mose,* Erträge der Forschung 191 (Darmstadt: Wissenschaftliche Buchgesellschaft, 1983), esp. 40–45. Supported by the inversion in Hos. 1:9, the suggested best translation is: "Ich will euch für mich als Volk annehmen und will für euch Gott sein"; Exod. 6:7. Schmidt, *Exodus: Teilband 1: Exodus 1–6,* Biblischer Kommentar: Altes Testament, vol. 2, pt. 1 (Neukirchen-Vluyn: Neukirchener Verlag des Erziehungsverein, 1988), esp. 175–177.

19. Jacques Lefèvre d'Étaples, *La Saincte Bible en Francoys* (Antwerp: Martin Lempereur, 1530); I have used the third edition (Antwerp, 1541), fo. 21^r. Francis M. Higman identified three copies of the first part of Lefèvre's Bible (the Books of Moses: April 30, 1528). Among the first translations of the Bible censured by the Sorbonne (November 6, 1525) and forbidden by decree of the Parlement of Paris (December 29, 1525) are Lefèvre's translations of the Letters, the Gospels, and the Psalms: "the censure did not prevent him from completing his translation." See Higman, *Censorship and the Sorbonne: A Bibliographical Study of Books in French Censured by the Faculty of Theology of the University of Paris, 1520–1551* (Geneva: Droz, 1979), 80–82, 81. The continued impact of the Vulgate can explain the fact that the Hebraist Sebastian Münster (d. 1552), eleven years after producing his valuable *Biblia Hebraica* (2 vols., Basel, 1534–1535), rendered Exod. 3:14 as

"ego sum, qui sum" in the Latin translation of his work (Basel, 1546). Cf. Pierre Robert Olivétan, *La Bible* (Neuchâtel: Pierre de Vingel, 1535): "Je suis qui je suis," with, in the margin, "Aucuns, je seray qui je seray; De ce mot est dict Eternal."

20. *D. Martin Luther: Die gantze Heilige Schrifft Deudsch: Aufs new zugericht, Wittenberg 1545*, ed. Hans Volz with Heinz Blanke (Munich: Rogner and Bernhard, 1972), 126. Whereas the King James (1611) and the New American Standard (1995) translations follow the ontological tradition (in contrast to the Dutch Statenvertaling, 1637), Martin Buber undertook to stay especially close to the Hebrew original: "Gott sprach zu Mosche: 'Ich werde dasein, als der ich dasein werde' "; *Die fünf Bücher der Weisung*, ed. Martin Buber with Franz Rosenzweig, Die Schrift 1 (Cologne: Hegner, 1954; 12th ed., Stuttgart: Deutsche Bibelgesellschaft, 1998), 158; Exod. 3:14.

21. Aquinas *Summa Theologiae*, 1, q. 2, art. 3, S*ed contra*.

22. See the thirty occurrences in the *Opuscula sancti patris Francisci Assisiensis*, ed. Kajetan Esser, Bibliotheca Franciscana ascetica medii aevi 12 (Grottaferrata: Editiones Collegii S. Bonaventurae ad Claras Aquas, 1978), 367.

23. For the reception of Saint Francis by Bonaventura, see the extensive introduction in Sophronius Clasen, ed., *Franziskus, Engel des sechsten Siegels: Sein Leben nach den Schriften des heiligen Bonaventura*, Franziskanische Quellenschriften 7 (Werl: Dietrich-Coelde-Verlag, 1962), 33–47, 54–64, 105–128.

24. *Sacrum commercium sancti Francisci cum Domina Paupertate*, ed. PP. Collegium S. Bonaventurae (Ad Claras Aquas, Florentine: Ex typographia Collegii S. Bonaventurae, 1929).

25. See the excellent comprehensive and topically well-ordered "Research Bibliography," in *Saint Francis of Assisi: Writings and Early Biographies: English Omnibus of the Sources for the Life of Saint Francis*, ed. Marion A. Habig (Chicago: Franciscan Herald Press, 1973), 1676–1760.

26. For the—nonmystical!—rendering of "commercium" as "Bund" (covenant), see Kajetan Esser, *Anfänge und ursprüngliche Zielsetzungen des Ordens der Minderbrüder*, Studia et Documenta Franciscana 4 (Leiden: E. J. Brill, 1966); cf. the convincing justification by Esser and Engelbert Grau for their rendering of the title in German as *Der Bund des Heiligen Franziskus mit der Herrin Armut*, in their introduction to the edition with this title, Franziskanische Quellenschriften 9 (Werl: Dietrich-Coelde-Verlag, 1966), 29–41.

27. For contemporary characterizations of nominalism and the via moderna see my *Werden und Wertung der Reformation: Vom Wegestreit zum*

Glaubenskampf, Spätscholastik und Reformation 2 (Tübingen: J. C. B. Mohr, 1977; 3d ed., Tübingen: J. C. B. Mohr, 1989), esp. 43–50.

28. "Hanc viam primus dicitur [Wilhelmus Ockam] purificasse." Stephan Hoest, *Reden und Briefe: Quellen zur Geschichte der Scholastik und des Humanismus im 15. Jahrhundert,* ed. and trans. Frank Baron, Humanistische Bibliothek, 2d ser., vol. 3 (Munich: Wilhelm Fink Verlag, 1971), 176, lines 210–221, 220 f.

29. See the Decree of March 1, 1473, in César É. Du Boulay [Bulaeus], *Ab anno 1400 ad annum 1500,* vol. 5 of *Historia Universitatis Parisiensis* (Paris, 1665–1673; Frankfurt: Minerva, 1965–1966), 706–710; text of the decree of repeal dated April 29–30, 1481; ibid., 739–741. (The year 1473 is according to the French calendar.)

30. A Nijmwegen research team under the guidance of H. A. G. Braakhuis has cleared the ground and reclaimed Albertinism as a distinct *via* in its own right. One of the finest fruits of international cooperation is the effective cosponsorship with Georg Wieland's Tübingen *sodalitas* in the joint edition of the Sentences Commentary of Marsilius of Inghen (d. 1396), the founding father of the *via Marsilii* in Heidelberg. Renowned as a spokesperson for the *via moderna* with support among early humanists (see n. 31 below), "Marsilius redivivus" documents in this new critical edition the extent to which the *moderni* prized inclusiveness, including the tradition of Albertus Magnus. See Marsilius of Inghen, *Quaestiones super quattuor libros Sententiarum,* ed. Georg Wieland, Maarten J. F. M. Hoenen, Manuel Santos Noya, and Manfred Schulze, vol. 1 of *Super Primum,* ed. Manuel Santos Noya, SHCT, 87–88 (Leiden: E. J. Brill, 2000), esp. the description of the "humanist" Strasbourg edition of Martin Flach (1501), 47–52; cf. the marking of the revealing subsequent "additiones"; ibid., vol. 2, 19. Schulze and Santos had already participated in the edition of that other spokesman for the via moderna, Gregory of Rimini, *Gregorii Ariminensis OESA Lectura super Primum et Secundum Sententiarum,* ed. A. Damasus Trapp, 6 vols., Spätmittelalter und Reformation, Texte und Untersuchungen 6–12 (Berlin: Walter de Gruyter, 1979–1987). For the *via Gregorii* see Manfred Schulze, "Via Gregorii in Forschung und Quellen," in *Gregor von Rimini: Werk und Wirkung bis zur Reformation,* ed. Heiko A. Oberman, Spätmittelalter und Reformation, Texte und Untersuchungen 20 (Berlin: Walter de Gruyter, 1981), 1–126. Moreover, Schulze edited (with Albert Czogalla) significant parts of the influential *Tractatus de Decimis* (1497) from the hand of the late-medieval commentator on Albertus, Conrad Summenhart (d. 1502), in Oberman, *Werden und Wertung,* 381–411.

31. For Wimpfeling, see the extensive entry by Barbara Könneker in *Contemporaries of Erasmus: A Biographical Register of the Renaissance and Reformation,* ed. Peter G. Bietenholz and Thomas B. Deutscher, vol. 3 (Toronto: University of Toronto Press, 1987), 447–450. In his oft reprinted influential *Adolescentia* (Strasbourg, 1500), Wimpfeling included a negative characterization of the *via antiqua* under his favorite heading of "Concord": "De concordantia antiquorum et modernorum." Whereas the Franciscans swear only by their Scotus, and the Dominicans are blinded by their Thomas, they fight one another with pen and fist. The secular scholars, however, pursue honest research by going with the evidence and weighing each case on its own merits—the best among them "in step with" the Heidelbergers (i.e., the via Marsilii). See the outstanding edition by Otto Herding, *Jakob Wimpfelings Adolescentia,* Jacobi Wimpfelingi opera selecta 1 (Munich: Wilhelm Fink Verlag, 1965), 381, lines 6–18. Wigand Trebellius, *Concordia curatorum et fratrum mendicantium* (n.p. [Strasbourg?], n.d. [1503?]), fol. b 2^r. Note that "Curati" is used instead of the technical neutral designation "seculars": not the friars but the secular clergy carry the burden of the *cura animarum,* the true pastoral care. In one of his precious "Miszellen," Nikolaus Paulus had already in 1903 identified Wimpfeling as the author behind the pseudonym Wigand Trebellius. See "Wimpfelingiana," *Zeitschrift für die Geschichte des Oberrheins* 18 (Karlsruhe, Germany: G. Braun Buchverlag, 1903), 46–57. In 1929 Paulus could correct Ritter and declared Wimpfeling responsible for the introduction, text, and conclusion of the edition of the Wesel interrogation; ibid., "Miszellen," vol. 42 (1929), 296–300. Gerhard Ritter conceded this point in a brief response in the same volume; ibid., 451–453. His insistence, against Paulus, on limiting Wimpfeling's part in the Wesel edition to the introduction and conclusion is convincing.

32. See the critical edition of the *Decisio quaestionis de audientia missae,* ed. Wolfgang Günter, in Johann von Staupitz, *Gutachten und Satzungen,* vol. 5 of *Sämtliche Schriften: Abhandlungen, Predigten, Zeugnisse,* ed. Lothar Graf zu Dohna and Richard Wetzel, Spätmittelalter und Reformation, Texte und Untersuchungen 17 (Berlin: Walter de Gruyter, 2001), 1–58.

33. WAT 1.135, 11 (no. 329; Veit Dietrich's *Nachschriften,* summer–fall 1532). In connection with the Wesel case we find eloquent documentation for this thrust. The Dominican Wigand Wirt in 1512 recanted his earlier *Dialogus Apologeticus contra Wesalianicam perfidiam* (Oppenheim, Germany, 1494), not because he came to doubt his critique of Wesel, as intimated by Otto Clemen, "Über Leben und Schriften Johanns von Wesel," *Deutsche*

Zeitschrift für Geschichtswissenschaft, N.S. 2, Vierteljahreshefte (1897–98), 143–173, 159: in his counterblast Wirt had questioned the Immaculate Conception of the Virgin Mary. In the revealing subtitle of his *Revocatio* he lists the offended parties—the Virgin Mary, Duns Scotus, *and* all the nominalists: "Ad Honorem totius familiae Franciscanae ceterorumque bonorum virorum eandem virginem ab originis labe immunem sentientium." *Apud Trebotes* (Strasbourg, n.d. [1513?]).

34. See Kaspar Elm, "Die Bedeutung Johannes Kapistrans und der Franziskanerobservanz für die Kirche des 15. Jahrhunderts," in *S. Giovanni da Capestrano nella Chiesa e nella Società del suo tempo: Convegno storico internazionale VI Centenario della nascita del Santo, 1381–1981, Capestrano—L'Aquila, 8–13 ottobre 1986,* ed. Edith Pásztor (L'Aquila: Da Arti Grafiche Aquilane, 1990), 100–120; cf. id., "Tod, Todesbewältigung und Endzeit bei Bernhardin von Siena: Ein Beitrag zum Verhältnis von italienischem Humanismus und franziskanischer Observantenpredigt," in *Conciliarismo, stati nazionali, inizi dell'umanesimo: Atti del XXV Convegno storico internazionale Todi, 9–12 ottobre 1988,* Atti dei Convegni dell'Academia Tudertina e del Centro di studi sulla spiritualità medievale 2 (Spoleto: Centro italiano di studi sull'alto Medioevo, 1990), 79–96.

35. See n. 7, above.

36. See the richly documented study of Christoph C. Burger, *Aedificatio, Fructus, Utilitas: Johannes Gerson als Professor der Theologie und Kanzler der Universität Paris,* Beiträge zur historischen Theologie 70 (Tübingen: J. C. B. Mohr, 1986).

37. "Der geistliche Verzicht auf Nachwuchs, der adelige auf die Güter der Kirche und der bürgerliche auf Wucher erübrigten sich alle gleichermassen. Die Vorliebe für die universale Hierarchie, die der gesellschaftlichen Struktur Früheuropas so ausgezeichnet entsprochen hatte, musste durch die Beschränkung auf jene territorialen Grenzen ersetzt werden, bis zu denen die neuartige Macht des ortsansässigen Monopolisten jeweils reichte." Constantin Fasolt, "Europäische Geschichte, zweiter Akt: Die Reformation," in *Die deutsche Reformation zwischen Mittelalter und Früher Neuzeit,* ed. Thomas A. Brady, Jr., with Elisabeth Müller-Luckner, Schriften des Historischen Kollegs, Kolloquien 50 (Munich: R. Oldenbourg Verlag, 2001), 231–250, 239, 241.

38. This aspect of confrontation and rejection is at once the main theme and conclusion of Leif Grane, *Contra Gabrielem: Luthers Auseinandersetzung mit Gabriel Biel in der Disputatio contra scholasticam theologiam, 1517,* Acta Theologica Danica 4 (Copenhagen: Gyldendal, 1962), esp. 380 f.

39. Despite the laborious punctuation of the text as a consequence of the nineteenth-century ideal of "diplomatische Treue," I refer here to the best-annotated edition of the disputation by Helmar Junghans, in *Martin Luther: Studienausgabe,* ed. Hans-Ulrich Delius (Berlin: Evangelische Verlagsanstalt, 1979), 1:169, line 16 f. = WA 1.226, Thesis 50.

40. *Disputatio Heidelbergae habita* (1518), Conclusio 19; WA 1.361, 32–36. = *Martin Luther,* Junghans, 1:207, 26 f.

41. WAT 1.330, 1 (no. 683). This high approval rating does not exclude the expression of acute disappointment that Bonaventure's *theologia affectiva* proved to be unable to replace the "elevator" of reason with the mystical ladder to God: "He drove me out of my mind, because I wanted to feel the union of God with my soul." WAT 1.302, 31–32 (no. 644); cf. WA 40 3.199, 32–36 (Ps. 126:6; 1532). See my "*Simul Gemitus et Raptus:* Luther and Mysticism," in Heiko A. Oberman, *The Dawn of the Reformation: Essays in Late Medieval and Early Reformation Thought* (Edinburgh: T. and T. Clark, 1986), 126–154.

42. The most reliable overview of the state of research is still to be found in the well-documented article by William J. Courtenay, "Nominalism and Late Medieval Religion," in *The Pursuit of Holiness in Late Medieval Religion,* ed. Charles Trinkaus and Heiko A. Oberman, SMRT 10 (Leiden: E. J. Brill, 1974), 26–59.

43. Though Scotus is the systematic propagator of God's covenantal action in justification, salvation, church, and sacrament, the father of *pactum* theology invoked to explain the connection between saving grace and the sacramental rite is the Parisian Bishop William of Auvergne (d. 1249). As Bonaventura recalls, William was the first to advance this concept in the Parisian Franciscan house in the presence of Alexander of Hales. See the conclusive documentation in Hamm, *Promissio, Pactum, Ordinatio,* esp. 483–486.

44. The *potentia ordinata* can be understood in two ways: what God can do "stante sua ordinatione qua eternaliter voluit se sic vel sic esse facturum," or (*magis large*) what he can do "stante veritate legis seu scripture divine." Pierre d'Ailly, *Quaestiones super libros Sententiarum* (Strasbourg, 1490; reprint, Frankfurt: Minerva, 1968), 1 Sent. q. 13, art. 1 D.

45. Cf. my essay *Contra vanam curiositatem: Ein Kapitel der Theologie zwischen Seelenwinkel und Weltall,* Theologische Studien 113 (Zürich: Theologischer Verlag, 1974). See esp. Burger, *Aedificatio, Fructus, Utilitas,* 110–125.

46. "[Monastica institutio] nullum habet testimonium de scriptura, neque ullum signum aut prodigium, quo sit coelitus comprobata." *De votis monasticis iudicium* (1521), WA 8.617, 17–35. These signs are ambivalent

insofar as false prophets are invoking their own *prodigia* in order to confuse the Christians. Ibid., 657, 16–19. Already in the Leipzig Disputation (1519) Luther explicitly grants the possibility of a "nova et probata revelatio"; WA 59.466, 1062.

47. The *Fasciculus morum* can serve as a telling example. Composed in England shortly after 1300, the Franciscan authorship and sympathies of this rich guide for preaching moral problem solving and pastoral counseling are clear from the beginning. Yet in the elaboration of the seven virtues and vices, the author does not hesitate to make use of Saint Thomas. See *Fasciculus Morum: A Fourteenth-Century Preacher's Handbook,* ed. and trans. Siegfried Wenzel (University Park, Pa.: Pennsylvania State University Press, 1989).

48. *Liber receptorum nationis Anglicanae (Alemanniae) in Universitate Parisiensi ab anno 1425 ad annum 1494,* ed. Astrik L. Gabriel and Gray C. Boyce, Auctarium chartularii Universitatis Parisiensis 6 (Paris: Marcel Didier, 1964), col. 331, n. 11. See Maarten van Rhijn, *Studiën over Wessel Gansfort en zijn tijd* (Utrecht: Kemink en Zoon N. V., 1933), 112–126, 124. Van Rhijn thinks Hoeck may have been among the *Signatores.* Ibid., 125 n. 2.

49. "Ante annum inceptae viae Scoti cum omni diligentia, quantum potui perspecte, graviores in ea quam in via Realium errores deprehendens, etiam corrigi paratus mutavi sententiam et Nominales adprehendi." *M. Wesseli Gansfortii Groningensis rarae et reconditae viri, qui olim Lux Mundi vulgo dictus sint, Opera* (Groningen, 1614; reprint, Nieuwkoop: n.p., 1966), 877.

50. See my "Wessel Gansfort: Magister contradictionis," in *Wessel Gansfort, 1419–1489, and Northern Humanism,* ed. Fokke Akkerman, Gerda C. Huisman, and Arie Johan Vanderjagt, Studies in Intellectual History 40 (Leiden: E. J. Brill, 1993), 97–121. In the same volume H. A. G. Braakhuis points to the abiding Albertinist tenets (see n. 30 above) in Gansfort's thought; "Wessel Gansfort between Albertism and Nominalism," 30–43. The same applies to the lasting impact of Scotus. This proud nominalist aspired to growth and a higher synthesis.

51. Gansfort, *Opera,* 419.

52. Ibid., 60. For the full quotation, see Oberman, "Wessel Gansfort," 115 n. 52. Cf. for the preceding period, the fine monograph of Caroline Walker Bynum, *Jesus as Mother: Studies in the Spirituality of the High Middle Ages,* Publications of the Center for Medieval and Renaissance Studies 16 (Berkeley, Calif.: University of California Press, 1982). Wessel's concern for the pastoral care of sisters, nuns, and tertiaries has not yet drawn the atten-

tion it deserves. For his friendship with Thomas of Kempen and his relationship with the Modern Devotion—which was a women's movement
to a larger extent than the usual name, "Brothers of the Common Life,"
suggests—see the history of Agnietenberg by B. J. Thüss and the extensive
literature appended to the Dutch translation of Thomas of Kempen's
Agnieten Chronicle (*Chronica montis sanctae Agnetis;* written in the years
1464–1471) by Udo de Kruijf, in *Een Klooster ontsloten: De Kroniek van
Sint-Agnietenberg bij Zwolle door Thomas van Kempen,* ed. Udo de Kruijf,
Jeroen Kummer, and Freek Pereboom, Publicaties van de IJsselacademie
124 (Kampen: IJsselacademie, 2000), 81–111, 127–196, 235–263.

53. Clemen, "Johanns von Wesel," 148–155; reedition, 108–115. In the ap-
pendix Clemen provides the interrogation record according to the Bonn
MS 747: 165–173, reedition, 125–133. (This version does not include
the revealing additions of Wimpfeling; see n. 31 above.) Two years later
Clemen published the list of articles Wesel recanted in Mainz on Sunday
Estomihi (Quinquagesima Sunday, February 21, 1479) in *Historische Vier-
teljahrschrift* 3 (1900), 521–523. For further literature, see Ludwig Hödl,
"J. Rucherat v. Wesel," in *Lexikon des Mittelalters* 5 (1991), col. 598; Win-
fried Eberhard, "Johannes v. Wesel," in *Lexikon für Theologie und Kirche,*
3d ed., vol. 5 (1996), col. 977; and most informative, Gustav Adolf
Benrath, "Johann Rucherat von Wesel," in *Theologische Realenzyklopädie,*
vol. 17 (1988), 150–153.

54. Gerhard Ritter, *Neue Quellenstücke zur Theologie des Johann von Wesel,*
vol. 3 of *Studien zur Spätscholastik,* Sitzungsberichte der Heidelberger
Akademie der Wissenschaften, Philosophische-historische Klasse 17, 5.
Abhandlung (Heidelberg: C. Winter Verlag, 1926–1927), 3–105.

55. Ibid., 24.

56. Ibid., 26. Ritter's critique of Wesel as "naïve" naively assumes that the
judges could not have come to any other conclusion than flagrant heresy:
"Wie hätte es auch anders sein sollen?" Ibid., 42. See, however, the reactions of Engelin of Braunschweig (d. 1481) and Geiler of Kaisersberg
(d. 1510) as reported by Wimpfeling; cf. Charles du Plessis d'Argentré, *Collectio judiciorum de novis erroribus,* vol. 1, pt. 2 (Paris: Andraem Cailleau,
1728; reprint, Brussels: Culture et Civilization, 1963), 298, left col. Like
Wimpfeling, both lived and died in Strasbourg and, more important for
us, both received their magister cap in Erfurt and belonged to the via moderna. The fundamental problem with Ritter's interpretation is that the
clash between via antiqua and via moderna is for him merely an intra-
mural "Schulstreit": "Sonderbar! War es denn wirklich erst nötig, dass

'Thomisten' kamen, um die Häresie der Weselschen Lehren zu entdecken?" Ibid., 41. Ritter's charge of naïveté is not without precedent. Earlier Clemen, quite tolerant of bold challenges throughout his productive life as a Luther scholar, suggested that Wesel himself evoked inquisitional action because of his "masslose Dreistigkeit." See Clemen, "Johannes von Wesel," 154; reprint, 114.

57. "Spitzfindigkeiten"; Ritter, *Neue Quellenstücke,* 17.

58. *Apologia Confessionis Augustanae* (Wittenberg, 1531), article 7 in *Die Bekenntnisschriften der evangelisch-lutherischen Kirche,* 12th ed. (1930; reprint, Göttingen: Vandenhoeck und Ruprecht, 1998), 238, line 21. For the formation of Melanchthon in Tübingen, see Heinz Scheible, *Melanchthon: Eine Biographie* (Munich: Verlag C. H. Beck, 1997), 20–27. Melanchthon received his magister degree on January 25, 1514, "in via moderna." Nominalism remained "zeitlebens seine philosophische Überzeugung." Ibid., 20.

59. "Sermones Iesu christi filii dei vivi, descriptos in evangeliis per scribas Iesu, Matthaeum, Marcum, Lucam et Ioannem legimus. In quibus mysteria salutis plurima, et fortassis omnia ad salutem necessaria continentur." John of Wesel, *Adversus indulgentias disputatio,* ed. Christian W. F. Walch, vol. 1, pt. 1 of *Monumenta Medii Aevi* (Göttingen, 1757), 111–156, 113. Whereas I will draw especially on what Wesel calls his "Compendium," the original *disputatio* later inserted in the treatise *Adversus indulgentias,* Gustav Adolf Benrath has provided an annotated modern edition of the entire treatise: *De indulgentiis,* in *Reformtheologen des 15. Jahrhunderts: Johann Pupper von Goch, Johann Ruchrath von Wesel, Wessel Gansfort* (Gütersloh: Gütersloher Verlagshaus G. Mohn, 1968), 39–60, 39.

60. "Sexta propositio: Quod poenae per hominem vel ius positivum indictae pro peccato, respondeant dei indictioni poenae, ita, quod illa soluta satisfactum sit deo, non est certum nec creditum, nisi cui deus revelavit. Claret hoc, quia divina voluntas hominibus est incognita nisi per sua sancta eloquia vel per revelationem specialem. In sacris autem eloquiis hoc non est expressum." Wesel, *Adversus indulgentias,* 117; *De indulgentiis,* Benrath, 41.

61. The concluding argument which for Wesel clinched the case against indulgences can therefore not come as a surprise. A real transfer of the merits of the saints from the "treasury of the Church" to the faithful would presuppose a covenantal sacrament; yet nothing in the Scriptures indicates that Jesus ever instituted such a pactum.

62. "Item esto quod beati, dum adhuc essent in miseria, meruerunt aliis, hoc non fuit, nisi per dei voluntatem distribuentem illis sicut placuit. Nam meritum nostrum non est ex voluntate nostra sed divina. Distribuere

autem illa merita nemo potest nisi deus principaliter. Si autem homo ministerialiter haec potuerit distribuere, hoc non erit nisi per divinum pactum, quod pepigerit deus cum hominibus, sicut de sacramentis dicunt doctores. Tale autem pactum esse factum cum ministris per Iesum in evangelicis scripturis non habetur." Wesel, *Adversus indulgentias,* 118; *De indulgentiis,* Benrath, 41.

63. Johannes von Paltz, *Supplementum Coelifodinae,* vol. 2 of *Werke,* ed. Berndt Hamm with Christoph Burger and Venicio Marcolino, Spätmittelalter und Reformation, Texte und Untersuchungen 3 (Berlin: Walter de Gruyter, 1983), 48, 17–21. Cf. Hamm, *Frömmigkeitstheologie,* 268, 291.

64. Gustav Adolf Benrath, *Wegbereiter der Reformation,* Klassiker des Protestantismus 1 (Bremen: Schünemann, 1967), 443–445.

65. Wesel, *Adversus indulgentias,* 119; *De indulgentiis,* Benrath, 42; Benrath, *Wegbereiter,* 445.

66. See n. 60 above.

67. WA 8.656, 25–27.

68. Ibid., 8.586, 30–32.

69. Ibid., 8.654, 9–11. Note that these *opera* have to be *certa,* interpreted at Leipzig as *probata;* cf. n. 46 above.

70. For documentation see my "Quo vadis, Petre? Tradition from Irenaeus to Humani Generis" [1962], in Oberman, *Dawn of the Reformation,* 269–296, esp. 286–289.

71. "Auf die lutherische Reformation übte Rucherat keinen Einfluß aus." Benrath, "Johann Rucherat von Wesel," 152, line 43.

72. Johannes Cochlaeus, *Commentaria de actis et scriptis Martini Lutheri Saxonis* (Mainz, 1549; reprint, Farnborough, England: Gregg, 1968), 7. In the subtitle Cochlaeus defines his task as covering the years 1517 through 1546. Note the unusual, indeed singular, identification of Luther as "Saxon." This devil-bred heretic should not be regarded as "Germanus"—as Johannes Eck had proudly ranked Albertus Magnus in his *Chrysopassus praedestinationis* (Augsburg, 1514), fol. b 2—but merely as a regional deviant.

73. From the immense literature, see esp. James H. Overfield, "A New Look at the Reuchlin Affair," *Studies in Medieval and Renaissance History* 8 (1971), 167–207.

74. On the function of the Magister Sacri Palatii as combining the two offices later distinguished as the departments for inquisition and censorship, see the frank analysis and extensive documentation by Peter Godman, *The Saint as Censor: Robert Bellarmine between Inquisition and Index,* SMRT 80 (Leiden: E. J. Brill, 2000).

75. See David V. N. Bagchi, *Luther's Earliest Opponents: Catholic Controversial-
ists, 1518–1525* (Minneapolis: Fortress Press, 1991); and Michael Tavuzzi,
Prierias: The Life and Works of Silvestro Mazzolini da Prierio, 1456–1527,
Duke Monographs in Medieval and Renaissance Studies 16 (Durham,
N.C.: Duke University Press, 1997), esp. 88–91, 104–115.

76. For a carefully documented reassessment of Gratius, see Walther Ludwig,
"Literatur und Geschichte: Ortwin Gratius, die 'Dunkelmännerbriefe' und
'Das Testament des Philipp Melanchthon' von Walter Jens," in *Mittella-
teinisches Jahrbuch* 34, no. 2 (1999), 125–167.

77. The title of this second edition with preface by Ortwin Gratius is: *Fasciculus rerum expetendarum ac fugiendarum* (Cologne, 1535); cf. Ritter,
Neue Quellenstücke, 37–40, 55. The *editio princeps* announces the history
of the Council of Basel proudly in its title: *Commentariorum Aeneae Sylvii
Piccolominei Senensis, de Concilio Basileae celebrato libri duo, olim quidem
scripti, nunc vero primum impressi* (n.p. [Cologne?]: n.d. [1521 or 1522?]).
This first edition contains a collection of reform-minded, conciliar, anti-
curial documents, chief among them the *Commentaria* on the Council of
Basel, completed in 1440 by Aeneas Sylvius Piccolomini, the later Pope
Pius II (1458–1464). The anonymous editors were probably Jacob Sobius
and Count Hermann of Neuenahr, supporters of Reuchlin against Hoogstraeten; Ritter, *Neue Quellenstücke,* 54. The anonymous introduction and
conclusion of the Wesel documentation were actually written by Jacob
Wimpfeling; cf. Paulus, "Miszellen," in *Geschichte des Oberrheins,* 296–300.
For Wimpfeling's description of Wesel's entry into the courtroom, see
Commentariorum, 338; for his concluding evaluation of the Wesel trial, see
ibid., 343. Only the devil himself could have sown so much hatred "inter
eos qui Thomam, qui Scotum, qui Marsilius imitantur." Ibid., 344.

78. O. G. [Ortwinus Gratius] Studioso Lectori S.P.D. [salutem plurimam
dicit], *Fasciculus rerum,* fol. 163^r.

79. Excerpts from the works of Wesel were published as *Paradoxa* by the
Cologne Inquisitors, Gerhard Elten and Jacob Sprenger, the (co)author of
the notorious "Witches hammer," the *Malleus Maleficarum* (advisedly not
"Maleficorum," thus gendering the term *witch*). I cite the reprint of the
first edition by Charles du Plessis d'Argentré, *Collectio judiciorum,* 291–
298. The editor, identified by Nikolaus Paulus as Wimpfeling ("Miszellen,"
in *Geschichte des Oberrheins*), notes that Wesel had to confront a solid pha-
lanx of Thomists: only one member on the board of investigation belonged
to the via moderna: "Nicolaus de Wachenheim, solus de via (ut dicunt)
Modernorum"; d'Argentré, *Collectio judiciorum,* 298, left col.

80. D'Argentré, *Collectio judiciorum,* 297, right col.; 293, left col.; 298, left col.

81. WA 9.23, 7. In 1517, Luther uses the near-synonymous term *illusor* in his letter to Johannes Lang of February 8, 1517; WABr, 1.88., no. 34. See also the finely nuanced argument of Gerhard Ebeling, "Philosophie und Theologie," in *Luther: Einführung in sein Denken* (Tübingen: J. C. B. Mohr, 1965), 79–99.

82. "Ex te primo omnium didici, solis canonicis libris deberi fidem, caeteris omnibus iudicium." WABr 1.171, 72, no. 74.

83. See n. 40 above.

84. Kenneth Hagen, *A Theology of Testament in the Young Luther: The Lectures on Hebrews,* SMRT 12 (Leiden: E. J. Brill, 1974), esp.117–119; Hamm, *Promissio, Pactum, Ordinatio,* esp. 361, 366, 375, 379. In pursuing the theological center of Luther's Reformation breakthrough, Oswald Bayer traces the significance of *pactum* (or *testamentum*) back to the early Luther and notes that a key text (Mark 16:16) is interpreted by Luther "im Einklang mit der nominalistischen Tradition"; *Promissio: Geschichte der reformatorischen Wende in Luthers Theologie,* Forschungen zur Kirchen- und Dogmengeschichte 24 (Göttingen: Vandenhoeck und Ruprecht, 1971), 119. For the function of pactum in the unfolding of Luther's doctrine of the Eucharist see Bayer, *Promissio,* esp. 241–253.

85. The pactum makes the sacramental element into a reliable sign "quo comprehenderet deum, nec vagaretur aut fluctuaret in suis speculationibus.... Nec est periculosius in homine aliquid ratione, quae pro sua curiositate non potest non evagari"; "Sermo de Testamento Christi" (April 8, 1520), WA 9.448; 9.35–449, 5. The covenantal view of God is already firmly in place with the earliest Luther: "Et hoc placitum: i.e., pactum," marginalium to Augustine *De Trinitate* 1.3 (ca. 1509), WA 9.16, 4; "pepigit nobiscum fedus," WA 4.350, 13 (Ps. 118:88; ca. 1514).

86. See my documentation in "Martin Luther: Vorläufer der Reformation," in *Verifikationen: Festschrift für Gerhard Ebeling zum 70. Geburtstag,* ed. Eberhard Jüngel, Johannes Wallmann, and Wilfrid Werbeck (Tübingen: J. C. B. Mohr, 1982), 91–119; English translation by Andrew Colin Gow in *Heiko A. Oberman, The Reformation: Roots and Ramifications* (Grand Rapids, Mich.: W. B. Eerdmans, 1994), 23–52. For Luther's conclusion that Hus is not to be regarded as his precursor, but rather that they are both precursors of Christ, see my "Hus and Luther: Prophets of a Radical Reformation," trans. John M. Frymire, in *The Contentious Triangle: Church, State, and University: A Festschrift in Honor of Professor George Huntston Williams,* ed. Rodney L. Petersen and Calvin Augustine Pater, Sixteenth

Century Essays and Studies 51 (Kirksville, Mo.: Thomas Jefferson University Press, 1999), 135–166.

87. "Confido enim instare diem illum," *De votis monasticis iudicium,* preface addressed to his father from the Wartburg ("ex eremo"), November 21, 1521; WA 8.576, 23.

88. WABr 10.554, 8, no. 3983; letter to Jacob Propst in Bremen, Wittenberg (ca. April 17, 1544).

89. E. Randolph Daniel's perceptive study, *The Franciscan Concept of Mission in the High Middle Ages* (Lexington, Ky.: University Press of Kentucky, 1975), has been reprinted with a survey of literature since 1975 (St. Bonaventure, N.Y.: Franciscan Institute, 1992). My colleague Helen Nader kindly called my attention to three sixteenth-century studies: John Leddy Phelan, *The Millennial Kingdom of the Franciscans in the New World: A Study of the Writings of Gerónimo de Mendieta (1525–1604),* University of California Publications in History 52 (1956; reprint, Berkeley, Calif.: University of California Press, 1980); Alain Milhou, *Colón y Su Mentalidad Mesiánica, en el Ambiente Franciscanista Español,* Cuadernos Colombinos 11 (Valladolid, Spain: Casa-Museo de Colón, Seminario Americanista de la Universidad de Valladolid, 1983); Joseph Perez, *La Revolución de las Comunidades de Castilla, 1520–1521,* Historia de los Movimientos Sociales (1970, French ed.; reprint, Madrid: Siglo Veintiuno de España, 1998).

90. The point of departure of a—for both parties—revealing disputation of October 3–4, 1519 (between representatives of the Saxon chapter of the Franciscan reformed conventuals, i.e., "Martinianer," convened in Wittenberg, and members of the Wittenberg theological faculty), is the fundamental *prima propositio* advanced by the Franciscan side: "Gratiose decrevit divina benignitas senescente mundo novam quandam ecclesiae suae militantis militiam demonstrare." See the exemplary edition by Gerhard Hammer, "Franziskanerdisputation" (1519), WA 59.678, 6 f. In the context of the ensuing debate about the stigmatization of Saint Francis, Luther returns to the opening thesis: "Martinus [Luther] opposuit quaerens sic, an ideo haereticus sit, si non credat Francisci religionem a deo esse institutam." Ibid., 686, 29 f.

91. "Non enim capit ratio, quid sit deus, certissime tamen capit, quid non sit deus. Ita licet non videat, quid rectum et bonum sit coram deo (nempe fidem), scit tamen evidenter infidelitatem, homicidia, inobedientia esse mala." *De votis monasticis iudicium* (1521), WA 8.629, 26–29.

92. 2 Pet. 3:3; as highlighted by Luther in 1521; WA 8.644, 2.

CHAPTER III: MARTIN LUTHER

1. AWA.

2. *Ernst Bizer, Luther und der Papst* (Munich: Chr. Kaiser, 1958); Bernhard Lohse, "Zur Lage der Lutherforschung heute," in *Zur Lage der Luther-forschung heute*, ed. Peter Manns (Wiesbaden: Steiner, 1982); Martin Brecht, *Sein Weg zur Reformation, 1483–1521*, vol. 1 of *Martin Luther* (Stuttgart: Calwer Verlag, 1981); Otto Hermann Pesch, *Gerechtfertigt aus Glauben: Luthers Frage an die Kirche* (Fribourg: Herder, 1982).

3. "Quae contra omnium hominum sensum, praesertim sapientium, sapiat. Sed primo grammatica videamus, verum ea theological." *Operationes in Psalmos*, Ps. 1:1a (1519); AWA 29, 2–4.

4. Charles Trinkaus, *In Our Image and Likeness: Humanity and Divinity in Italian Humanist Thought*, 2 vols. (London: Constable, 1970), esp. vol. 1; and Helmar Junghans, *Der junge Luther und die Humanisten* (Weimar: H. Böhlau, 1985).

5. "Fidei oculis et auribus opus est, ut haec verba spiritus ['Beatus vir qui non abiit in consilio impiorum et in via peccatorum non stetit, in cathedra derisorum non sedit,' Ps. 1:1] audias et eorum rem videas. Homo enim non potest ea intelligere." WA 5.31, 11–12 = AWA 2.37, 5.

6. WA 9.23, 7. In 1517, Luther uses the seemingly synonymous term *illusor;* letter to Johannes Lang of February 8, 1517; WABr 1.88, no. 34. It is to be noted, however, that the illusor is the characteristic Gestält of the devil in the end time. Though not established for 1517, in 1521 Luther repeatedly suggests this identification by invoking 2 Pet. 3:3: "Venient in novissimis diebus in deceptione illusores," WA 8.644, 1–3; "O tempora, o regna, o facta et omnia Satanae!" WA 8.651, 3.

7. As Adolar Zumkeller has shown, sharp criticism of Aristotle is a strong tenet in the Erfurt studium, the seminary of Luther's order, the Augustin-ian Observants; Zumkeller, *Erbsünde, Gnade, Rechtfertigung und Verdienst nach der Lehre der Erfurter Augustinertheologen des Spätmittelalters*, Cas-siciacum 35 (Würzburg, Germany: Augustinus-Verlag, 1984). Cf. the sub-stantial review by Wolfgang Urban in *Theologische Revue* 83 (1987), 37–40; see particularly the documentation for the via Gregorii, and for the impact of Gregory of Rimini as the *doctor authenticus* on the Erfurt Augustinian Johannes Klenkok (d. 1374), the renowned blaster of the Sachsenspiegel. For the history of the via Gregorii, see Manfred Schulze, "Via Gregorii in Forschung und Quellen," in *Gregor von Rimini: Werk und Wirkung bis zur*

Reformation, ed. Heiko A. Oberman, Spätmittelalter und Reformation, Texte und Untersuchungen 20 (Berlin: Walter de Gruyter, 1981), 1–126.

8. For the context of this attack, see chap. 2.

9. "Ex te primo omnium didici, solis canonicis libris deberi fidem, caeteris omnibus iudicium." WABr 1.171, 72, no. 74 (May 9, 1518). Luther's second most important Erfurt teacher in philosophy, Bartholomäus Arnoldi von Usingen (1464/65–1532), was inspired by Luther to join the Augustinian Observants in Erfurt. However, he did not follow Luther's "second turn," and died as a convinced opponent of the Reformation. For a biography and bibliography on Usingen, see the introduction to *Bartholomaei Arnoldi de Usingen OSA: Responsio contra Apologiam Philippi Melanchthonis*, ed. Primoz Simoniti, Cassiciacum, Supplementband 7 (Würzburg: Augustinus-Verlag, 1978), esp. xii.

10. "Fuisti tu sane organum consilii divini, sicut tibi ipsi incognitum, ita omnibus purae theologiae studiosis expectatissimum; adeo longe alia fiebant a Deo, et alia videbantur geri per vos." Letter to Reuchlin, December 14, 1518; WABr, Bd. 1 (2d ed., St. Louis: 1986), 286. On Luther's estimation of Erasmus's biblical work, see his letter to Oecolampadius, June 20, 1523; WABr, Bd. 3, 96. See also Siegfried Raeder, *Das Hebräische bei Luther untersucht bis zum Ende der ersten Psalmenvorlesung* (Tübingen: J. C. B. Mohr), 5–6.

11. J[ohannes] P. Boendermaker, *Luthers Commentaar op de Brief aan de Hebreeën, 1517–1518*, Van Gorcum's Theologische Bibliotheek 28 (Assen, The Netherlands: Uitgeverij Van Gorcum, 1965); Kenneth Hagen, *A Theology of Testament in the Young Luther: The Lectures on Hebrews*, SMRT 12 (Leiden: E. J. Brill, 1974), esp. 117–119. In pursuing the theological center of Luther's Reformation "breakthrough," Oswald Bayer traced the significance of *pactum* (or *testamentum*) back to the early Luther and noted that a key text (Mark 16:16) is interpreted by Luther "im Einklang mit der nominalistischen Tradition"; *Promissio: Geschichte der reformatorischen Wende in Luthers Theologie*, Forschungen zur Kirchen- und Dogmengeschichte 24 (Göttingen: Vandenhoeck und Ruprecht, 1971), 119. For the function of *pactum* in the unfolding of Luther's doctrine of the Eucharist see ibid., esp. 241–253. I have already cited the work of Berndt Hamm extensively in chap. 2: *Promissio, Pactum, Ordinatio; Frömmigkeitstheologie*; and "Normative Centering."

12. The *pactum* makes the sacramental element into a reliable sign "quo comprehenderet deum, nec vagaretur aut fluctuaret in suis speculationibus. . . . Nec est periculosius in homine aliquid ratione, quae pro sua curiositate

non potest non evagari"; "Sermo de Testamento Christi" (April 8, 1520), WA 9.448, 9.35–449, 5. The covenantal view of God is already firmly in place with the earliest Luther: "Et hoc placitum: i.e., pactum," marginalium to Augustine *De Trinitate* 1.3 (ca. 1509), WA 9.16, 4; "pepigit nobiscum fedus," WA 4.350, 13 (Ps. 118:88; ca. 1514).

13. See my "Iustitia Christi and Iustitia Dei: Luther and the Scholastic Doctrines of Justification," *Harvard Theological Review* 59 (1966), 1–26. Reprinted in German translation: "Iustitia Christi und Iustitia Dei: Luther und die scholastischen Lehren von der Rechtfertigung," in *Der Durchbruch der reformatorischen Erkenntnis bei Luther*, ed. Bernhard Lohse, Wege der Forschung 123 (Darmstadt: Wissenschaftliche Buchgesellschaft, 1968), 413–444.

14. Though I limited my purview to the yield of Luther scholarship in the second half of the twentieth century, I must make an exception for the groundbreaking work of the immensely learned Dominican Heinrich Denifle: his whole oeuvre testifies to the fact that Luther-hatred can be as fruitful as the love motivating the majority of Luther scholars. Because of the understandable need to counter his—indeed vicious—personal attacks on the reformer, his richly documented illumination of Luther's *Sitz im Leben,* specifically his analysis of Luther's spirituality as a member of Augustinian Observants, has not been sufficiently "received." Heinrich Denifle OP died June 10, 1905, just two weeks after completing the preface to his *Quellenbelege: Die abendländischen Schriftausleger bis Luther über Iustitia Dei (Rom. 1,17) und Iustificatio,* vol. 1 of *Ergänzungen zu Denifle's Luther und Luthertum* (Mainz: Verlag von Kirchheim, 1905).

15. Still fundamental is the study of Bernhard Lohse, *Mönchtum und Reformation: Luthers Auseinandersetzung mit dem Mönchsideal des Mittelalters*, Forschungen zur Kirchen- und Dogmengeschichte 12 (Göttingen: Vandenhoeck und Ruprecht, 1963). See further the descriptive chronological listing of Luther's treatment of the vows by Heinz-Meinolf Stamm, *Luthers Stellung zum Ordensleben*, Veröffentlichungen des Instituts für Europäische Geschichte Mainz 101 (Wiesbaden, Germany: Franz Steiner Verlag, 1980).

16. "Ideale und Hoffnungen, die einstmals den Einsatz des ganzen Lebens wert gewesen waren, galten nun als obsolet, ja der Kampf gegen sie konnte als neue Lebensaufgabe erscheinen." Bernd Moeller, "Die frühe Reformation in Deutschland als neues Mönchtum," in *Die frühe Reformation in Deutschland als Umbruch: Wissenschaftliches Symposion des Vereins für Reformationsgeschichte 1996*, ed. id. with Stephen E. Buckwalter, Schriften des

Vereins für Reformationsgeschichte 199 (Gütersloh: Gütersloher Verlagshaus, 1998), 76–91. For a critical evaluation and further literature, see my review article in ARH 91 (2000), 396–406.

17. WA 1.44–52, 50, 12–20. See my article "Teufelsdreck: Eschatology and Scatology in the 'Old' Luther," *Sixteenth Century Journal* 19 (1988), 435–450. Cf. my *Luther: Man between God and the Devil*, trans. Eileen Walliser-Schwarzbart (New Haven: Yale University Press, 1989), 106–110.

18. "*In tempore suo*. O aureum et amabile verbum, quo asseritur libertas iustitiae Christianae! Impiis stati sunt dies, stata tempora, certa opera, certa loca, quibus sic inhaerent, ut, si proximus fame esset moriturus, non ab illis divelli possint." AWA 2.49, 7–10. Otto Hermann Pesch called attention to Luther's nearly contemporary *Taufsermon* of 1519 in a theologically perceptive evaluation of his position on monasticism. Pesch follows received opinion when he regards Luther's position in 1521 as the endpoint: "Luthers Kritik am Mönchtum in katholischer Sicht," in *Strukturen Christlicher Existenz: Beiträge zur Erneuerung des geistlichen Lebens*, ed. Heinrich Schlier et al. (Würzburg, Germany: Echter-Verlag, 1968), 81–96, 371–374. For the *Taufsermon*, see WA 2.727–737.

19. "At beatus hic vir liber in omne tempus, in omne opus, in omnem locum, in omnem personam. Utcumque sese obtulerit casus, tibi serviet; quodcumque invenerit manus eius, hoc faciet. Non est Judaeus neque gentilis neque Graecus neque Barbarus, nullius prorsus personae, sed *dat fructum suum in tempore suo*, quoties opus sit eius opera deo et hominibus. Ideo neque fructus eius habet nomen, neque tempus eius habet nomen, neque ipse habet nomen, neque rivi aquarum eius habent nomen; unus non uni nec uno tempore, loco, opere, sed omnibus ubique per omnia servit estque vere vir omnium horarum, omnium operum, omnium personarum et imagine sui patris omnia in omnibus et super omnia." AWA 2.49, 10–19.

20. "Impii vero, sicut Ps 17[, 46] dicitur: 'Clauduntur in angustiis suis,' seipsos captivant et in operibus, temporibus, locis a se electis torquent, extra quae nihil rectum geri putant. Unde suorum fructuum aestimatores nihil faciunt, quam ut alienos fructus mordeant, iudicent, damnent, liberrimi, et in quocumque tempore prompti alios reprehendere, et omnino tales in malo faciendo, quales pii sunt in bono. Sunt enim et ipsi omnium horarum viri, non uno modo, non uno tempore, non uni homini, sed utcumque sors obtulerit, aliis detrahentes ac nocentes. Quae studia si verterent ad bona, nullo meliore compendio pii fierent." AWA 2.49, 20–50, 4.

21. Marius, *Martin Luther: The Christian between God and Death;* see my criti-

cal review article under the gentle title "Varieties of Protest," *The New Republic* 221 (August 16, 1999), 40–45.

22. *Constitutiones fratrum Eremitarum sancti Augustini apostolicorum privilegiorum formam pro reformatione Alemanniae,* ed. Wolfgang Günter, in Johann von Staupitz, *Gutachten und Satzungen,* vol. 5 of *Sämtliche Schriften: Abhandlungen, Predigten, Zeugnisse,* ed. Lothar Graf zu Dohna and Richard Wetzel, Spätmittelalter und Reformation, Texte und Untersuchungen 17 (Berlin: Walter de Gruyter, 2001). For a well-documented reconstruction of what it meant to belong to the *Ordo Eremitarum Sancti Augustini* (OESA, today OSA), particularly in Germany and specifically in late-medieval Erfurt, see Eric Leland Saak, "The Creation of Augustinian Identity in the Later Middle Ages," *Augustiniana* 49 (1999), 109–164, 251–286. Though I received this two-part article after completion of the present essay, I should like to acknowledge that my understanding of daily life in the Order was much enhanced by directing Saak's dissertation entitled "Religio Augustini: Jordan of Quedlinburg and the Augustinian Tradition in Late Medieval Germany" (Ph.D. diss., University of Arizona, 1993), now published as *Highway to Heaven: The Augustinian Platform between Reform and Reformation, 1292–1524,* SMRT (2002).

23. "Non sane haec dico, quod caerimonias ecclesiarum et monasteriorum reprobem, immo haec fuit prima religiosorum institutio, ut, qui monasterium ingressus esset, maiori subiectus disceret nihil proprie operari, sed promptus omnibus servire. Erantque monasteria vere quaedam gymnasia Christianae libertatis exercendae et perficiendae, sicut adhuc sunt, sicubi priscam servant institutionem; hic, inquam, erat finis et modus caerimoniarum." AWA 2.50, 5–10.

24. "Nam quid sunt ipsa quoque caritatis et misercordiae opera quam liberae quaedam caerimoniae, cum et ipsa sint externa et corporalia? Et veteris legis caerimoniae itidem erant utilissimae exercitationes verae et liberae pietatis. At ubi coeperunt perversitatis studio in libertatis iniuriam usurpari, et earum praetextu vera pietas exstingui, iamque pro libertate servitus tyrannisaret, opus erat, ut universae tollerentur, sicut et nunc quoque pastorum piae sollicitudinis esset tumultus caerimoniales abrogare, ubi nonnisi in laqueos animarum et in offendicula liberae pietatis grassantur." AWA 2.50, 11–18.

25. WA 8.578, 4 f. For Luther's characteristic use of "immo," see my article "Immo: Luthers reformatorische Entdeckungen im Spiegel der Rhetorik," in *Lutheriana: Zum 500. Geburtstag Martin Luthers von den Mitarbeitern*

der Weimarer Ausgabe, ed. Gerhard Hammer and Karl-Heinz zur Mühlen, Archiv zur Weimarer Ausgabe der Werke Martin Luthers 5 (Cologne: Böhlau, 1984), 17–38.

26. On February 24, 1520, Luther shared with his intimate friend, Georg Spalatin, a breathtaking, chilling thought. He had just completed reading the annotated edition (Mainz: [1520?]) by the poet laureate Ulrich von Hutten of Lorenzo Valla's 1440 treatise (distributed originally in Italy in just a few manuscript copies) in which the *Donation of Constantine* was unmasked as forgery. At that point a horrifying awareness dawned on him: "I am filled with deep anxiety that there is hardly any reason to doubt that the Pope is really the Antichrist so widely expected"; "Deus bone, quante seu tenebre seu nequitie Romanensium & quod in Dei iuditio mireris per tot secula non modo durasse. Sed etiam prevaluisse ac inter decretales relata esse, tam Impura tam crassa tam impudentia mendacia inque fidei articulorum (nequid monstrosissimi monstri desit) vicem successisse. Ego sic angor, ut prope non dubitem papam esse proprie Antichristum illum, quem vulgata opinione expectat mundus." WABr 2.48, 22–49, 28, no. 257. Though Luther refers explicitly only to Valla, the Hutten edition entitled *De Donatione Constantini quid veri habeat* (n.p.: n.d.) also contained the critique advanced by Nicholas of Cusa and Antoninus of Florence; see *Ulrichi Hutteni Equitis Germani Opera quae reperiri potverunt omnia,* ed. Eduard Böcking, Ulrichs von Hutten Schriften 1 (Leipzig: Verlag B.G. Teubner, 1859), 18. Cf. WA 50.65 f. Whereas Böcking surmises ("wie ich glaube") that the year of publication is early 1518 in Mainz, the WA editor can establish—on the basis of the Adelmann correspondence—that the first edition (2d ed., 1522) is to be set in "Anfang, 1520." See the quoted letter no. 257, WABr 2.51 n. 14.

27. For the origins of the systematic neglect of Luther's realistic eschatology, see n. 73 below. For the presentation of Luther as harbinger of modernity, see Moeller, "Die frühe Reformation," 89. As concerns Moeller's related suggestion that the Reformation can be characterized as a new form of monasticism ("neues Mönchtum"; ibid., 88) based on the contention that Protestantism in all its variances would display congregational features ("in jeder seiner Spielarten ein kongregationalistischer Zug zu eigen ist"; ibid., 89), it is relevant to recall the sustained, pan-European effort of the mendicant orders to challenge the parish, its cohesion, and privileges. Whereas in Moeller's view of fifteenth-century piety there is hardly any place for heresy, the escalation of the public debate about the Inquisition cases brought against John of Wesel, Wessel Gansfort, and Johannes Reuchlin—

not to mention Martin Luther—feeds on the constantly fermenting tension between *fratres* and *curati;* cf. chap. 2, 38. See the ample evidence presented in a rich scholarly tradition reaching from Luzian Pfleger (*Die elsässische Pfarrei: Ihre Entstehung und Entwicklung: Ein Beitrag zur kirchlichen Rechts- und Kulturgeschichte*, Forschungen zur Kirchengeschichte des Elsass 3 [Strasbourg: Gesellschaft für Elsässische Kirchengeschichte, 1936], esp. 146–179) through Wolfgang Günter's careful *Einleitung* to Johannes Staupitz' *Decisio quaestionis de audentia misse* [*sic*] (1500). Staupitz breaks mendicant ranks by defending the rights of the parish priest, only to be attacked by the Franciscan Caspar Schatzgeyer, later a vocal opponent of Luther; see Staupitz, *Gutachten und Satzungen*, 5–8. Though uncomfortable with—and indeed, apologizing for—Luther's identification of the papacy with the Antichrist, Bernhard Lohse's impressive grasp of the morphology of Luther's thought allowed him to highlight the central role of the Last Judgment, so that at least the end of the rule of the Antichrist is done full justice; Lohse, *Luthers Theologie in ihrer historischen Entwicklung und in ihrem systematischen Zusammenhang* (Göttingen: Vandenhoeck und Ruprecht, 1995), 276; cf. 345. See also the excellent survey by Willem van 't Spijker in *Eschatologie: Handboek over de christelijke Toekomstverwachting*, ed. W[illem] van 't Spijker (Kampen: De Groot Goudriaan, 1999), 201–242; cf. the essay on the eschatology of the "Zestiende-eeuwse Radicalen" by Willem Balke, ibid., 243–258.

28. "Confido enim instare diem illum," *De votis monasticis iudicium*, preface addressed to his father from the Wartburg ("ex eremo"), November 21, 1521; WA 8.576, 23. For the popular impact of this Latin treatise for the well-trained, particularly through the elaboration in the German Epiphanias sermon published in the sought-after *Christmaspostille*, see the well-documented essay by Hans-Christoph Rublack, "Zur Rezeption von Luthers *De votis monasticis iudicium*," in *Reformation und Revolution: Beiträge zum politischen Wandel und den sozialen Kräften am Beginn der Neuzeit: Festschrift für Rainer Wohlfeil zum 60. Geburtstag*, ed. Rainer Postel and Franklin Kopitzsch (Stuttgart: Franz Steiner Verlag, 1989), 224–237.

29. "O vere tempora periculosa, de quibus Paulus praedixit. Nunc vero, cum votum et institutum suum in hoc verbum dei: 'Vovete et reddite,' fundent, ego pronuncio, morem istum dispensandi esse impium, et perditionis et operationis errorem. Vel eo tandem cogam, ut vota omnia prohibita et libera esse evincam, quod ut plenius et copiosius faciam, videamus primum causas levissimae suae dispensationis in aliis partibus regulae et rigoris

crudelis in retinendae castitatis voto." WA 8.635, 15–21. Cf. the discourse on 2 Tim. 3:1–9 in the German *Weihnachtspostille*, wherein the vices and problems of the clergy are listed from the pope down to the parish priests. The main thrust is less anticlerical than anti-Roman, antimendicant, and critical of cathedral chapters. Throughout, though only until 1540 (see n. 73, below), the meaning of 2 Tim. 3 is interpreted in the context of the end time (*in novissimis diebus*): "Ich meyne, S. Paulus hatt alhie keyn blat fur den mund genommen und gleych mit fingern auff unser geystliche herrnn und Herodis heyligis gesind zeyget. Ist doch keyn buchstab hie gesetzt, den nitt yderman sihet offentlich ym geystlichen stand weldigen. . . . Drumb mussen wyr den reychen text Pauli eyn wenig bedencken und eben ansehen, das wyr den Herodem recht wol erkennen." WA 10 1.1.634, 20–635, 7. I.e., "syn [Paul's] wort sind klar und dringen auff das platten- unnd kappenvolck, auff das geystliche regiment"; ibid., 635, 13 f. "Wo ist geystlich leben, gottisdienst, heylige stend, denn bey den stifften und klostern? Item, das er sagt, sie lauffen durch die hewsser und furen die weyber gefangen und leren sie ymer, ist yhe klerlich von den lerern und predigern gesagt, ssondern von den bettellorden und landleuffernn. Item, das sie der warheytt widerstehen, wie Jannes und Mambres Mosi"; ibid., 635, 17–21. The extensive application of 2 Tim. 3 in the *Weihnachtspostille* presents the abomination of the Mass as the climax of the millennial horrors: "Ich acht, das solcher missprauch des hohen sacraments dissem stand halten ist, als dem ergisten, vorderblichsten und grewlichsten, der auff erden komen ist, und unter den bossen der grossist und letzt seyn wirtt"; ibid., 706, 20–22.

30. "Et Petrus: 'Venient in novissimis diebus, in deceptione illusores, secundum propria desideria ambulantes.' " WA 8.644, 1–3.

31. Ibid., 8.635, 15–18.

32. We can identify one of those very first readers of the Latin original of *De votis monasticis*. Thanks to a 1540 transcript of Luther's *Tischreden* (Table Talk) by Johannes Mathesius, we learn that immediately upon receipt Prince Frederick, as Luther vividly recalled, read the whole treatise throughout the night so assiduously that he was knocked out for two days: "nam meum librum de votis legit per totam noctem, ita ut biduum esset infirmus." WAT 4.624, 19 f., no. 5034. The Elector's command of Latin was better than rusty—fair and usable, though not displaying any humanist splendor; see Ingetraut Ludolphy, *Friedrich der Weise: Kurfürst von Sachsen, 1463–1525* (Göttingen: Vandenhoeck und Ruprecht, 1984), 46. In contrast to most other German princes of his time, the Elector could therefore

grasp forthwith (*statim*) what evangelical freedom implied for the reformer's appearance in the public forum, sending Luther a fine piece of cloth for a new robe: for once the Elector thought faster than Luther could act. Until his death in 1525, Frederick the Wise continued to enact the traditional Saxon policy of support for the conciliar program of reformation in head and members by seizing initiative to reorder church and society, consistently favoring the growth of observance in the Order of Augustinian Hermits. For this strategy as well as its significance for the state of the German Empire on the eve of the Reformation, see the documentation provided by Manfred Schulze, *Fürsten und Reformation: Geistliche Reformpolitik weltlicher Fürsten vor der Reformation*, Spätmittelalter und Reformation, Neue Reihe 2 (Tübingen: Mohr Siebeck, 1991).

33. "Ita si voveas religionem, ut cum hominibus eiusmodi vivas ea conscientia, ut nihil hinc commodi vel incommodi petas apud deum, sed quod vel casus hoc vitae genus obtulerit amplectendum vel ita visum tibi sit vivere, nihilo te meliorem hinc arbitratus eo, qui vel uxorem duxerit vel agriculturam apprehenderit, neque male voves neque male vivis quantum ad voti rationem attinet. Nam quo casu charitas exigat cadere votum, non sine peccato in voto pertinax fueris, ut dicemus." WA 8.610, 5–12. Cf. "Er spricht [2 Tim. 3:5]: 'hutte dich und meyde dieselbigen', darynn er uns warnett, das wyr uns fur dem geystlichen regiment und stand fursehen, und gibt urlaub, ia gepeutt eraussztulauffen, wer auff yhre weysse drynnen ist, wie wyr horen werden, sperret alle stifft und klöster auff, macht pfaffen unnd munche loss. Wie auch Christus Matt. 24 [:23, 26]: man soll von yhn flehen unnd sie meyden." Turning to 2 Tim. 3:6–7: "Wer mag das anders deutten, denn auff die bettelorden, wilch der Apostel hie klerlich vorsehenn hatt, sie sind es yhe, die durch die hewsser lauffen." WA 10 1.1.662, 5–15. Cf. "O herrgott, wie sicher blind ist die wellt! Wie ists vorkeret, die wellt ist izt geystlich, die geystlichen sind die wellt. Wie starck ist des Endchrists regiment!" Ibid., 688, 11–13. At the same time evangelical monasticism is still an option: "Darumb allen den tzu ratten ist, das sie platten und kappen, stifft unnd kloster lassen und auffhoren yhr gelubd zu hallten, odder fahen von newes an, ynn Christlichem glawben unnd meynung tzu geloben solchs leben." Ibid., 687, 20–23.

34. "Rursum fieri potest ut aliqui spiritu fidei haec apprehendant citra scandalum at foeliciter impleant, ut de sanctis credimus. Et cum hos non liceat damnare nec illos laudare, fit ut periculosa sint omnia et nihil possit certo definiri." WA 8.652, 23–26. Cf. "Ach gott, hymlischer vatter, deyness grewlichen tzornss und schrecklichen gerichts ubir die welt yn dissen

ferlichen, elenden zeytten, und leyder das niemandt erkennen will." WA 10
1.1.640, 1–3. The possibility of an evangelical monastic life is articulated in
the section of the *Weihnachtspostille* suppressed in 1540: "auff das wyr allen
iungen munchen und nonnen mugen weyber und menner geben und
widerumb weltlich machen, wo es yhn nott ist und nit halten konnen mit
gutem gewissen und gottlichem gefallen und willen, damit wyr die klöster
widderumb bringen ynn yhr allt, erst, ursprunglich reformacion und
wessen, das sie seyen Christlich schulen, darynnen man die knaben und
meydlin lere tzucht, ehre und den glawben, darnach sie drynnen mugen
frey bleyben biss ynn den todt, oder wie lang sie wollen, und gott hatt sie
auch nie anders angesehen noch gewolt." Ibid., 700, 13–20.

35. For the introduction to the fifteen theses, see WA 59.93–103. For Luther's
postscript to the "Apology" of Duchess Ursula, see WA 26.623–625.

36. "Das sie den wercken gerechtigkeit für Got geben wider den glauben und
auff ihr leben sich verlassen mehr den auff Christum. Das sie wider die
Christliche freyheit sünde und gewissen machen yn speise, kleider, stet,
wercken, da keine für Got sind." WA 59.101, 10–13.

37. Martin Brecht, *Ordnung und Abgrenzung der Reformation, 1521–1532*,
vol. 2 of *Martin Luther* (Stuttgart: Calwer Verlag, 1986), 99, 453 n. 2.

38. WAT 5.657, 19 f., no. 6430.

39. WAT 5.303, 16 f., no. 4414; for these statuta, see n. 22 above.

40. "Nam et ego incipiam tandem etiam cucullum reiicere, quem ad sustenta-
tionem infirmorum et ad ludibrium pape hactenus retinui." WABr 3.299,
23–25, no. 748.

41. Far from being omitted in 1521, the educational function of monasticism
is elaborated and presented as *conditio sine qua non* for its genuine Christian character exemplified by the *Vitas Patrum* (not identified as that influential collection of saints' lives in the various editions consulted). "Proinde
ego ausim pronunciare cum fiducia: Nisi monastica obedientia voveatur et
servetur temporaliter tanquam rudimentum ad Christianam et Evangelicam obedientiam, ut iuvenilis aetas in ea exercitata discat sic omnibus in
omnibus cedere, sicut per votum cedit suo maiori in monasterio in ali-
quibus, quemadmodum in Vitis Patrum quaedam etiam probant exempla,
esse plane impiam et mox deserendam. Sic et puerorum paupertas est, ne
res administrent, quo discant frugales esse qui propter aetatem prodigi et
dissoluti fierent, si statim in manu eorum res traderentur." WA 8.646, 39–
647, 6. For the Praemonstratensian ideal of teaching as the combination
of the *vita contemplativa* and the *vita activa,* see Caroline Walker Bynum,
Docere verbo et exemplo: An Aspect of Twelfth-Century Spirituality, Harvard

Theological Studies 31 (Missoula, Mont.: Scholars Press, 1979); quoted in Saak, "Creation of Augustinian Identity," 118.

42. For the function of the *Vitasfratrum* as the Augustinians' *Legenda aurea*, see Saak, "Creation of Augustinian Identity," esp. 269–286. For the lectio in the refectorium, see the "Constitutiones," in Staupitz, *Gutachten und Satzungen*, cap. 21, 12 n. 7.

43. Staupitz was not mentioned at this time, perhaps because he had already stepped down as vicar-general at the chapter meeting in Eisleben on Saint Augustine's Day, August 28, 1520. See the still most reliable reconstruction by Theodor Kolde, *Die deutsche Augustiner-Congregation und Johann von Staupitz: Ein Beitrag zur Ordens- und Reformationsgeschichte* (Gotha, Germany: Friedrich Andreas Perthes, 1879). Cf. my articles "Captivitas Babylonica: Die Kirchenkritik des Johann von Staupitz," in *Reformatio et Reformationes: Festschrift für Lothar Graf zu Dohna zum 65. Geburtstag*, ed. Andreas Mehl and Wolfgang Christian Schneider, THD-Schriftenreihe Wissenschaft und Technik 47 (Darmstadt, Germany: Technische Hochschule Darmstadt, 1989), 97–106; and "Duplex misericordia: Der Teufel und die Kirche in der Theologie des jungen Johann von Staupitz," *Theologische Zeitschrift* 45 (1989), 231–243.

44. "[J]uxta formam Evangelii"; WA 8.578.20. For the momentous pilgrimage of Staupitz from Eisleben (Order of Augustinian Hermits) to Salzburg (ultimately Order of Saint Benedict) as well as the continuity in Staupitz' theological position, see Johann von Staupitz, *Sämtliche Schriften*, vol. 2, *Lateinische Schriften 2: Libellus de exsecutione aeternae praedestinationis*, ed. Lother Graf zu Dohna and Richard Wetzel (1979), 8 f. nn. 30 f. Cf. zu Dohna in his *Einleitung* to the *Consultatio super Confessione Fratris Stephani Agricolae*, ibid., vol. 5.

45. The formulation in the Franciscan Rule, "sanctum Evangelium observare," is rendered by Luther as: "Regulam suam esse Evangelium Ihesu Cristi." WA 8.579, 26.

46. Ibid., 8.380, 13–15.

47. The point of departure of the amazing, recently discovered Disputation of October 4, 1519 (between representatives of the Saxon chapter of the Franciscan reformed conventuals, i.e., the "Martinianer," convened in Wittenberg, and members of the Wittenberg theological faculty), is the fundamental *prima propositio* advanced by the Franciscan side: "Gratiose decrevit divina benignitas senescente mundo novam quandam ecclesiae suae militantis militiam demonstrare." See the exemplary edition by Gerhard Hammer, "Franziskanerdisputation" (1519), WA 59.678–697. In

the context of the ensuing debate about the stigmatization of Saint Francis, Luther returns to the opening thesis: "Martinus [Luther] opposuit quaerens sic, an ideo haereticus sit, si non credat Francisci religionem a deo esse institutam." Ibid. 686, 29–30. It is noteworthy that on the far-advanced age of the world (*senescente mundo*), Luther and his Franciscan opponents were in full agreement.

48. WA 8.590, 18–21.

49. Dan. 6; cf. Dan. 3:19–23.

50. The monastic life is as risky as the Babylonian pit: "in qua electi miraculose, ceu tres pueri in fornace, serventur." WA 8.586, 30–32. In his *Weihnachtspostille* Luther unfolds the "den" in a series of exempla: "Eyns haben sie, das sie auffwerffen: Es seyen heylige vetter ynn geystlichem stand gewessen. Aber dagegen sollt sie erschrecken, das Christus spricht, die ausserweleten mugen vorfurett werden von yhn (Matt. 2:2, 1–10), wie alhie die Magi von Herodes vorfurett wurden. Und der exempell viell mehr: die drey kinder Ananias, Azarias, Misael blieben ym fewroffen Babylonis, Naaman auss Syrien bleyb frum ym tempell des abtgotts alleyn. Joseph bleyb frum ynn Aegypto. Was soll ich sagen: sanct Hagnes bleyb keusch ym gemeynen frawenhawss, und die merterer blieben heylig yn kerkern, und noch teglich bleyben Christen frum, ym fleysch, ynn der wellt, mitten unter den teuffelln; *sollt er denn nitt auch Francis, Bernhard und yhr gleychen mitten ym yrthum behalten haben kunden, und ob [sie] mitunter geyrret hetten, widder eraussss furen?* [my italics] Er hatt fast keynen grossen heyligen on yrthum leben lassen, Mosen unnd Aaron und Mariam, David, Salomon, Ezechias und viel mehr hatt er lassen strauchlen, auff das yhe niemandt auff die blosse exempell der heyligen unnd werck on schrifft sich vorlassen sollt, aber wyr plumpen eynhynn, was wyr nur sehen und horen von heyligen, da fallen wyr auff und treffen gemeynicklich das, da sie als menschen geprechlich geyrret haben. Da muss denn der yrthum uns eyn grundliche warheytt seyn." WA 10 1.1.705, 21–706, 12. God does not always intervene *miraculose*. See in the *Weihnachtspostille*: "der Bapst lest sie fliessen, brennen und martern, wie sie konnen, das ich acht, es sind die kinder, die dem fewrigen abgott Moloch ym volck Israel geopffert und vorbrennet wurden." WA 10 1.1.693, 20–22.

51. "Non enim in sermone, sed in virtute regnum dei habebant." WA 8.587, 39.

52. "Atque demus, ut fide pura miraculose serveris vovens et vivens in votis, sicut Bernhardus et multi alii servati sunt, quibus propter fidem Christi, qua pleni erant, venenum hoc non nocuit." WA 8.600, 26–29. For

Bernard of Clairvaux, see Erich Kleineidam, "Ursprung und Gegenstand der Theologie bei Bernhard von Clairvaux und Martin Luther," in *Dienst der Vermittlung: Festschrift zum 25-jährigen Bestehen des philosophisch-theologischen Studiums im Priesterseminar Erfurt*, Erfurter Theologishe Studien 37 (Leipzig: Saint Benno-Verlag, 1977), 221–247; Theo Bell, *Divus Bernhardus: Bernhard von Clairvaux in Martin Luthers Schriften*, Veröffentlichungen des Instituts für Europäische Geschichte Mainz, Abteilung für Religionsgeschichte 148 (1989, Dutch ed.; Mainz: Phillip von Zabern, 1993); Franz Posset, "Saint Bernard's Influence on Two Reformers: John von Staupitz and Martin Luther," *Cistercian Studies* 25 (1990), 175–187; id., "Bernhard von Clairvauxs Sermone zur Weihnachts-, Fasten- und Osterzeit als Quellen Luthers," *Luther Jahrbuch* 61 (1994), 93–116; and Bernhard Lohse, "Luther und Bernhard von Clairvaux," in *Bernhard von Clairvaux: Rezeption und Wirkung im Mittelalter und in der Neuzeit*, ed. Kaspar Elm, Wolfenbütteler Mittelalter-Studien 6 (Wiesbaden: Harrassowitz, 1994), 271–301.

53. My italics. "Non disputo, ut sancti vixerint sub instituto isto, sed de ipso instituto." WA 8.617, 27.

54. Craig Hairline and Eddy Put, *A Bishop's Tale: Mathias Hovius among His Flock in Seventeenth-Century Flanders* (New Haven: Yale University Press, 2000), 10. For a critical assessment of recent research, see Craig Hairline, "Official Religion: Popular Religion in Recent Historiography of the Catholic Reformation," *Archive for Reformation History* 81 (1990), 239–262.

55. "Difficulter cucullam meam deposui"; WAT 5.657, 19, no. 6430; cf. "aegre et difficulter deposuisset habitum"; WAT 4.303, 17, no. 4414.

56. "Ego ipse in me et multis aliis expertus sum, quam pacatus et quietus soleat esse Satan in primo anno sacerdocii et monachatus, ut nihil iucundius esse videatur castitate, sed hoc in tentationem et in laqueum insidiosissimus hostis facit, cui cooperantur insani monastici et annum probationis non solum non ex spiritu, sed neque ex re ipsa, verum ex calendario et numero dierum metiuntur, ut probent nihil sani neque pensi apud se esse, incedentes in rebus istis spiritualibus et periculosissimis ceu bruta (ut Petrus ait [2 Pet. 2:12]) irrationalia, naturaliter in mactationem genita." WA 8.660, 31–38. Cf. his striking frankness in the *Weihnachtspostille:* "verleucke du nur nit, das du eyn mensch seyest, der fleysch und blutt hatt, lass darnach gott richten tzwisschen den Engelischen starcken hellten unnd dyr krancken, vorachten sunder! Ich hoff, ich sey tzo fernn kommen, das ich von gottis gnaden bleyben werd, wie ich bynn, wiewol ich noch nit byn ubirn berg und den keuschen hertzen mich nit traw tzuvorgleychen, were

myr auch leydt, und gott wollt mich gnediglich dafur behutten." WA 10
1.1.707, 24–708, 4.

57. WA 8.586, 30–32.

58. "Licet in sanctis sub votorum instituto captivis operatus sit et locutus mirabiliter sine votis." WA 8.656, 26–27.

59. Ibid., 8.660, 6. To put this in the vocabulary of the via moderna so familiar
to him, Luther argues that the exceptional intervention of God *de potentia
absoluta* does not delegitimize the established order (*lex stans*) *de potentia
ordinata*. See chap. 2.

60. "Es hat die wahrheit das sprichwort erfunden: vortzweyffeln macht eyn
munch; denn wieviel ist yhr, die nit alleyn darumb geystlich werden, das
sie ssorgen, sie mugen sich nit erneeren oder musten mit erbeyt und muhe
sich erneeren?" WA 10 1.1.639, 6–9; cf. WA 10 3.229, 20 (Sermon 1522);
WA 29.65, 12–13 (Sermon 1529); and WA 32.319, 35 (Sermon 1530/32).
One year earlier Luther had invoked this proverb in a comparatively milder
version, confirming our findings as to the stage Luther reached in 1520
(*adhuc*—"das mehrer teyl"—[not all monks—deemphasizing the sole focus
on the cowl by the inclusion of the parish priests]): "Ich befind das sprichwort warhafftig, das vorzweyffeln machet das mehrer teyl munch unnd
pfaffen: drumb gaht und staht es auch, wie wir sehen." *An den christlichen
Adel deutscher Nation* (1520), WA 6.468, 5–7. For "Verzweiflung macht
Münch," see *Deutsches Sprichwörter-Lexikon: Ein Hausschatz für das
Deutsche Volk*, ed. Karl Friedrich Wilhelm Wander, vol. 4 (Leipzig, 1876;
Darmstadt: Wissenschaftliche Buchgesellschaft, 1964), col. 1625. Luther
admired the wisdom of vernacular marketplace proverbs as much as
Erasmus treasured his classical *adagia*. Although a timeless favorite, this
genre is particularly precious for the historian of late-medieval and early-
modern mentality as a revealing form of communication. Proverbs can
best be characterized as vivid caricatures transporting information in the
abbreviated, suggestive form of modern cartoons or television spots. It is
interesting that in the Latin version our proverb has a wider societal scope,
reflecting perhaps its urban-civic matrix: "Desperation produces three M's:
a Monk, a Medical aide, and a Military man" (Desperatio facit tria 'M':
Monachum, Medicum, Militem); ibid., s.v. "Verzweiflung." In spotting the
monk, Luther can employ a reductionist caricature because he has amply
articulated the basis of his critique in assailing monasticism as the final and
ultimate outgrowth of justification by works. At the same time we should
note the other side of the coin, the mentality and response of those who
read and pondered Luther but decided to remain in their cloisters. For fur-

ther literature, see my review of "Die frühe Reformation in Deutschland,"
by Bernd Moeller, ARH 91 (2000), 396–406. Since the myth of the mass
movement has tended to drown out the numerous decision makers on the
other side, it is pertinent to give voice to at least one eloquent and influential member of the opposition: Johann Justus Landsberg, a member of the
Carthusian Order (which, when compared with the Augustinian Hermits
and Franciscans, proved strikingly impervious to Lutheran "poison"). This
younger contemporary (1490–1539) of Luther entered the Cologne "Car-
thuse" in 1509 and was a mighty voice in that crucial region which in the
1540s stood between the confessions. For background see Karl-Heinz zur
Mühlen (editor of the "Akten der Reichsreligionsgespräche" in 1540–1541,
1546, and 1557), "Die Edition der Akten und Berichte der Religionsge-
spräche von Hagenau und Worms 1540/41," in *Reformatorisches Profil:
Studien zum Weg Martin Luthers und der Reformation*, ed. Johannes
Brosseder and Athina Lexutt (Göttingen: Vandenhoeck und Ruprecht,
1995), 310–324. In one of his many tracts and sermons dedicated to the
monastic life, Landsberg provided a sober answer to the widely circulated
criticism of the "vorzweiffelte munch": "Meministis ut olim ex Aegypto
eduxerit Deus filios Israel, et quoties in veteri lege praeceperit, ut essent
memores tanti beneficii. Idem facit Deus, quando hodie certos quosdam
electos suos ex hoc seculo nequam vocat ad vitam monasticam quae sanc-
torum virorum testimonio velut quaedam paradisus terrestris est: esto
quod quidam illic non bene vivant; quod nihil illi vitae derogat, quando
etiam nemo propterea damnat matrimonium, quod multi sint adulteri."
"In solemnitate SS. Apostolorum Petri et Pauli," in *D. Joannis Justi Lans-
pergii Cartusiani opera omnia: In quinque tomos distributa juxta exemplar
Coloniense anni 1693 editio nova et emendata*, vol. 2 (Monsterolii: Typis
Cartusiae Sanctae Mariae de Pratis, 1889), "Sermo secundus," 404–408,
405, cols. 1–2. John Frymire kindly called my attention to the impressive
nineteenth-century edition of this widely read opponent of Lutheranism.
For further literature on Landsberg (Landsberger), see Joseph Greven, *Die
Kölner Kartause und die Anfänge der katholischen Reform in Deutschland*,
ed. Wilhelm Neuss, Katholisches Leben und Kämpfen im Zeitalter der
Glaubenspaltung 6 (Münster: Aschendorff, 1935), 27–49; for Landsberg's
writings, see Wilbirgis Klaiber, ed., *Katholische Kontroverstheologen und Reformer des 16. Jahrhunderts: Ein Werkverzeichnis*, Reformationsgeschicht-
liche Studien und Texte 116 (Münster: Aschendorff, 1978), 164–166, nos.
1753–1766. The Carthusians were well prepared to function as "coun-
terelite" when the pivotal Cologne Archdiocese was kept in the Catholic

camp after Emperor Charles V tipped the scales by conquering Guelders and Zutphen (1543). For the influence of the Cologne Carthusians, see Gérald Chaix, *Réforme et contre-réforme catholiques: Recherches sur la Chartreuse de Cologne au XVI siècle*, Analecta Cartusiana 80 (Salzburg, Austria: Institut für Anglistik und Amerikanistik, Universität Salzburg, 1981), 1:157–163, 175–202; and the lucid interpretation by Sigrun Haude, *In the Shadow of "Savage Wolves": Anabaptist Münster and the German Reformation during the 1530s*, Studies in Central European Histories (Boston: Humanities Press, 2000), 60–69.

61. "Darumb sage ich: der Bapst nympt yhm fur auss lautterm frevel munch und nonnen auss den klosternn tzihen und hatt seyn nitt macht; Die eltern haben des macht und mugen yhr kind lassen drynnen odder erauss nehmen, wenn und wie sie wollen, odder wie sie sehen, das den kindern nutz ist." WA 10 1.1.641, 12–16. Cf. "Sso mach nur nit viel disputirnss, gang frey hyn und tzeuch das kind auss dem kloster, auss kutten, auss blatten, und woreyn es geschlossen ist. Sihe nit an, wenn es hunderttausent gelubd than hette, und alle Bischoffe auff eynen hawffen dran gesegnet hetten! Deyn kind ist dyr befolhen von gott tzu regirn"; ibid., 640, 28–641, 4. For the growing emphasis on paternal authority and civic obedience in the later Middle Ages and early-modern period, see Robert James Bast, *Honor Your Fathers: Catechisms and the Emergence of a Patriarchal Ideology in Germany, 1400–1600*, SMRT 63 (Leiden: Brill, 1997).

62. Rom. 7:14–20.

63. "Propter fidem in spiritu repugnantem ignoscitur et non imputatur"; WA 8.653, 30–32. Luther can be quite frank—amazingly frank as compared with our modern times—about the application of these words to himself: WA 10 1.1.707, 24–708, 4; see n. 56 above. As compared to the medieval, consistently negative view of "libido"—located in the lower, "female" part of the soul—Luther's reevaluation has unexpected implications that call for further treatment.

64. Acts 15:6–30; the First Council of the Church.

65. Acts 15:12.

66. "Apostolus Paulus Act. xv. [15:12] ex operibus dei demonstravit libertatem Evangelicam, quod spiritus dabatur gentibus absque circuncisione et lege Mosi, licet tota ferme Ecclesia illa primitiva erronea conscientia contrarium sentiret, solus autem Petrus, Paulus et Barnabus autoritate divinorum operum, libertatis sententiam tulerunt et firmaverunt adversus omnes." WA 8.654, 5–9.

67. Luther "Disputatio contra scholasticam theologiam, 1517," WA 1, 221–228.

68. "In qua re nos erudimur ut, ubi scripturae testimonia non suffragantur, illic certis operibus dei nos niti oportere et vice testimoniorum ea sequi." WA 8.654, 9–11. We touch here upon an aspect of Luther's thought that proved to be highly explosive in the decisive years at the end of the Weimar Republic and the rise of Adolf Hitler, when this "God-given reversal" turned into a central plank in the platform of the *Deutsche Christen*. Divorced from a firm grasp of the biblical Luther of the Last Days, such extrascriptural revelation can feed into a malleable doctrine of Providence that not only the Führer liked to invoke but that paved the path of such an influential Luther scholar as Emanuel Hirsch to a Nazi ideology he would never forswear. The key words signifying for him the mighty hand of Providence ("Gottes Lenkung") are *Volksschicksal* and *nationale Wiedergeburt*—entailing the recovery of a "Deutscher Volksordnung und Volksart" as the basis of a virtue designated by Hirsch as "Deutsche Humanität," not easy to translate yet soon afterward spelled out throughout Europe. For the explicit appeal to extrascriptural revelation, see Emanuel Hirsch, *Das kirchliche Wollen der Deutschen Christen*, 3d ed. (Berlin-Steglitz: Evangelischer Pressverband für Deutschland, 1933), 6. For his unmitigated, profound account ("Rechenschaft") after the end of the Thousand Years, see "Meine theologische Anfänge," *Freies Christentum* 3, no. 10 (1951), 2–4; "Mein Weg in die Wissenschaft, 1911–1916," no. 11, 3–5; and "Meine Wendejahre, 1916–1921," no. 12, 3–6. Hirsch saw more clearly than his modern admirers that scholarship and politics are closely, in this case indissolubly, intertwined. *Initiis obsta!* Beware! Luther's doctrine of justification is abused when invoked to justify a person, his thoughts, his generation, his country—or anyone, anywhere in space or time.

69. "[Monastica institutio] nullum habet testimonium de scriptura, neque ullum signum aut prodigium quo sit coelitus comprobata"; WA 8.617, 18 f.

70. Ibid., 59.466, 1062.

71. WABr 2.404, 6 f., no. 404; November 22, 1521, Luther (from the Wartburg) to Spalatin. Luther wrote his *De votis monasticis* in response to reports from Wittenberg that a considerable number of his confratres (probably as many as thirteen) had shed the cowl. The WA editor quotes Kaspar Cruciger as reporting that monks "everywhere" (*passim*) had left their monasteries; ibid., n. 4. These must have seemed "mighty acts" to Luther even while being so concerned (*timor*) about the right motivation that he took up his pen and started writing. The exclamation "wonderfully" (*mirifice, wunderbarlich*) pertains to the progress of the Reformation in south Germany and the Alsace three years later, yet articulates

exactly the surprised joy that Luther associates with the mighty acts of God: "Mirifice placent nuptie sacerdotorum et monachorum et monalium apud vos; placet appellatio maritorum adversus satane episcopum, placent vocati ad parochias." WABr 3.299, 16–18, no. 748, to Capito and Bucer. The "mass movement" that Protestant historians later were to hail as the measure of Luther's success is exactly—and properly—what Luther was originally concerned about most. As he wrote on the High Feast of the Assumption of the Virgin Mary, a conscientious decision is not easily reached in a crowd (*turba*). WABr 2.380, 33–36; August 15, 1521, Luther (from the Wartburg) to Spalatin.

72. Luther took up his pen to write *De votis monasticis* on the basis of "vague and unverified rumors" that "some of ours [Augustinian Friars]" have shed their cowl [*vaga et incerta relatione didici deposuisse*]: "I am filled with fear [*timui*] that their action might not have been taken with that profundity which makes for a firm decision [*forte non satis firma conscientia*]. It is this grave concern which forced my hand to write this treatise [*Hic timor extorsit mihi eum libellum*] . . . in the hope that they themselves take heart and those of goodwill are heartened." Cf. n. 38 above. WABr 2.404, 6–405, 11, no. 441; November 22, 1521, Luther (from the Wartburg) to Spalatin. Cf. n. 71 above.

73. "In novissimis diebus"; 2 Tim. 3:1–9. In the wide vernacular popularization of *De votis* the horrors of the end times are spelled out in the application of 2 Tim. 3:1–9—only to be suppressed in 1540. Cf. "Das Evangelium am tage der heyligen drey künige. Matthei 2[:1–13]"; WA 10 1.1.555, 16–728, 24, *Weihnachtspostille*, 1522; then in *Predigten von Advent bis auf Ostern*, 1525 (at least twenty-three editions were circulating by 1544). Together with the extensive discussion of the monastic vows (WA 10 1.1.681, 24–709, 9) this section was *not* included in the Wittenberg editions by Hans Luft, 1540, and Nikolaus Wolrab, 1544. See WA 10 1.1.8–11. Significantly, there is evidence that in England the original intention of Luther was "received." See Frank Engehausen, "Luther und die Wunderzeichen: Eine englische Übersetzung der Adventspostille im Jahre 1661," ARG 84 (1993), 276–288. In the context of his discussion of radical "Puritanismus," Engehausen refers to an English version of excerpts from Luther's *Adventspostille* (1522): *Signs of Christ's Coming, and of the Last Day* . . . (London, 1561). It should be noted that this translation is based not on the purged German text but on the unpurged Latin Basel edition of 1546: *Enarrationes seu Postillae . . . maiores, in Lectiones, quae ex Evangelicis historijs.*

This English version highlighted the sermon for 2. Advent, based on Luke 21:21–33 (WA 10 1.2, 93–120).

74. See Hubert Jedin, *A History of the Council of Trent,* trans. Ernest Graf, 2 vols. (London: Thomas Nelson, 1957), vol. 2, chap. 2, esp. 74. Cf. my "Quo vadis, Petre? Tradition from Irenaeus to Humani Generis" [1962], in *The Dawn of the Reformation: Essays in Late Medieval and Early Reformation Thought,* ed. Heiko A. Oberman (Edinburgh: T. and T. Clark, 1986), esp. 286–289.

CHAPTER IV: REFORMATION

1. For a brief discussion of universals, see Marilyn McCord Adams, "Universals in the Early Fourteenth Century," in *The Cambridge History of Later Medieval Philosophy: From the Rediscovery of Aristotle to the Disintegration of Scholasticism, 1100–1600,* ed. Norman Kretzmann et al. (Cambridge: Cambridge University Press, 1982; rev. ed., Cambridge: Cambridge University Press, 1997), 411–439.

2. Emanuel Hirsch, *Lutherstudien,* vol. 3, ed. Hans Martin Müller, *Gesammelte Werke/ Emanuel Hirsch* 3 (Waltrop, Germany: Hartmut Spenner, 1999), 327.

3. Emanuel Hirsch, *Das kirchliche Wollen der deutschen Christen,* 3d ed. (Berlin-Steglitz: Evangelischer Pressverband für Deutschland, 1933), 6–8.

4. See particularly Emanuel Hirsch, "Meine theologische Anfänge," *Freies Christentum* 3 no. 10 (1951), 2–4; "Mein Weg in die Wissenschaft, 1911–16," no. 11, 3–5; and "Meine Wendejahre, 1916–21," no. 12, 3–6.

5. *Martin Luther: Studienausgabe,* ed. Hans-Ulrich Delius (Berlin: Evangelische Verlagsanstalt, 1979), 3.77, 20.

6. *Studienausgabe,* Delius, 3.79, 4; WA 11.411, 26.

7. Martin Luther, *De captivitate,* WA 6, 497–573. On the Babylonian Captivity of the church, see G[uillaume] Mollat, *The Popes at Avignon, 1305–1378,* trans. Janet Love (New York: Harper and Row, 1963); and Yves Renouard, *The Avignon Papacy: The Popes in Exile, 1305–1403,* trans. Denis Bethell (Hamden, Conn.: Archon Books, 1970).

8. WA 10 1.2.95, 18.

9. *De votis monasticis iudicium,* preface addressed to his father from the Wartburg ("ex eremo"), November 21, 1521; WA 8.576, 23.

10. WABr 10.554, 8, no. 3983; letter to Jacob Propst in Bremen, Wittenberg (ca. April 17, 1544).

11. Amos 5:18; Apocalypse of Baruch 30.1; *Assumptio Mosis,* 10:12.

12. In his often reprinted *Adventspostille* of 1522.

13. WA 10 1.2.95–97; 97, 25.

CHAPTER V: FROM LUTHER TO HITLER

1. Daniel J. Goldhagen, *Hitler's Willing Executioners: Ordinary Germans and the Holocaust* (New York: Alfred A. Knopf, 1996).

2. Joachim C. Fest, *Fremdheit und Nähe: Von der Gegenwart des Gewesenen* (Stuttgart: Ullstein, 1996); Klaus Scholder, *The Churches and the Third Reich,* trans. John Bowden, vol. 1 (Philadelphia: Fortress Press, 1988).

3. Wolfgang von Buch, *Wir Kindersoldaten* (Berlin: Siedler Verlag, 1998).

CHAPTER VI: THE CONTROVERSY OVER IMAGES AT THE TIME OF THE REFORMATION

1. After graduating from Magdalen College, Oxford, John Colet (1466/7– 1519) spent three years of study in France and Italy. Returning to England, probably in 1496, he lectured in Oxford on the Epistles of St. Paul, but after 1504, when he was appointed Dean of St. Paul's Cathedral, he spent most of his career as a scholar, preacher, ecclesiastical reformer and writer in London. In 1509 he founded St. Paul's School there. His works include *An Exposition of St. Paul's Epistle to the Romans, A ryght fruitfull monicion concernynge the order of a good christen mannes lyfe,* and *Two Treatises on the Hierarchies of Dionysius.* (DW)

2. ASD, 1, 156, line 215.

3. Eamon Duffy, *The Stripping of the Altars: Traditional Religion in England, c. 1400–c. 1580* (New Haven: Yale University Press, 1992), 591.

4. Text: WA 10–3, 18, lines 10–19, 28–35 and 19, ll. 1–7. Translation: LW 51, 77–78.

5. TRE VI, 546, line 42.

6. Ibid., 547, lines 11–12.

7. Ibid, 547, lines 6–17.

8. "Die Bilderfrage in der Reformationszeit," *Blätter fur Württembergische Kirchengeschichte* (1990), 38–64, esp. 38.

9. Ibid., 38, n. 2.

10. Ibid., 38–39.

11. "Sponte sua caderent, si populus institutus sciret eas nihil esse coram deo." To Nikolaus Hausman, WABr 2 (no. 459), 474, lines 23–24. Translation: LW 48, 401.

12. WA 56, 493, lines 15–16.

13. WA, 56, 494, line 17.

14. Ibid., 497, lines 19–32, 498, lines 1–12. Translation: LW 25, 491–492.

15. WA, 10–1, 253, lines 3–4. Translation: LW 39, 253

16. Lorenzo Valla, *De falso credita et ementita Constantini donatione declamatio* (1440). The *Donation* purported to record the deathbed legacy of the Emperor Constantine upon which the papacy based its claims to temporal rule over the Empire. Using humanist methods of textual criticism, Valla demonstrated that the document was a forgery originating in papal circles in the eighth century. (DW)

17. Ulrich von Hutten (1488–1523), German humanist, defender of knightly prerogatives against the princes, and one of the authors of *Letters of the Obscure Men* (1515–1517), a satire of scholasticism and monastic obscurantism. Hutten's edition of Valla's *Donation* (Basel: Cratander, 1518) is the second. The first edition is Strasbourg: Johann Grüninger, 1506. (DW)

18. "Ego sic angor, ut prope non dubitem papam esse proprie Antichristum illum, quem vulgata opinione expectat mundus." WABr 2, 48, 26–27; 2, 49, 1–2.

19. "In medium filiorum Dei" (no. 313). Ibid., 2, 145, line 21.

20. "Opus itaque erit non prudentia nec armis, sed humili oratione, et forti fide quibus obtineamus Christum pro nobis: alioquin vere actum est, si viribus nostris nixi fuerimus. Itaque ad orationem mecum confuge, ne ex scintilla late incendium conflet spiritus Domini malus. Non sunt contemnenda parva praesertim quae autore Satana exordium sumunt." Ibid., 145, 31–36.

21. Emil Egli, *Aktensammlung zur Geschichte der Zürcher Reformation* (1879; Nieuwkoop repr., 1973), 126, p. 24.

22. Following Adolf Laube, *Flugschriften der frühen Reformationsbewegung* (1518–1524), 2 vols. (Vaduz-Berlin, 1983), 1, 281.

23. J. F. Gerhard Goeters, *Ludwig Hätzer (ca. 1500 bis 1529) Spiritualist und Antitrinitarier: Eine Randfigur der frühen Täuferbewegung* (Gutersloh: C. Bertelsmann, 1957).

24. Ibid., 2, 272.

25. Ibid., 1, 281; 2, 278.

26. ZW 2, 654, lines 14–16.

27. Among their works, see Berndt Hamm, *Bürgertum und Glaube: Konturen der städtischen Reformation* (Göttingen: Vandenhoeck and Ruprecht, 1996); Peter Blickle, *From the Communal Reformation to the Revolution of the Common Man,* trans. Beate Kümin (Leiden: Brill, 1998).

28. ZW 2, 757, lines 23–25.

29. ASD 5–5, 98, lines 889–898.

30. ZW 2, 658, lines 8–14.

31. *Defensio adversus axioma catholicum,* ed. William Ian P. Hazlett, in *Martini Buceri Opera Latina,* SMRT 83, Bd. 5 (2000).

32. *The Christian Tradition: A History of the Development of Doctrine,* 2 vols. (Chicago: University of Chicago Press, 1989), vol. 2, 92–130.

CHAPTER VII: TOWARD THE RECOVERY OF THE HISTORICAL CALVIN

1. Epigraph: A verse of the earliest known Huguenot song (ca. December 1525): "Stop preaching the truth, / Maître Michel! / The Gospel's Truth, / Too great is the danger / of being locked up. / Read, read, and pass this on." Henri-Léonard Bordier, *Le chansonnier Huguenot du XVIᵉ siècle* (Paris, 1969; reprint, Geneva: Slatkine Reprints, 1969), xv. Maître Michel is Michel d'Arande, a friend of Guillaume Farel, and like Farel was called by Bishop Briçonnet to serve as a preacher in Meaux. Stefan Zweig, *Castellio gegen Calvin oder ein Gewissen gegen die Gewalt* (Vienna: Herbert Reichner Verlag, 1936), esp. 322–325. In his autobiography, Zweig provides the larger framework by articulating his intention to favor the victims rather than the victors, i.e., "the morally just rather than the historically successful": "Erasmus und nicht Luther, Maria Stuart und nicht Elisabeth, Castellio und nicht Calvin." *Die Welt von Gestern: Erinnerungen eines Europäers* (Stockholm, 1944; reprint, Berlin: Fischer Verlag, 1968), 159.

2. Johan Huizinga, "De Wetenschap der Geschiedenis" (lecture written in 1934; rev. ed., 1937), in *Verzamelde Werken,* vol. 7 (Haarlem: Tjeenk Willink, 1950), 129.

3. František Graus, *Das Spätmittelalter als Krisenzeit: Ein Literaturbericht als Zwischenbilanz,* Medievalia Bohemica, Suppl. 1 (Prague: Historický útsav CSAV, 1968). In the tragic aftermath of the "Prague Spring" this important essay received only limited circulation. It is no. 82 in the bibliography attached to *Spannung und Widersprüche: Gedenkschrift für František Graus,* ed. Susanna Burghartz et al. (Sigmaringen, Germany: Jan Thorbecke Verlag, 1992), 315–324, 319.

4. As Wolfgang J. Mommsen put it: "Die Gestaltungen und Ereignisse der Vergangenheit sind, für sich genommen, tot und sinnlos"; *Die Geschichtswissenschaft jenseits des Historismus* (Düsseldorf: Droste Verlag 1971; rev. ed., Düsseldorf: Droste Verlag, 1972), 45.

5. See Bernd Moeller, "Was wurde in der Frühzeit der Reformation in den deutschen Städten gepredigt," *Archiv für Reformationsgeschichte* 75 (1984), 176–193, 193. Ten years later Moeller tried to avoid misunderstandings by replacing "Lutherische Engführung" with "Evangelische Engführung,"

retaining the real crux: "Engführung"; Berndt Hamm, Bernd Moeller, and Dorothea Wendebourg, *Reformationstheorien: Ein Kirchenhistorischer Disput über Einheit und Vielfalt der Reformation* (Göttingen: Vandenhoeck und Ruprecht, 1995), 21 n. 22. For a balanced analysis of the striking variety of lay carrier groups in terms of programmatic differences and common convictions, see Miriam Usher Chrisman, *Conflicting Visions of Reform: German Lay Propaganda Pamphlets, 1519–1530,* Studies in German Histories (Atlantic Highlands, N.J.: Humanities Press, 1996).

6. Thomas A. Brady, Jr., *The Politics of the Reformation in Germany: Jacob Sturm (1489–1553) of Strasbourg* (Atlantic Highlands, N.J.: Humanities Press, 1997), 3.

7. See Scholder, *Die Kirchen und das Dritte Reich.*

8. G. W. Locher, "Festvortrag: Reformation als Beharrung und Fortschritt: Ein Votum Calvins gegen Ende des 20. Jahrhunderts," in *Calvinus Theologus,* ed. Wilhelm H. Neuser (Neukirchen-Vluyn: Neukirchener Verlag, 1976), 3–16.

9. William J. Bouwsma, *John Calvin: A Sixteenth-Century Portrait* (New York: Oxford University Press, 1988). In addition to its other merits, Bouwsma's book presents a sensitive cultural history of the sixteenth century.

10. E. William Monter, *Calvin's Geneva,* New Dimensions in History: Historical Cities (New York: John Wiley, 1967; reprint, Huntington, N.Y.: R. E. Krieger, 1975); Robert McCune Kingdon, *Geneva and the Coming of the Wars of Religion in France, 1555–1556,* Travaux d'humanisme et renaissance 22 (Geneva: Librairie E. Droz, 1956); Francis M. Higman, *La diffusion de la réforme en France, 1520–1565,* Publications de la Faculté de théologie de l'Université de Genève 17 (Geneva: Labor et Fides, 1992); Henry Heller, *The Conquest of Poverty: The Calvinist Revolt in Sixteenth Century France,* Studies in Medieval and Reformation Thought 35 (Leiden: E. J. Brill, 1986); note esp. the finely chiseled entry by Bernard Roussel in *The Oxford Encyclopedia of the Reformation,* vol. 1, ed. Hans Joachim Hillerbrand (New York: Oxford University Press, 1996), 132–133, s.v. "Béarn"; Harro Höpfl, *The Christian Polity of John Calvin,* Cambridge Studies in the History and Theory of Politics (Cambridge: Cambridge University Press, 1982); and Philip Benedict, *Rouen during the Wars of Religion,* Cambridge Studies in Early Modern History (Cambridge: Cambridge University Press, 1981).

11. Charlotte C. Wells, *Law and Citizenship in Early Modern France* (Baltimore: Johns Hopkins University Press, 1995).

12. See Schilling's even-handed discussion of the state of scholarship in "Dis-

ciplinierung oder Selbstregulierung der Untertanen? Ein Plädoyer für die Doppelperspektive von Makro- und Mikro-historie bei der Erforschung der frühmodernen Kirchenzucht," *Historische Zeitschrift* 264 (1997), 675–691.

13. Heinz Schilling, *Civic Calvinism in Northwestern Germany and the Netherlands: Sixteenth to Nineteenth Centuries*, Sixteenth Century Essays and Studies 17 (Kirksville, Mo.: Sixteenth Century Journal Publishers, 1991). Cf. the more comprehensive and richly documented presentation in his *Religion, Political Culture, and the Emergence of Early Modern Society: Essays in German and Dutch History*, SMRT 50 (Leiden: E. J. Brill, 1992).

14. Wolfgang Reinhard, review of Heinz Schilling, *Religion, Political Culture, and the Emergence of Early Modern Society, Zeitschrift für historische Forschung* 22 (1995), 265–267.

15. Volker Press, "Stadt und territoriale Konfessionsbildung," in *Kirche und gesellschaftlicher Wandel in deutschen und niederländischen Städten der werdenden Neuzeit,* ed. Franz Petri, Städteforschung, Reihe A, Darstellungen 10 (Cologne: Böhlau Verlag, 1980), 251–296; id., "Soziale Folgen der Reformation in Deutschland," in *Schichtung und Entwicklung der Gesellschaft in Polen und Deutschland im 16. und 17. Jahrhundert: Parallelen, Verknüpfungen, Vergleiche,* ed. Marian Biskup and Klaus Zernack, Vierteljahresschrift für Sozial- und Wirtschaftsgeschichte, Beiheft 74 (Wiesbaden, Germany: Franz Steiner Verlag, 1983), 196–243.

16. Heinz Schilling, ed., *Die reformierte Konfessionalisierung in Deutschland: Das Problem der Zweiten Reformation: Wissenschaftliches Symposion des Vereins für Reformationsgeschichte 1985,* Schriften des Vereins für Reformationsgeschichte 195 (Gütersloh: Gütersloher Verlagshaus Gerd Mohn, 1986). In its application to Germany, it can indeed clarify aspects of the ensuing confessionalization. See Schilling, "Nochmals zweite Reformation in Deutschland: Der Fall Brandenburg in mehrspektivisher Sicht," *Zeitschrift für Historische Forschung* 23 (1996), 501–524.

17. Martin Heckel, "Die reichsrechtliche Bedeutung des Bekenntnisses," in *Bekenntnis und Einheit der Kirche: Studien zum Konkordienbuch,* ed. Martin Brecht and Reinhard Schwarz (Stuttgart: Calwer Verlag, 1980), 57–88. Cf. id., "Konfession und Reichsverfassung: Bekenntnisbildung und Bekenntnisbindung in den Freiheitsgarantien und der Verfassungsorganisation des Reichs seit der Glaubensspaltung," in *Glaube und Eid,* ed. Paolo Prodi with Elisabeth Müller-Luckner, Schriften des Historischen Kollegs, Kolloquien 28 (Munich: R. Oldenbourg Verlag, 1993), 69–96.

18. It is important to point out that Heinz Schilling is well aware of the distort-

ing potential of the process of confessionalization as ideology; instead it should be regarded as an interpretive model ("Erklärunsparadigma"). See Wolfgang Reinhard and Heinz Schilling, eds., *Die katholische Konfessionalisierung: Wissenschaftliches Symposium der Gesellschaft zur Herausgabe des Corpus Catholicorum und des Vereins für Reformationsgeschichte,* Schriften des Vereins für Reformationsgeschichte 198 (Gütersloh: Gütersloher Verlagshaus, 1995).

19. See my academy address, "The Devil and the Devious Historian: Reaching for the Roots of Modernity," in *Koninklijke Nederlandse Akademie van Wetenschappen: Heineken Lectures, 1996* (Amsterdam: Royal Netherlands Academy of Arts and Sciences, 1997), 33–44.

20. Thomas F. Mayer and Peter E. Starenko, "An Unknown Diary of Julius III's Conclave by Bartolomeo Stella, a Servant of Cardinal Pole," *Annuarium Historiae Conciliorum* 24 (1992), 345–375. Cf. Thomas F. Mayer, "Il fallimento di una candidatura: Il partito della riforma, Reginald Pole e il conclave di Giulio III," *Annali dell'Istituto storico italo-germanico in Trento* 21 (1995), 41–67.

21. See Colin Martin and Geoffrey Parker, *The Spanish Armada* (London: Hamish Hamilton, 1988), 23–66.

22. Bernard Chevalier, "France from Charles VII to Henry IV," in *Handbook of European History.* vol. 1, 395.

23. When the Parisians awoke on the morning of August 30, 1590, they were surprised to see that Henry had withdrawn his troops just when major concessions were considered. See Leopold von Ranke, *Französische Geschichte vornehmlich im 16. und 17. Jahrhundert,* 6 vols. (1852; 4th ed., Leipzig: Duncker und Humboldt, 1876), vol. 1, 366.

24. See my review article, "The Present Profile and Future Face of Reformation History," *Sixteenth Century Studies Journal* 28 (1997), 163–171.

25. For the rehistorization of the Whig fear of the repressive antiliberal potential of political papalism, see Patrick Collinson, "The Elizabethan Exclusion Crisis and the Elizabethan Polity," *Proceedings of the British Academy* 84 (1994), 51–92.

26. Mario Scaduto, "La Ginevra di Teodoro Beza nei ricordi di un gesuita lucano, Luca Pinelli, 1542–1607," *Archivum Historicum Societatis Jesu* 20 (1951), 117–142. Quoted in Scott Manetsch, *Theodore Beza and the Quest for Peace in France, 1572–1598,* SMRT 79 (Leiden: E. J. Brill, 2000).

27. Dale K. Van Kley, *The Religious Origins of the French Revolution: From Calvin to the Civil Constitution, 1560–1791* (New Haven: Yale University Press, 1996), 53. As A. Lynn Martin has pointed out, the head-on conflict

between Calvinists and Jesuits broke out relatively late, only in 1559, when the "Jesuits finally awakened to the Calvinist threat"; *The Jesuit Mind: The Mentality of an Elite in Early Modern France* (Ithaca: Cornell University Press, 1988), 89. The thoroughly partisan identification of this author with the Jesuit perspective documents another revealing parallel: e.g., in contrast with modern Luther studies, both Jesuit and Calvin research are still dominated by "disciples" and have not yet outgrown the "in-group" phase.

28. WA 10 3.9, 1 f.

CHAPTER VIII: TOWARD A NEW MAP OF REFORMATION EUROPE

Epigraph: A verse of the earliest known Huguenot song (ca. December 1525): "Let us pray to the King of Heaven / that by His benevolence / He sends us His Light / And that He writes in our hearts / By His sweetness / All that the Gospel contains / Read, read, and pass it on." Henri-Léonard Bordier, *Le chansonnier Huguenot du XVIe siècle* (Paris, 1969; reprint, Geneva: Slatkine Reprints, 1969), xvii–xviii.

1. Brian Tierney, *Foundations of the Conciliar Theory: The Contribution of the Medieval Canonists from Gratian to the Great Schism*, SHCT 81 (Cambridge, England, 1955; rev. and enl. ed., Leiden: E. J. Brill, 1998), xx.

2. In any modern reconstruction, the extensive literary study of Raymond Lebèque should not be overlooked: *La tragédie religieuse en France: Les débuts, 1514–1573* (Paris: Librairie Honoré Champion, 1929).

3. Philip Benedict, "Settlements: France," in *Handbook of European History,* vol. 1, 423. For the influence of Marguerite de Navarre, see Jonathan Reid, "King's Sister, Queen of Dissent: Marguerite de Navarre, 1492–1549, and Her Evangelical Network" (Ph.D. diss., University of Arizona, 2001).

4. Karen Lindsey may be right that Henry was unable to love, but by ignoring the wider constitutional issues of Tudor politics at the time she reduces dynastic politics to bedroom dynamics. *Divorced, Beheaded, Survived: A Feminist Reinterpretation of the Wives of Henry VIII* (Reading, Mass.: Addison-Wesley, 1995).

5. See my *Luther: Man between God and the Devil*, trans. Eileen Walliser-Schwarzbart (New Haven: Yale University Press, 1989; reprint, New York: Doubleday, 1992), 49.

6. Carlos M. N. Eire, *From Madrid to Purgatory: The Art and Craft of Dying in Sixteenth-Century Spain* (Cambridge: Cambridge University Press, 1995).

7. Manfred Schulze, *Fürsten und Reformation: Geistliche Reformpolitik weltlicher Fürsten vor der Reformation,* Spätmittelalter und Reformation, Neue Reihe 2 (Tübingen: Mohr Siebeck, 1991). See also Erwin Iserloh, "Die

protestantische Reformation," in *Reformation, Katholische Reform und Gegenreformation,* ed. Erwin Iserloh, Josef Glazik, and Hubert Jedin, Handbuch der Kirchengeschichte 4 (Fribourg: Herder Verlag, 1967), 145.

8. Peter Blickle, *Communal Reformation: The Quest for Salvation in Sixteenth-Century Germany,* trans. Thomas Dunlap, Studies in German Histories (Atlantic Highlands, N.J.: Humanities Press, 1992), 193; originally published as *Gemeindereformation: Die Menschen des 16. Jahrhunderts auf dem Weg zum Heil* (Munich: R. Oldenburg Verlag, 1985).

9. Brady, *Handbook of European History,* Introduction, xvii–xx.

10. See my "Tumultus rusticorum: Vom Klosterkrieg zum Fürstensieg: Beobachtungen zum Bauerenkrieg unter besonderer Berücksichtigung Zeitgenössischer Beurteilungen," in *Deutscher Bauernkrieg 1525,* ed. Heiko A. Oberman, *Zeitschrift für Kirchengeschichte* 85, Heft 2 (Stuttgart: Kohlhammer Verlag, 1974), 301–306. English translation in *Harvard Theological Review* 69 (1976), 103–129.

11. Already during the Diet at Worms Erasmus had expressed his disapproval of Luther: "non probavi seditiose clamores apud populum"; Erasmus to Luigi Mariano, March 25; letter 1195 [1521]. *Opus epistolarum Desiderii Erasmi Roterodami,* ed. P. S. Allen et al., 11 vols. (Oxford: Clarendon, 1906–1958), vol. 3, 459.

12. Max Steinmetz, *Thomas Müntzers Weg nach Allstedt: Eine Studie zur siener Frühentwicklung* (Berlin: Deutscher Verlag der Wissenschaften, 1988).

CHAPTER IX: THE CUTTING EDGE

Epigraph: A verse of the earliest known Huguenot song (ca. December 1525): "Be patient, / You servants of the Lord, / Put your hope / In our sweet Savior. / The one and only mediator, / All power is His. / The one and only mediator, / Let us render Him all honor." Henri-Léonard Bordier, *Le chansonnier Huguenot du XVIᵉ siècle* (Paris, 1969; reprint, Geneva: Slatkine Reprints, 1969), xx.

1. CO, 6.510 A, B.

2. "Ecclesiae instaurationem . . . opus esse Dei, quod a spe opinioneque hominum nihilo magis pendeat, quam aut mortuorum resurrectio, aut aliud miraculum ex eo genere"; CO 6.510 C.

3. "Vult Dominus evangelium suum praedicari. Huic mandato pareamus, et sequamur, quo nos vocat. Quis futurus sit successus, inquirere, non est nostrum: nisi quod eum quam optimum et votis optare et precibus a Domino postulare debemus: eniti etiam omni studio, sollicitudine, diligentia, ut talis contingat: interea tamen qualiscunque erit, aequo animo ferre." CO 6.511 A.

4. WA 10 3.18, 15 f.

5. See Susan E. Schreiner, *The Theater of His Glory: Nature and the Natural Order in the Thought of John Calvin* (Durham, N.C.: Labyrinth Press, 1991).

6. Philip Benedict, *Rouen during the Wars of Religion*, Cambridge Studies in Early Modern History (Cambridge: Cambridge University Press, 1981), 109.

7. Willem van 't Spijker, "Prädestination bei Bucer und Calvin: Ihre gegenseitige Beeinflussung und Abhängigkeit," in *Calvinus Theologus*, ed. Wilhelm H. Neuser (Neukirchen-Vluyn: Neukirchener Verlag, 1976), 85–101, 106.

8. See my "Europa Afflicta: The Reformation of the Refugees," ARG 83 (1992), 91–111.

9. See my *De Erfenis van Calvijn: Grootheid en Grenzen* (Kampen: J. H. Kok, 1988).

10. For the explosive context of iconoclasm, see Denis Crouzet, *Les guerriers de Dieu: La violence au temps des troubles de religion, vers 1525—vers 1610,* 2 vols. (Seyssel, France: Éditions Champ Vallon, 1990).

11. Carlos M. N. Eire, *From Madrid to Purgatory: The Art and Craft of Dying in Sixteenth-Century Spain* (Cambridge: Cambridge University Press, 1995).

12. Carlos M. N. Eire, *War against the Idols: The Reformation of Worship from Erasmus to Calvin* (New York: Cambridge University Press, 1986).

13. In an audacious intellectual history of iconoclasm, Alain Besançon has argued that Calvin did not change the image of God but of the world. The term "le monde dé-divinisé" is acceptable for this view, provided it is interpreted in the sense that God is "de-localized." *L'image interdite: Une histoire intellectuelle de l'iconoclasme* (Paris: Librairie Fayard, 1994), 255.

14. See my "Calvin and Farel: The Dynamics of Legitimation in Early Calvinism," *Journal of Early Modern History* 2 (1998), 32–60.

15. For the iconoclastic outbreak in the Netherlands, see David Freedberg, *Iconoclasm and Painting in the Revolt of the Netherlands, 1566–1609* (New York: Garland, 1988).

CHAPTER X: CALVIN'S LEGACY

A revised version of the Kuyper Lectures of 1986 at the Free University of Amsterdam, 23, which were originally presented as "De Erfenis van Calvijn: Grootheid en Grenzen" and later published as *Calvin's Legacy: Its Greatness and Limitations*, trans. John Vriend (Grand Rapids: Eerdmans, 1990).

1. Allard Pierson, *Onuitgegeven Manuscripten* (not available commercially), Introduction by J. L. Pierson (Amsterdam: P. N. van Kampen, 1919), 202.

2. The passage is quoted from C. Augustijn's carefully nuanced characterization "kerk en godsdienst 1879–1890," in *De Doleantie van 1886 en haar geschiedenis,* ed. W. Bakker et al. (Kampen: Kok, 1986), 40–75.

3. Hugo Grotius, *Meletius, sive De iis quae Christianos convenient Epistola,* critical edition with translation, commentary, and introduction by Guillaume H. M. Posthumus Meyjes, Studies in the History of Church Theology 40 (Leiden: Brill, 1988).

4. Commentary on Jer. 22:28: "Et scimus hoc esse durius, ubi quis longe abstrahitur a patria"; John Calvin, *Commentaries on the Book of the Prophet Jeremiah and the Lamentations,* trans. John Owen, 3 vols. (Edinburgh: Calvin Translation Society, 1850), vol. 1; reprint, *Calvin's Commentaries,* 22 vols. (Grand Rapids: Baker Book House, 1984), vol. 9, 123–134, lecture 84.

5. Jer. 20:47; *Calvin's Commentaries,* vol. 10.

6. In accordance with W. F. Dankbaar, *Calvijn: Zijn weg en werk* (Nijkerk, The Netherlands: Callenbach, 1957), 215–217.

7. André M. Hugo, *Calvijn en Seneca: Een inleidende studie van Calvijns Commentaar op Seneca, "De clementia," anno 1532* (Groningen: Wolters, 1957), 43–45.

8. Jean Calvin, *Institutes of the Christian Religion,* ed. John T. McNeilll, trans. Ford Lewis Battles, 2 vols. (Philadephia: Westminster Press, 1960), bk. 2, chap. 2, sec. 18.

9. Abraham Kuyper, *Calvinism: Six Stone Foundation Lectures* (Grand Rapids, Mich.: Eerdmans, 1943), 40.

10. Allard Pierson, *Studiën over Johannes Kalvijn, eerst reeks, 1527–1536* (Amsterdam: P. N. van Kampen, 1881), 8.

11. The *Reveil* was the Dutch manifestation of the evangelical revival of Restoration Europe. It "stemmed directly from currents in Switzerland and England and appealed most to the best born and educated." James D. Bratt, *Dutch Calvinism in Modern America: A History of a Conservative Subculture,* trans. John Vriend (Grand Rapids: Eerdmans, 1984), 10; cf. 10–13, 20, 29, 31, 44.

12. Pierson, *Johannes Kalvijn,* 12.

13. *Responsio ad Sadoleti Epistolam* (1539); OS 1, 460.

14. CR 79, 532.

15. Ibid., 82, 5.

16. *Epistola ad Genevates:* OS 1, 451.

17. *Responsio ad Sadoleti Epistolam* (1539); OS 1, 460.

18. OS 1, 482.

19. Ibid., 1, 485.

20. OS 1, 482; *A Reformation Debate: Sadoleto's Letter to the Genevans and Calvin's Reply*, ed. John C. Olin (New York: Harper & Row, 1966), 85.

21. Otto Weber, *Die Treue Gottes in der Geschichte der Kirche* (Neukirchen-Vluyn: Neukirchener Verlag des Erziehungsvereins, 1968).

22. They all occur together in Calvin's interpretation of 2 Thess. 2:6; CR 80, 199.

23. *Calvin's Commentaries*, on 2 Thess. 2:7; CR 80, 200.

24. The Consensus Tigurinus, the Latin name of the Zürich Consensus negotiated by Calvin and Heinrich Bullinger, Zwingli's successor in Zürich, on the issue of the Lord's Supper. The compromise was intended to provide a unifying confession of faith for reformed churches in Switzerland and had considerable success. (DW)

25. OS 1, 463; *Reformation Debate*, ed. Olin, 58.

26. Cf. Otto Weber, *Die Treue Gottes in der Geschichte der Kirche*, Gesammelte Aufsätze 2 (Neukirchen-Vluyn: Neukirchener Verlag, 1968), 59.

27. OS 1, 463.

28. Pierson, *Johannes Kalvijn*, 105.

29. Umberto Eco, "In praise of Thomas Aquinas," *Wilson Quarterly* (fall 1986), 78–87; taken over from *Travels in Hyperreality* (San Diego: Harcourt Brace Jovanovich, 1986).

30. Eco, "Thomas Aquinas," 83.

31. On April 1, 1572, the Spanish military commander Alva lost control of the fortified city Den Briel to the Dutch Sea Beggars. This proved to be a key event in the subsequent liberation of the Dutch from Spanish rule. The joke was—with a pun on the name of the city—that Alva had thereby lost his "bril," or glasses. He was relieved of his command soon afterward. (John Vriend, trans.)

32. See E. William Monter, *Calvin's Geneva*, New Dimensions in History: Historical Cities (New York: Wiley, 1967), esp. 139; Robert M. Kingdon, "The Deacons of the Reformed Church in Calvin's Geneva," in *Mélanges d'histoire du seizième siècle à Henri Meylan*, Travaux d'humanisme et renaissance 110 (Geneva: Librairie Droz, 1970), 81–87; William C. Innes, *Social Concern in Calvin's Geneva*, Pittsburgh Theological Monographs 7 (Allison Park, Pa.: Pickwick Publications, 1983), 103–120. See Kingdon's conclusion: "In working out these specifications, however, Calvin was not creat-

ing a new institution. He was rather providing a religious warrant, drawn from the Bible, for a program of social work that already existed. . . . In other words in his discussions of the diaconate, Calvin may have been describing an institution which he had seen operating in Geneva"; ibid., 82, 87. Innes prefers to think of the influence of a theological tradition, particularly of Bucer's *Von der wahren Seelsorge* (1538); cf. ibid., 106.

33. See *Extraits . . . Registres publiques de Genève par Jacques Flournois, 1522– 1536*, 137, published in Anthoine Fromment, *Les Actes et Gestes merveilleux de la cité de Genève* (Geneva: I. G. Fick, 1854).

34. A. A. van Schelven, *Kerkeraads-Protocollen der Nederduitse Vluchtelingen-Kerk te Londen, 1560–1563* (Amsterdam: J. Müller, 1921), 28. For the years 1569–1571 they were edited by Abraham Kuyper: cf. *Kerkeraads-Protocollen der Hollandsche Gemeente te Londen, 1569–1571*, Werken der Marnix-Vereeniging, ser. 1, bk. 1 (Utrecht: Kemink, 1870).

35. For this phase, cf. my *Die Reformation: Von Wittenberg nach Genf* (Göttingen: Vandenhoeck und Ruprecht, 1986), 296–299.

36. CR 81, 273.

37. Pierson, *Johannes Kalvijn, derde reeks, 1540–1542* (1891), 160 f.

38. Ibid., 180.

39. Ibid., 183.

40. Cf. Karsien Hendrik Boersema, *Allard Pierson: Eene Cultuur-Historische Studie* ('s-Gravenhage, The Netherlands: Martinus Nijhoff International, 1924), 11; quoted by P. L. Schram, "Een huisvrouw uit het Réveil—Ida Pierson-Oyens, 1806–1860," in *Aspecten van het Réveil: Opstellen ter gelegenheid van het vijftigjarig bestaan van de Stichting Het Réveil-Archief*, ed. Johannes van den Berg, P. L. Schram, and Simon Leendert Verheus (Kampen: Kok, 1980), 224.

41. Jan Romein, "Abraham Kuyper: De klokkenist der kleine luyden," in *Erflaters van onze beschaving: Nederlandse gestalten uit zes eeuwen*, ed. Jan Romein and Anna Romein-Verschoor (Amsterdam: HVO-Querido, 1938– 1939; 9th ed., rev., Amsterdam: HVO-Querido, 1971), 747–770.

42. The Nadere Reformation of the seventeenth century was a renewal movement which stressed the subjective and ethical side of Christian faith and life. (John Vriend, trans.)

43. Stefan Zweig, *Castellio gegen Calvin: Oder ein Gewissen gegend di Gewalt* (Vienna: Herbert Reichner Verlag, 1936); American ed: *The Right to Heresy: Castellio against Calvin*, trans. Eden and Cedar Paul (New York: Viking, 1964). On Castellio's writings, including an extensive bibliography, see Heinz Liebing, "Die Schriftenauslegung Sebastian Castellios," *Huma-*

nismus, Reformation, Konfessionen: Beiträge zur Kirchengeschichte, ed. Heinz Liebing et al., Marburger theologische Studien 20 (Marburg: Elwert, 1986), 11–24. The quotation is in part an improvisation by EZ.

44. Wilhelm Neuser, *Calvin* (Berlin: Walter de Gruyter, 1971), 8a.

45. *Calvin's New Testament Commentaries,* ed. T. H. L. Parker (Grand Rapids, Mich.: Eerdmans, 1964), on Timothy, 314, 315.

46. Ibid., 315.

47. See, e.g., Johann Gerhard's summary of the convictions of all who sub-scribe to the Augsburg Confession: "Evangelical ministers are the suc-cessors of the apostles," *Loci Theologici,* vol. 5 (Berolini, 1867), locus 22, 199, 3, p. 449; locus 23, 87, 2, p. 57.

48. See Hans Scholl, *Reformation und Politik: Politische Ethik bei Luther, Calvin und den Frühhugenotten,* Urban-Taschenbücher 616 (Stuttgart: Kohlham-mer, 1976), 87–102.

49. Ibid., 102.

50. Ibid., 102.

51. Thus we sense no inconsistency in our own idiom when in true democratic fashion we insist on freedom of thought and assembly, freedom to organize and to agitate, but exclude terrorism from the claims of tolerance as sub-versive of the state.

52. The Canons of Dordt were promulgated by the international Synod held in Dordt, or Dordrecht, 1618–1619, to resolve doctrinal conflicts in the Reformation churches of the Netherlands. The Canons endorsed the strict predestinarian views of the Counter Remonstrants, or Calvinists, and the Synod went on to exclude the Remonstrants, or Arminians, from eccle-siastical offices and condemn their teachings. (DW)

53. G. H. M. Posthumus Meyjes, *Verdrukking, vlucht en toevlucht: Het dagboek van Jean Migault over de geloofsvervolging onder Lodewijk XIV* (Kampen: Kok, 1985).

54. Ibid., 53.

55. Ibid., 55.

56. *Calvin's New Testament Commentaries,* 344. CR 80, 396: "toto vitae curri-culo nos eius manu regi, donec tota militia perfuncti, victoria potiamur."

57. CR 80, 355.

58. Iohannis Calvini, *Commentarius in epistolam Pauli ad Romanos,* ed. T. H. L. Parker, SHCT 22 (Leiden: E. J. Brill, 1981), 182, 69: "aeternum Dei consilium."

59. *Calvin's New Testament Commentaries,* on Eph., 144.

60. Ibid., 147.

61. See note 42.

62. CR 80, 355. Cf. Matt. 16:18 (Vulgate).

63. *Calvin's New Testament Commentaries*, on 2 Tim., 316.

64. Ibid., 324.

65. Ibid., on 2 Tim. 3:2.

66. Ibid., on 2 Tim. 3:12: "exilium, carcerem, fugam"; CR 80, 380. Note the order.

67. My italics. *Calvin's New Testament Commentaries*, on 2 Tim. 2:19, 316.

68. Ibid.

69. See Karl Barth, *Church Dogmatics*, vol. 2, pt. 2; Otto Weber, *Die Treue Gottes in der Geschichte der Kirche*, Gesammelte Aufsätze 2, Beiträge zur Geschichte und Lehre der Reformierten Kirche 29 (Neukirchen-Vluyen: Neukirchener Verlag des Erziehungsvereins, 1968), 21. Among Calvin's medieval precursors the name of Duns Scotus must not be overlooked. It would be profitable to examine this parallel.

70. Heinrich Denzinger, *The Sources of Catholic Dogma* (St. Louis: B. Herder, 1957), 253.

71. Jürgen Moltmann, "Erwählung und Beharrung der Gläubigen," in *Calvin-Studien 1959*, ed. Jürgen Moltmann (Neukirchen-Vluyen: Neukirchener Verlag des Erziehungsvereins, 1960), 43–61:50.

72. *Calvin's New Testament Commentaries*, on 2 Tim. 2:19, 316–317.

73. Ibid., on 2 Tim. 2:12, 327.

74. Pierson, *Studien over Johannes Kalvijn*, 176.

75. *Calvin's New Testament Commentaries*, on 2 Tim. 3:16, 330.

76. Assen, site of the Reformed Synod of 1926, where a literal interpretation of Gen. 3 was upheld.

77. *Johannes Calvins Auslegung der Heiligen Schrift* (in deutscher Übersetzung), ed. Karl Müller, trans. Samuel Engels, Neukirchen z. j., Bd 10. (Leer, Ost-friesland: n.p., n.d.), 135.

78. Ibid., 330.

79. Ibid., 329.

80. Ibid., 330.

81. WAT [1919], Nr. 5468, 5.168.30–32: "Scripturas sanctas sciat se nemo degustasse satis, nisi centum annis cum Prophetis, ut Elia et Elisaeo, Ioanne Baptista, Christo en Apostolis Ecclesias gubernarit."

INDEX